Paolo Attivissimo

MOON HOAX: DEBUNKED!

Dispelling doubts about the Moon landings,
celebrating courage and ingenuity

First edition

Updates to this book can be downloaded
from *MoonHoaxDebunked.com*.

Cover: Gene Cernan during his third moonwalk, Apollo 17, December 1972. NASA image AS17-140-21391. The image has been cropped and the sky has been extended digitally to fit the book layout. Credit: NASA.

Back cover photo: Andrea Tedeschi Photography (www.andreatedeschi.ch).

Copyright notice

Preface

It is now over forty years since man first set foot on the Moon. Many of us, including myself, experienced that extraordinary moment as amazing news that filled the papers and magazines and gave us an unforgettable, sleepless night spent gazing at the ghostly live television pictures that reached our homes from another world.

Today, however, to a growing number of people that memorable achievement is literally history: blurred, distant, known only through second-hand stories and often reported tiredly and superficially by mainstream media. Even today, going to the Moon is still an incredible, mythical and unreal challenge, and the idea that we went there in the 1960s – and then *stopped going* – is, for many, understandably hard to accept.

I offer this book to anyone who honestly seeks to understand what really happened and rightly demands answers to his or her reasonable doubts. To hardcore Moon hoax believers, those who are impervious to any argument and think that they have it all figured out, I offer only my pity. They are unable to enjoy this amazing adventure, which is one of the few peaceful endeavors for which the twentieth century stands a chance of being remembered as something more than a heartbreaking series of wars, devastations and genocides.

However, this book is not just a pedantic refutation of a set of eccentric claims. It's a celebration of a moment in time that can never be equaled or repeated. Yes, there will be other destinations, other missions, other landings on distant worlds, but the Moon landing of July 1969 will be forever mankind's first contact with another world. It will always be the first time that humanity proved, albeit for a brief moment, that it is capable of crawling out of its fragile cradle.

What an incredible privilege it is to be alive in that unique, minuscule slice of history in which all this happened, and to be able to personally thank, talk and shake hands with those who accomplished a voyage that for countless centuries was merely a dream beyond the power of even the mightiest king, emperor or pharaoh. *To walk on the Moon.* This book is my small homage to the courage and ingenuity of all those who contributed to turning that dream into reality. In peace, for all mankind.

Acknowledgments

I would like to thank all the people who patiently read and checked the drafts of this book and debugged them as they grew online. I am especially indebted to Luca Boschini, John H. Cato, jr, Epsilon, Cesare Guariniello, Hammer, Martin Keenan, Massy, Naomi, Razvan Neagoe, Papageno, Giuseppe Regalzi, Luigi Rosa, Claudio Severi, Linden Sims, Roland Suhr, Trystero, Tukler and Larry Turoski for their tireless fact-checking and proofreading. Any surviving mistakes are solely mine.

I am also very grateful to Terry Watson (Apollo GNC), Eric Jones of the *Apollo Lunar Surface Journal*, and to all the members of the *Project Apollo* online forum, for helping me through the maze of jargon and technical minutiae and for unerringly answering the bizarre questions of a fellow space geek; to Nicola Colotti, Fabio Letta, Milco Margaroli, Rodri Van Click, Andrea Tedeschi, Luigi Pizzimenti, Roberto Crippa, Guido Schwartz and Lukas Viglietti, for organizing amazing encounters and interviews with Apollo astronauts Buzz Aldrin, Charlie Duke and Walt Cunningham and with Mission Control EECOM Sy Liebergot; to Diego Cuoghi, for kindly sharing his research; to Elena Albertini, for keeping the e-book and paper editions in sync; and to my daughters Lisa and Linda, who helped me with the technical process of creating the digital edition of this book.

This book is dedicated to my parents, who woke me up when I was six years old so that I could watch the Apollo 11 Moon landing live on TV in sleepy amazement (it was nighttime in Europe), and to my aunt Iris, who in the early 1970s gave me a copy of Peter Ryan's enthralling account of the first Apollo missions, *The Invasion of the Moon 1957-70*. I never recovered from this double bite of the space bug. That dog-eared paperback is still here with me as I write these words. Its pages are fading, but the passion and wonder they have fed for all these years are certainly not.

Free distribution

However, writing a technical book takes time and hard work; buying manuals and DVDs and documents takes money. So if you like what you read and you feel like lending me a hand on this project, you're welcome to point out errors or unclear language, help me with research, buy me space reference books from my Amazon.com wish list or donate the equivalent of a genuine Italian pizza and a good beer via my Paypal account as an incentive for me to keep on writing. You can also help me by buying the Amazon Kindle edition or the printed edition of this book, if you haven't already (if you have, consider buying one for a friend). All the details are on the *MoonHoaxDebunked.com* website.

Units of measurement

Throughout this book, all measurements are given in both metric units and US customary units. Unless otherwise specified, *mile* is understood to reference a statute mile and *ton* is understood to be a metric ton (1,000 kg). Some rounding may be introduced to avoid unnecessarily pedantic conversion results; e.g., 100,000 feet will be converted to 30,000 meters instead of 30,480. Also, idiomatic expressions such as *a couple of inches* or *a few feet*, which suggest a very approximate measurement, will not be converted.

Links to source documents

To avoid long and cumbersome Internet links in the text, links to all the source documents referenced in this book that can be downloaded from the Internet are available in the *Links to source documents* section of the *MoonHoaxDebunked.com* website.

Comments, corrections and updates

This book is a work in progress. Apollo's science and documentation are still being studied today and new Moon probes are providing updates and new opportunities for cross-checking that are included here as they become available. Also, conspiracy theorists concoct new "evidence" and claims all the time, so you might find that a specific claim hasn't yet been debunked specifically in this book. You might also find mistakes or typos. If so, let me know by e-mail at *paolo.attivissimo@gmail.com*, so that the next edition of this book will be updated and corrected. The *MoonHoaxDebunked.com* website lists the changes introduced in the various editions.

Additional photographs, videos and documents

Some of the technical explanations given in these pages become clearer with the aid of high-resolution scans of photographs and digitized samples of footage from the Apollo TV broadcasts and 16 mm color films. This additional material can be downloaded at *Moon-HoaxDebunked.com*.

In memoriam

This book wishes to honor those who paid the highest price in order to reach and extend the new frontier, sometimes in secret and often without being remembered even as a footnote of history. The story behind each one of the names that follow is given in the *Remembering the fallen* chapter. Let's not ever forget that anyone who denies the Moon landings is sullying the memory of these brave people, of their families and of everyone who worked hard for the exploration of space.

Michael J. Adams	Robert H. Lawrence, Jr.
Michael P. Anderson	Christa McAuliffe
Charles A. Bassett II	William C. McCool
Valentin Bondarenko	Ronald McNair
David M. Brown	Ellison Onizuka
Roger Chaffee	Viktor Patsayev
Kalpana Chawla	Ilan Ramon
Laurel B. Clark	Judith Resnick
Georgi Dobrovolski	Francis "Dick" Scobee
Theodore C. Freeman	Elliot McKay See, Jr.
Edward G. Givens, Jr.	Michael J. Smith
Virgil "Gus" Grissom	Vladislav Volkov
Rick D. Husband	Ed White
Gregory Jarvis	Clifton C. Williams, Jr.
Vladimir Komarov	

Ad astra per aspera.

1. Race for the Moon

The time is the 1950s. The United States and the Soviet Union are intently playing history's most dangerous game of chicken, aiming thousands of nuclear bombs at each other's cities, according to a doctrine aptly named *MAD*. As in *Mutual Assured Destruction*. They both know that if one of them decides to attack, the other's nuclear retaliation will lead to utter annihilation.

This fragile balance of terror will last forty-five years and will end with the breakup of the Soviet Union in 1991. But at the time of the Moon race, the Soviet Union is a powerful, secretive superstate that includes the countries now known as Russia, Armenia, Azerbaijan, Belarus, Estonia, Georgia, Kazakhstan, Kyrgyzstan, Latvia, Lithuania, Moldova, Tajikistan, Turkmenistan, Ukraine and Uzbekistan.

Figure 1-1. The United States and the Soviet Union. Image source: Wikipedia.

These two military superpowers are vying for control of the ultimate high ground: space. They both view spaceflight as an opportunity to lob atomic annihilation more efficiently and to prove to the world their technological prowess and the superiority of their social system. Space is propaganda.

On October 4, 1957, the Soviet Union stuns the world by launching the world's first artificial satellite, Sputnik 1. The fact that Sputnik overflies the US and the rest of the world with absolute impunity, and has been hurled into the sky on one of the intercontinental missiles that the Soviets (like the Americans) are building to deliver nuclear warheads in mere minutes onto enemy targets, is not lost on Western public opinion.

The United States launches a crash federal program to recover from the political humiliation of being beaten by what was considered by many a backward country. It belatedly accelerates its fledgling space program, which had already achieved remarkable results, such as the first photographs taken from space.[1] The program also seeks to close the academic, military and technological gap that Sputnik has so eloquently exposed. But at first the only result of this effort is further embarrassment.

One month after Sputnik 1, on November 3, 1957, the Soviets set another record with Sputnik 2, taking the first living being into orbit around the Earth, the dog Laika, before the United States has placed anything at all in orbit. Laika dies a few hours later from overheating and stress, but this is kept secret. The flight has been planned as a one-way mission anyway, because the technology for returning from space is not yet available.

Figure 1-2. Kaboom.

Finally, on December 6, the US makes its first orbital launch attempt. The Navy's Vanguard TV3 rocket rises a few feet and then explodes dishearteningly on the pad, in front of a television audience of millions (Figure 1-2).

The United States manages to place a satellite in orbit on January 31, 1958: Explorer 1 is launched on a Jupiter-C/Juno-I, a US Army Redstone rocket designed and modified by Wernher Von Braun, creator of the infamous Nazi V-2 rockets that had been used to bomb London and other cities during the Second World War. Von Braun had defected from Germany in 1945 and is now working for the US military.

---

1   Towards the end of the 1940s, the United States had modified German V-2 rockets to perform brief vertical flights to altitudes of 160 kilometers (100 miles), carrying scientific instruments and cameras into space. In the early 1950s, the US, like the Soviet Union, had developed missiles to deliver nuclear warheads. However, in 1957 US rockets were not as powerful as Soviet ones because American nukes were lighter. The Soviets, saddled with heavier warheads, simply built bigger rockets, which happened to be easily adaptable for spaceflight. Thus, ironically, part of the Soviets' space success was due to their *inferior* military technology.

America is in space at last. Nevertheless, the measly 14 kilograms (31 pounds) of Explorer 1 are nothing compared to the over 500 kilos (1,100 pounds) of Sputnik 2 and the over 1,300 kilos (2,900 pounds) carried into space by Sputnik 3 on May 15.

1.1 The Soviet lead

In August 1958, the United States tries to get ahead of the Russians with an attempt to be the first to reach the Moon with an automatic probe, Able 1, but the launch fails 77 seconds after liftoff and the next three attempts (Pioneer 1, 2 and 3) suffer a similar fate.

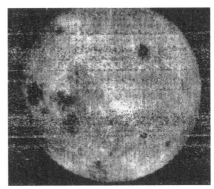

On January 2, 1959, the Soviets launch the Luna 1 probe, which two days later achieves the first lunar flyby, getting as close as 6,000 kilometers

Figure 1-3. The far side of the Moon, imaged by the Soviet probe Luna 3 in 1959.

(3,700 miles) to the Moon, and becomes the first vehicle to go into orbit around the Sun.

America's fifth lunar attempt, Pioneer 4, achieves solar orbit but fails to get any closer than 60,000 kilometers (37,000 miles) to the Moon on March 4.

The Soviets achieve another first on September 13, 1959: their Luna 2 probe crash-lands on the Moon. Less than a month later, Luna 3 reveals to the world the very first pictures of the far side of the Moon (Figure 1-3).

It will take the US five more years, and nine more attempts, to reach the Moon with a space probe. For the time being, America has to make do with science missions in Earth orbit, such as Explorer 6, which provides an almost complete map of the Van Allen radiation belts that encircle our planet and returns the first television pictures of Earth from space. Two monkeys, Able and Baker, are recovered successfully after suborbital flights into space. But the headline-grabbing space launches are all Soviet.

1.2 The US catches up

In 1960 the United States achieves several records: first imaging weather satellite (TIROS-1, April 1), first electronic intelligence satellite (GRAB 1, July 5), first recovery of a satellite after reentry from Earth orbit (Discoverer 13, August 11) and first imaging spy satellite (Discoverer 14, August 18). These are mostly military achievements, prompted by the need to replace urgently with satellites the top-secret U-2 spy planes that had been conducting covert reconnaissance flights over Soviet territory, taking detailed pictures of the country's most secret facilities. On May 1, 1960, one of these planes had been shot down and the pilot captured, causing huge diplomatic embarrassment to the United States.

Once again the Soviet Union grabs the space headlines: in August, Sputnik 5 carries plants and animals (two dogs, Belka and Strelka, forty mice and two rats) into space and for the first time returns them safely from orbit.

1.3 The first man in space

1961 sees a new Soviet shocker: on April 12, Yuri Gagarin becomes the first man to fly in space. Not as a brief up-and-down hop beyond the atmosphere, but as an orbital flight aboard Vostok 1.

Americans are stunned (Figure 1-4) and beaten to the draw once again. The best response they can muster is a fifteen-minute suborbital flight with Alan Shepard in a Mercury spacecraft on

Figure 1-4. Shock in USA.

May 5, because US rockets powerful enough to carry an astronaut into Earth orbit have the unpleasant tendency to explode during test launches. Russian rockets, instead, appear to be outstandingly reliable, also thanks to the fact that their failures are not disclosed.

So with a grand total of fifteen minutes of suborbital human spaceflight on its track record and a bunch of exploding rockets as its current assets, the United States throws down a daring gauntlet: on May 25, 1961, President John Fitzgerald Kennedy challenges the Soviet Union to a race to the Moon.

> *I believe that this nation should commit itself to achieving the goal, before this decade is out, of landing a man on the Moon and returning him safely to the earth. No single space project in this period will be more impressive to mankind or more important for the long-range exploration of space; and none will be so difficult or expensive to accomplish.*

The President's strategy is as simple as it is ambitious: set a grandiose goal that will impress the world, boost America's morale and is far enough in the future to give the US aerospace industry the time to get its act together, close the rocket reliability gap and do better than the Russians. Kennedy, however, will not live to see the outcome of his challenge. He will be assassinated in Dallas, Texas, two years later, on November 22, 1963.

Meanwhile the Russians march on relentlessly. Before America manages to achieve a single human orbital flight, Gherman Titov repeats and extends Gagarin's mission, performing seventeen Earth orbits in early August 1961 aboard Vostok 2.

Gus Grissom performs another suborbital flight on July 21, 1961, and finally, on February 20, 1962, nearly one year after the Russians, John Glenn becomes the first American to orbit the Earth aboard the Friendship 7 spacecraft.

But the Soviet Union ups the ante: in August, two spacecraft (Vostoks 3 and 4) fly simultaneously and cosmonauts Nikolayev and Popovich are briefly less than 5 km (3 miles) apart. The double flight is not a rendezvous, but that's how Soviet propaganda presents it. Nikolayev also sets a new endurance record: four days in space. His picture is broadcast by onboard television cameras to Russian viewers.

In June 1963, Valentina Tereshkova becomes the first woman in space, aboard Vostok 6. She is also the first civilian spacefarer, since all previous astronauts and cosmonauts have been members of the US or Soviet military. On its own, her 48-orbit flight lasts longer than the combined times of all the American astronauts that have flown until then. No other woman will fly in space for the next 19 years: the second woman to do so will be Russian cosmonaut Svetlana Savitskaya in 1982, aboard Soyuz T-7, and the first American woman in space will be Sally Ride in 1983, aboard Space Shuttle Challenger (STS-7).

On October 12, 1964, the Soviet Union accomplishes the first multimanned spaceflight: Voskhod 1 carries into orbit three men before the US is able to fly even two. The flight is essentially a propaganda stunt: in order to cram three astronauts into a vehicle designed for two, they are recklessly required to fly without spacesuits.

The first spacewalk is also a Russian record, set on March 18, 1965 by Alexei Leonov aboard Voskhod 2. All the US can do is send the first successful probe to Mars (Mariner 4). The first soft landing of a space probe and the first pictures from the surface of the Moon are also a Soviet achievement, with Luna 9 in February 1966.

In the meantime, however, the US space program has been acquiring experience with human spaceflight and with the techniques required for a manned Moon landing. Between 1965 and 1966, the spacecraft of the Gemini program (Figure 1-5) carry two-man crews that achieve orbit changes, long-duration flights (up to 14 days), spacewalks and rendezvous with dockings and set a new altitude

Figure 1-5. The Gemini 7 spacecraft.

record for human spaceflight: during the Gemini 11 mission (September 12-15, 1966), Charles "Pete" Conrad and Richard F. Gordon fly to a distance of 1374 kilometers (854 miles) from the Earth's surface and become the first human beings to see their home planet as a sphere.

Meanwhile, the Lunar Orbiter robot probes take detailed photographic surveys of the Moon's surface and the Surveyor spacecraft land on it, testing its nature and consistency. By and large, the US has caught up with the Russians.

But the Apollo program, meant to put an American on the Moon, is in deep trouble. On January 27, 1967, Gus Grissom, Ed White and Roger Chaffee die in the fire of their Apollo 1 command module during a routine test on the launch pad (Figure 1-6). A substantial redesign was already in progress, but the nationwide shock prompts a drastic rethinking of the ill-conceived spacecraft.

Figure 1-6. The charred Apollo 1 crew module.

1967 is a tragic year also for Russian space endeavors. On April 24, Vladimir Komarov becomes the first person to die during spaceflight. His Soyuz 1, prepared hastily to appease the Soviet government's craving for propaganda coups, crashes fatally upon return from space.[2]

2   Some researchers (such as the Italian Judica Cordiglia brothers) claim that they intercep-

1.4 Apollo gets up to speed

The massive US investments in space begin to bear fruit. The huge Kennedy Space Center at Cape Canaveral has risen from the Floridian swamps in record time. Several unmanned flights test the Apollo spacecraft, the giant Saturn V Moon rocket designed by Wernher Von Braun, and the ground support hardware and staff.

Meanwhile the Soviet space program nets another first: on September 18, 1968, the Zond 5 automatic probe takes the first living beings around the Moon. Turtles, wine flies, meal worms, plants, seeds and bacteria are returned safely to Earth, apparently none the worse for the trip. What's more, the spacecraft is clearly big enough to carry a man.

Figure 1-7. The cover of Time, *December 6, 1968.*

On October 11, Walter Schirra, Donn Eisele and Walter Cunningham perform the first manned flight of the redesigned Apollo spacecraft, testing Apollo 7 in Earth orbit for eleven days.

Their flight is also the first American mission with a crew of three and the first manned test of the Saturn IB rocket, Saturn V's smaller brother. There's no time to waste: the US government knows that the Soviets are secretly getting ready to beat America to the Moon.

So two months later, Apollo 8 is the first manned flight of a Saturn V, and although the giant booster has only flown twice previously the goal is already tremendously bold: to travel three hundred times farther than anyone has ever done and take three American astronauts around the Moon.

On December 24, 1968, for the first time in history, human beings see the Moon with their own eyes from as little as 110 kilometers (69 miles) and fly over its far side, which is forever hidden from view from Earth.

The worldwide emotional impact of this mission is huge, not least because it is shown live on TV. Much of mankind is able to share the view of the cratered surface of the Moon rolling past as astronauts Frank Borman, James Lovell and William Anders read verses from the Book of Gen-

---

ted radio signals from other Soviet manned flights that ended tragically and were kept secret. However, so far the cross-checks of spaceflight historians (James Oberg and others) have found no evidence to support these claims and have pointed out their inconsistencies.

esis. The Christmas Eve broadcast from the Moon is the most watched TV event up to that time.

The Apollo 8 astronauts also take unforgettable photographs of their destination and of our home planet as a distant, delicate blue marble suspended in the blackness of the cosmos. The contrast with the harsh, lifeless lunar horizon could not be more eloquent and striking in its message to mankind (Figure 1-8).

Figure 1-8. Us. NASA photograph AS8-14-2383.

At least in the eyes of public opinion, the flight is an unmitigated American triumph that marks the defeat of the Soviet space propaganda machine. Little is said, at the time, about the disastrous conditions aboard the spacecraft: vomiting and diarrhea caused by space sickness, outgassing of sealant that fogged up the windows and hindered star sighting for navigation, water pooling dangerously in the crew cabin, and more.

But the race to the Moon isn't over yet. The actual landing is yet to be achieved, and the Soviet Union secretly hasn't given up on its ambitions to be the first to land a human being on the Moon.

1.5 The real conspiracy: secret Soviet moonshots

The Soviet Union has secretly been developing the N1-L3 system: a giant rocket, the N1 (Figure 1-9), as big as a Saturn V and capable of sending two cosmonauts towards the Moon in a vehicle, known as L3, that includes a lunar lander designed to carry one Russian to the surface of the Moon.

The N1, however, is underfunded and plagued by interpersonal rivalries among top Soviet

Figure 1-9. Preparing the N1 rocket.

rocket engineers. The thirty engines of its first stage are a nightmare to coordinate and control. The Soviet military oppose the project because they see it as an expensive propaganda gimmick with no practical military use, differently from all of Russia's previous space rockets, which were derived from nuclear weapon-carrying missiles.

The giant booster flies for the first time in February 1969 for an unmanned test and explodes 66 seconds after liftoff. The failure is kept secret, and in May the Soviet Union officially states that it does not intend to send cosmonauts to the Moon because it will not risk human lives in such an endeavor and will use only robot probes instead.

Figure 1-10. The Soviet lunar module (Lunniy Korabl).

The second launch is an even worse disaster. On July 3, 1969, days before the American Moon landing, an unmanned N1 falls back onto the launch pad moments after ignition. The explosion of its 2,600 tons of fuel is the most violent in the history of rocketry. This failure, too, is silenced.

Officially, for the Soviet Union the N1-L3 project never existed. It will continue in total secrecy for a few more years, testing the lunar lander (Figure 1-10) in Earth orbit, but after two more disastrous launch failures the N1 will be abandoned. No Soviet cosmonaut will ever walk on the Moon.

None of this will be known to the public for more than twenty years, but the US government is well aware of the Soviet attempt thanks to spy satellite

Figure 1-11. An N1 rocket on its launch pad, caught by a KH-4 Corona spy satellite. Credit: C. P. Vick.

photographs of the massive rocket and of its launch facilities at the Baikonur Cosmodrome (Figure 1-11). Other pictures also reveal the devastation of the pad after the second launch failure of the N1.

The US government, in other words, knows that Russia is out of the Moon race, but can't tell the public, because this would reveal the capabilities of its spy satellites and the political grounds for the Moon shots would vanish.

Secretly, there's no more rush to get to the Moon, but there's still a murdered president's pledge to be kept, and for public opinion, unaware of the N1 disasters, the race is still on.

1.6 Dress rehearsals, then the real thing

Kennedy's deadline is looming and the Apollo project advances at full speed. In March 1969, Apollo 9 flies in Earth orbit to test the lunar module, the navigation systems, the lunar spacesuits and the docking maneuvers.

In May, Apollo 10 soars to the Moon and rehearses every step of a Moon landing mission except for the touchdown itself. Apollo 10's lunar module carries Thomas Stafford and Gene Cernan to within 14.45 kilometers (47,400 feet) of the lunar surface.

The next mission, Apollo 11, takes mankind to the Moon, live on worldwide TV, landing there on July 20, 1969. Commander Neil Armstrong cautiously sets his left foot on the surface of the Moon at 10:56 EDT (July 21 2:56 UTC).

Lunar Module Pilot Edwin "Buzz" Aldrin then joins him (Figure 1-12) and together they plant the flag of the United States on the surface, conduct scientific experiments, collect Moon rock samples and take historic photographs while the third crew member, Command Module Pilot Michael Collins, waits in lunar orbit to take

Figure 1-12. Buzz Aldrin on the Moon. Detail of NASA photo AS11-40-5946.

them home and join them in the history books.

The Soviets make one last attempt to steal the show by trying to retrieve a lunar soil sample with the Luna 15 unmanned probe just before the American astronauts return home. But Luna 15 crashes on the

Moon while Armstrong, Aldrin and Collins are getting ready to return with 21.5 kilograms (47.5 pounds) of Moon rocks.[3]

Between 1969 and 1972, the United States lands astronauts on the Moon six times, with increasingly advanced, extended and complex missions. Apollo 11, 12, 14, 15, 16 and 17 carry twelve men to the surface of the Moon and return over 382 kilograms (842 pounds) of carefully selected lunar rocks and a wealth of scientific data that is still being used and analyzed today.

Figure 1-13. The Apollo 11 crew: Neil Armstrong, Michael Collins and Buzz Aldrin. Official NASA portrait, March 1969.

Apollo 13, too, is planned as a lunar landing mission but has to be aborted due to an oxygen tank rupture on the way to the Moon. The crewmembers (James Lovell, John "Jack" Swigert and Fred Haise) narrowly escape death, brilliantly aided by their skills and by the resourcefulness of Mission Control on Earth. Their space Odyssey captures the world's attention, highlighting the perils of space travel that the success of previous missions had caused many to underestimate.

The Apollo project was originally scheduled to end with Apollo 20, but political issues and the Apollo 13 near-disaster led to the gradual cancellation of the last three planned missions when their vehicles had already been built.

Since December 14, 1972, when geologist Harrison Schmitt and Commander Eugene Cernan climbed back up the ladder of

Figure 1-14. Aldrin, Armstrong and Collins in 2009, during a visit to the Smithsonian.

Apollo 17's lunar module and closed the hatch behind them after three days of lunar surface exploration, no human being has set foot on the Moon.

---

3   The Luna 1969B and 1969C missions, in April and June 1969, may also have been failed attempts to retrieve lunar soil samples (*Tentatively Identified Missions and Launch Failures*, Nasa.gov, 2005).

1.7 Post-Apollo explorations

After the Apollo missions, the Moon has been visited by many other unmanned spacecraft of various countries.

Between 1970 and 1976, Soviet automatic probes of the Luna series landed on the Moon, brought back small rock samples and traveled extensively over its surface, analyzing its soil and transmitting thousands of pictures.

Apart from the Soviet Union and the United States, no other country so far has achieved a soft landing of a manned or unmanned vehicle on the Moon. However, Japan, the US, Europe, China and India have explored the Moon in detail, and are still doing so, by means of Moon-orbiting probes such as Muses-A, Clementine, Lunar Prospector, Smart 1, Selene/Kaguya, Chang'e, Chandrayaan and Lunar Reconnaissance Orbiter.

Japan, India and the US have also crashed space probes intentionally into the Moon (Selene/Kaguya, Chandrayaan, LCROSS), creating artificial craters and generating debris clouds that have allowed remote analysis of the surface of the Moon.

Thanks to the vast amount of science data gathered by these probes, today we have an extremely detailed altimetric map of the entire lunar surface and know its geology in detail. For example, their ongoing work has allowed scientists to confirm the presence of water on the Moon.

The exploration of our satellite continues: several national and private missions with robotic landers are planned for the near future. However, there are no solid plans for manned trips back to the Moon.

In the decades after Apollo, human presence in space has been frequent, with Russian, American and Chinese flights which also carried astronauts from other countries and used advanced vehicles such as the US Space Shuttle, but it has remained very close to Earth.

Shifting from competition to cooperation, Russia, the United States, Canada, Europe and Japan have carried out joint missions and built the International Space Station, which has now been inhabited uninterruptedly for over twelve years and orbits the Earth at an altitude of approximately 400 km (250 miles). Nobody, however, has ventured as far as the Apollo crews.

The six Moon landings were seen at the time as a prelude to ongoing, ever-expanding manned space exploration, but today they appear to be destined for many more years to remain unrivaled adventures, extraordinary leaps forward whose early promise was later abandoned.

2. How we went to the Moon

Understanding the claims of Moon hoax theorists and the reasons why they're wrong requires at least a smattering of knowledge of the jargon, technology and stages of an Apollo moonshot. This chapter is mostly based on the Apollo 11 mission, the first Moon landing, but the basic concepts presented here apply to all the lunar flights.

2.1 The Saturn V rocket

The Saturn V-Apollo stack (Figure 2-1) stood 111 meters (363 feet) tall and weighed almost 3,000 tons (6.5 million pounds). Even today it is still the most powerful operational rocket ever built; only the failed Soviet N-1 exceeded it in terms of total thrust.

The Saturn V consisted of three stages, topped by the Apollo spacecraft, which carried three astronauts. The very tip of this stack was the Launch Escape System, a high-acceleration rocket designed to whisk the crew compartment with the astronauts to safety in case of an emergency during liftoff.

The first stage, known as S-IC and manufactured by Boeing, was 42 meters (138 feet) tall, had a diameter of 10 meters (33 feet) and was equipped with five enormous F-1 engines that

Figure 2-1. Apollo 11's Saturn V on the launch pad. Detail of NASA photo S69-38660.

gulped 13.3 tons (29,300 pounds) of kerosene and liquid oxygen *per second* at liftoff, lifting the entire rocket to an altitude of about 67 kilometers (220,000 feet) and accelerating it to a speed of approximately 9,900 km/h (6,180 mph) in a little over two and a half minutes. The spent S-IC stage was then jettisoned and fell into the Atlantic Ocean.

The S-II second stage used liquid hydrogen and oxygen to fuel its five J-2 engines and continue the climb to space, reaching a speed of almost 24,000 km/h (14,800 mph) and an altitude of approximately 182 kilometers (600,000 feet) nine minutes after liftoff. It was then jettisoned like the previous stage. Together, these two stages constituted nine tenths of the total weight of a Saturn V.

To reach the speed of 28,000 km/h (17,400 mph) required to orbit the Earth at an altitude of 190 kilometers (617,000 feet), the Saturn V needed the extra kick of its third stage, the S-IVB, which had a single restartable J-2 engine.

Less than twelve minutes after launch, the astronauts were already in a parking orbit around the Earth, where they checked the onboard systems. The spacecraft at this point had the configuration shown in Figure 2-3.

After one orbit and a half, two hours and forty-four minutes after liftoff from Florida, the third-stage engine was restarted and burned for almost six minutes, accelerating the spacecraft to 39,000 km/h (24,200 mph) towards the Moon, which was approximately 400,000 kilometers (250,000 miles) away: measured center to center, the Earth-Moon distance varies every 27.3 days from 363,100 to 405,700 kilometers (225,600 to 252,000 miles).

The spacecraft began coasting with its engines off towards its destination, gradually slowing down due to the Earth's gravitational attraction.

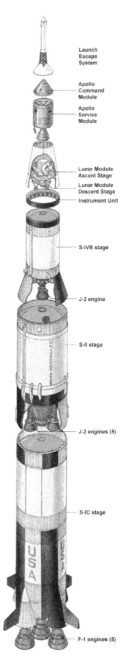

Figure 2-2. The Saturn V-Apollo stack components.

2.2 The Apollo spacecraft

The crew traveled in the pressurized cone-shaped Command Module (CM), shown at the top in Figure 2-3. The CM was 4 meters (13 feet) wide at the base and 3.5 meters (11.5 feet) tall, with a total cabin volume equal to the cargo body of a small van – and no toilet (bags were used for solids; liquids were dumped overboard through a tube).

It had small maneuvering thrusters, a heat shield to protect it from the heat of reentry, and three parachutes, as it was the only part of the giant rocket that returned to Earth.

Behind the astronauts there was the Service Module (SM), the cylindrical part near the top in Figure 2-3, which held the fuel for the main rocket engine of the Apollo spacecraft and for the sixteen maneuvering rockets (arranged in four cross-like clusters of four) and most of the oxygen, water, electric power and communication systems required for the mission.

A conical aerodynamic fairing, shown in phantom lines in Figure 2-3, connected the command and service modules to the third stage of the Saturn rocket (S-IVB) and enclosed the Lunar Module (LM), the spider-like spacecraft that would be used by two of the three astronauts to land on the Moon while the third waited for them in the Command Module.

Since the Lunar Module was to be used only in the vacuum of space, it didn't need to be streamlined and instead had to be as light as possible in order to reduce the fuel requirements and maximize its payload. Accordingly, it was stripped down to the absolute minimum: even the seats were sacrificed, so the astronauts flew the LM while standing.

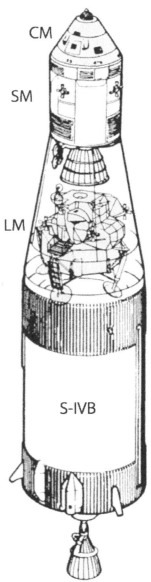

Figure 2-3. From the top: Command Module, Service Module, Lunar Module and S-IVB stage. Source: Apollo 11 Press Kit (enhanced).

The LM was 7.3 meters (23 feet) tall, weighed approximately 15 tons (33,000 lb) and was divided into two stages, shown separately in Figure 2-4.

The *descent stage* was the lower octagonal part, which had a single engine to brake the descent to the Moon, four shock-absorbing landing legs and storage compartments for scientific equipment, water, fuel and (from Apollo 15 onwards) an electric Moon buggy (the Lunar Roving Vehicle).

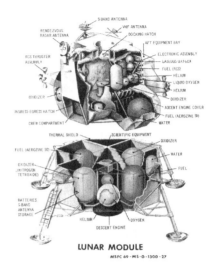

Figure 2-4. Cutout view of the Lunar Module.

The top part of the Lunar Module, known as *ascent stage*, contained the cramped crew cabin, some oxygen, food and water supplies, the onboard computers, the radio and television equipment and the single rocket engine used to climb back to orbit from the Moon. The ascent stage was equipped with sixteen attitude control thrusters (in four clusters of four, as in the Service Module) with their propellant tanks.

The astronauts viewed the lunar surface during landing through two small sloping triangular windows at the front of the ascent stage. After touchdown, they exited the vehicle by crawling backwards in their bulky spacesuits through a narrow square hatch and then climbed down along a ladder attached to one of the legs of the descent

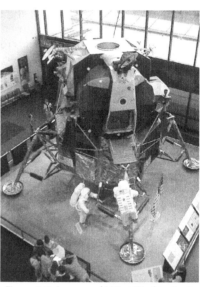

Figure 2-5. An unused LM at Washington's National Air and Space Museum. Credit: Wikipedia.

stage, as shown by the LM on display at the National Air and Space Museum in Washington, D.C. (Figure 2-5), and began their exploration of the Moon.

At the end of their stay on the Moon, the astronauts lifted off in the ascent stage and used the descent stage as a launch pad. The descent stage was left on the Moon.

2.3 Crucial maneuvers

Success of the mission and survival of the astronauts depended on some very tricky undocking and redocking maneuvers during the outbound journey and on a vital rendezvous while in orbit around the Moon.

A few hours after liftoff, the crew separated the Command and Service modules (CSM) from the rest of the spacecraft and positioned them slightly ahead by using the SM's maneuvering thrusters. The four panels of the fairing were released, exposing the lunar module. The astronauts then turned the CSM around, docked with the LM and extracted it from

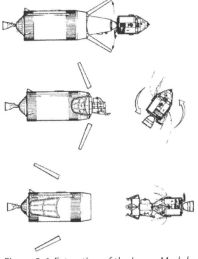

Figure 2-6. Extraction of the Lunar Module. Source: NASA Press Kit.

the S-IVB, the third stage of the Saturn V rocket (Figure 2-6).

The CSM and the LM then continued their flight towards lunar orbit, while the S-IVB rocket motor was restarted to nudge the spent stage away into an orbit around the Sun or, from Apollo 13 onwards, to crash into the Moon and produce a man-made moonquake, which was picked up by the seismometers placed on the lunar surface by previous missions, allowing scientists to probe the interior structure of the Moon.

The docked Lunar Module was linked to the CSM by a tunnel, through which the astronauts crawled to power up and check the vehicle and prepare it for descent to the Moon. As the spacecraft approached the Moon, the drag of Earth's gravity that had been gradually slowing it began to fade and Apollo's speed started to increase due to the pull of lunar gravity.

The astronauts turned the spacecraft around so that the Service Module's powerful main engine was pointing forwards. They had to achieve multiple carefully timed burns of this engine, as they swung repeatedly around the far side of the Moon, out of radio contact with Earth, in order to slow down and gradually achieve a stable, almost circular orbit around their destination, at an altitude of 100 to 120 kilometers (54 to 65 nautical miles) and a speed of approximately 5,900 km/h (3,700 mph).

The two astronauts that would walk on the Moon transferred into the lunar module, while their colleague stayed in the Command Module, and the two vehicles undocked. After flying in formation to visually inspect each other and run a final check of all onboard systems, the LM pointed its descent engine forward and fired it to begin the landing phase.

On the Moon there's no atmosphere to glide through with wings or parachutes. Descent depended entirely on the flawless operation of the descent stage's single rocket engine, which had to reduce the spacecraft's speed from 5,900 km/h (3,700 mph) to zero in about twelve minutes and then allow the LM to hover just above the lunar surface long enough to find a safe landing spot. Fuel reserves were tight and left little margin for error.

After landing, the astronauts performed one or more moonwalks (*Extravehicular Activities* or *EVAs*; Figure 2-7 shows Buzz Aldrin during the Apollo 11 EVA) to gather science data and samples under the watchful eye of a television camera that broadcast their activities live to Mission Control and to a worldwide audience back on Earth.

Figure 2-7. Buzz Aldrin on the Moon. Detail of NASA photo AS11-40-5872.

The Apollo moonwalkers had fully autonomous spacesuits, with oxygen, cooling systems and radio links in their backpacks. In the more advanced missions, they also used an electric car, the *Lunar Roving Vehicle* or *Rover*, to cover distances of as much as 35 kilometers (22 miles) during Apollo 17, the lunar mission which also set the total EVA duration record, with over 22 hours spent outside the Lunar Module during three moonwalks.

Once their lunar excursion was complete, the astronauts threw out all unnecessary weights and lifted off in the ascent stage of the LM. The timing and execution of this liftoff had to be very accurate in order to rendezvous with the Command and Service Module, in which the third crewmember was waiting for them in lunar orbit.

If the single ascent engine failed to fire, the lunar astronauts would be trapped on the Moon, with no chance of rescue. With narrow margins for error, If the engine didn't fire at the right time, with the right thrust and for the right duration, or if the trajectory was incorrect, they would not achieve the rendezvous and would perish in orbit or crash back onto the Moon. The third astronaut would have no choice but to abandon them and return to Earth alone.

The final rendezvous between the Command Module and the ascent stage of the Lunar Module (Figure 2-8) required docking the two spacecraft so that the moonwalkers could return to the Command Module with their priceless cargo of science data, Moon rocks, photographs and film footage.

The ascent stage of the LM was then jettisoned, subsequently crashing onto the Moon, while the instruments placed by the astronauts on the lunar surface radioed their data to scientists back on Earth.

The astronauts then rested, checked all the spacecraft's systems, and fired the Service Module's main engine again to accelerate and leave lunar orbit, heading home to Earth. The return journey took approximately three days.

Figure 2-8. The LM climbs back from the Moon. NASA photo AS11-44-6643 (cropped).

2.4 Fiery return

Shortly before contact with the Earth's atmosphere, the Service Module, too, was jettisoned. Of the 111-meter (363-foot) behemoth that had left Earth a few days earlier, only the small conical Command Module remained. It hurtled into the Earth's atmosphere at about 38,000 km/h (23,600 mph) with no braking rockets.

Air resistance slowed the spacecraft but also generated tremendous heat. Its heat shield had to cope with temperatures up to 2,700°C (5,000°F), and reentry had to occur at a very precise angle, between 5.5 and 7.5 degrees.

If the reentry angle was too shallow, the CM would slice through the thin upper layers of the atmosphere without losing enough speed and would end up in space again, with no chance of safe return. An excessively steep angle would overload the heat shield, turning the spacecraft and its occupants into a deadly fireball.

The astronauts also had to deal with violent deceleration (up to 7 g, which is equivalent to having seven times one's own weight).

The heat of high-speed reentry also produced a wall of ionized air, which blocked radio communications. The people in Mission Control, who had guided and supported the entire flight with their vast technical skills and resources, had no way to know the outcome of reentry until the spacecraft slowed sufficiently to resume radio contact.

Small drogue parachutes opened at an altitude of 7,000 meters (23,000 feet), followed by the main chutes at 3,000 meters (10,000 feet).

The Apollo capsule splashed down in the Pacific Ocean (Figure 2-9), where it was reached by a recovery helicopter, which hoisted up the astronauts on a winch with the aid of frogmen and then flew the returning spacefarers to a nearby aircraft carrier. Another chopper later recovered the spacecraft and its precious science cargo.

At the end of the early Moon landing missions, the astronauts donned airtight suits when they exited the Apollo spacecraft and were then quarantined in sealed quarters to guard against the remote chance of Moon germs (Figure 2-10). From

Figure 2-9. Splashdown. NASA photo AP16-S72-36293 (cropped).

Apollo 15 onwards, this precaution was dropped and the astronauts were free to join the celebrations for their safe return from a fantastic voyage.

Figure 2-10. Armstrong, Collins and Aldrin with US President Richard Nixon.

2.5 The true cost of Apollo

The manned Moon landings did not come cheap. In 1973, the total cost of the Apollo program was reported as 25.4 billion dollars over a ten-year period. In 2004, the Congressional Budget Office estimated this cost to be equivalent to roughly 170 billion in 2005 dollars.[4]

The Apollo project was widely perceived as an unsustainable and exorbitantly costly endeavor, despite the fact that the money was all spent on Earth and helped to train a whole generation of scientists and engineers and to develop countless technologies that we still use today.

---

4   *House Subcommittee on Manned Space Flight of the Committee on Science and Astronautics, 1974 NASA Authorization, Hearings on H.R. 4567, 93/2, Part 2*, page 1271; *A Budgetary Analysis of NASA's New Vision for Space*, Congressional Budget Office, September 2004.

This misperception contributed to the early cancellation of the project once its primary political goal had been achieved.

Through the years, the cost of Apollo and of space ventures in general has been consistently and greatly overestimated by American public opinion. For example, a 1997 poll reported that Americans believed on average that NASA drained 20% of the entire US budget, although the actual figure has always been less than 1%, with the exception of the Apollo era, when it peaked at 2.2% in 1966.[5]

By way of comparison, in 2005 the total expenditure for US defense was 493.6 billion dollars, social security outlays were 518.7 billion and Medicare/Medicaid outlays totaled 513 billion, according to the Congressional Budget Office. In other words, in recent years the US spent on defense *each year* three times the cost of the entire Apollo program.

Looking at it another way, getting to the Moon cost each one of the 202 million Americans alive in 1969 the grand sum of 84 dollars a year for ten years (in 2005 dollars). That's roughly equivalent to twenty packets of cigarettes per year per person. In fact, two years of US consumer spending on tobacco products, which is 90 billion dollars per year according to 2006 CDC estimates, would pay for the entire Apollo project.[6]

But in politics as in public opinion, perception often matters far more than reality.

* * *

This, in summary, is how a Moon mission was accomplished with 1960s-era technology: high costs, minimal margins for error, high chances of failure, no rescue options, with the whole world watching live on TV and a nation's prestige at stake. No wonder nobody has gone back to the Moon since.

---

5   *Public Opinion Polls and Perceptions of US Human Spaceflight*, Roger D. Launius (2003); *The Manhattan Project, Apollo Program, and Federal Energy Technology R&D Programs: A Comparative Analysis*, Deborah D. Stine (2009).

6   *Economic Facts About U.S. Tobacco Production and Use*, Centers for Disease Control and Prevention, Cdc.gov (2012).

3. The best evidence of the Moon landings

Moon hoax supporters claim to have countless items of evidence to back their views. In a face-to-face discussion it's often impossible to debate and debunk each item, as the second part of this book will do. However, there's another, more feasible approach: provide the clearest evidence of the fact that we *did* go to the Moon.

If we have simple, clear, bulletproof evidence that we actually landed on the Moon in 1969 and went back five more times, then all the conspiracy theorists' objections and items of alleged "evidence" must be wrong. End of story. Exactly *why* they're wrong is another question, which has a very revealing answer, but at least we can start on a very firm footing.

So is there any such clear, hard evidence of the Moon landings that can be understood by a non-expert? It might seem difficult to prove something that took place over forty years ago, on another world 400,000 kilometers (250,000 miles) away, since we can't go there and check – not yet, anyway – and most of the evidence comes from a single source, i.e., NASA, which clearly might have some interest in self-promotion.

But the answer is *yes*: there is hard, independent evidence of the Moon landings. However, it's not the kind of evidence you might expect and it provides a great opportunity to become better acquainted with the many fascinating aspects of space exploration..

3.1 Documentation

The United States' manned Moon landing program generated an immense amount of documents: technical manuals, plans and blueprints for even the tiniest spacecraft part, thousands of science articles, checklists, procedures, measurements, budgets, audits, contracts, purchase orders, inspection reports, press kits, mission reports, medical reports, experience reports, sample analyses, full transcripts of communications, and much more (Figures 3-1 and 3-2).

This documentation includes high-quality photographs, radio and television broadcasts, color film footage and telemetry data, as well as ground-to-air and onboard audio recordings.

The six Apollo Moon landings generated more than 6,500 photos and dozens of hours of TV recordings and movie camera footage. That's just the pictures and footage *on the lunar surface*, excluding the rest of the trip, which would bring the total to roughly 20,000 photographs.

NASA TECHNICAL NOTE   NASA TN D-2999

NASA TN D-2999

LUNAR LANDING AND
SITE SELECTION STUDY

by James L. Lewis and Charles D. Wheelwright

Manned Spacecraft Center
Houston, Texas

NATIONAL AERONAUTICS AND SPACE ADMINISTRATION • WASHINGTON, D. C. • SEPTEMBER 1965

Figure 3-1. An example of the vast documentation of the Moon missions: a landing site selection study dated 1965.

All this material has been publicly available for decades to anyone who asked for it and paid for duplication costs. Today it's also available on the Internet, on digital media or on paper (see the *References* section at the end of this book). Apart from occasional typos and minor errors, it is all completely self-consistent and in agreement with the space research conducted by other countries.

These documents have been studied for forty years by the world's leading researchers and are the basis for countless science and technology innovations that we use every day, from GPS navigation to mobile phones.

Today NASA's reports and data can be analyzed with techniques that didn't even exist at the time and that any 1969 fakery accordingly would have been unable to preempt. *If they were forged, the world's experts would know.*

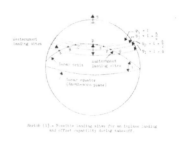

Figure 3-2. Another example of the publicly available Apollo documents.

Moreover, achieving such a massive, perfectly consistent and future-proof forgery would have been probably harder than actually going to the Moon.

Cross-checks

Rather amusingly, the most significant technical error found in forty years of expert examination of the Moon landing documents is that NASA claimed incorrectly that there were no photographs of Neil Armstrong walking on the Moon and that all the photos of the historic first moonwalk of Apollo 11 showed his crew mate Buzz Aldrin. Quite an embarrassment, considering that Armstrong was the commander of the mission and the first man to set foot on the Moon's surface (Aldrin joined him a few minutes later).

But in 1987 two researchers, H. J. P. Arnold and Keith Wilson, cross-checked the Apollo 11 radio communication transcripts and the astronauts' reports and realized that some of the photographs actually showed Armstrong and not Aldrin as NASA had claimed.[7]

The mistake was partly due to the fact that the moonwalk plan explicitly prescribed that only Armstrong would take photographs of Aldrin, but not vice versa. Moreover, the astronauts' spacesuits had no identifying markings apart from small name tags (starting with Apollo 13, this was fixed by providing the commander's suit with conspicuous red bands).

Thanks to this research, today we know that there are six full-figure or partial photographs of Neil Armstrong on the Moon: the best one is AS11-40-5886 (of which Figure 3-3 is a detail). Not much of a snapshot, but it's better than nothing. Most of all, it shows that independent cross-checks on mission data are feasible and effective and that NASA's word is not accepted unquestioningly.

It's also worth noting that NASA's error was found not by Moon hoax theorists, but by expert researchers, well-versed in spaceflight history, who patiently checked their sources and facts.

Unfortunately, this mislabeling went uncorrected for eighteen years, allowing it to spread and fueling the conjecture that Aldrin refused to take photographs of Armstrong out of spite because he had not been chosen to be the first man to set foot on the Moon.

The other photographs of Neil Armstrong on the lunar surface are AS11-40-5894 (in shadow, underexposed), AS11-40-5895 (just his legs),

---

7   *Spaceflight*, August and December 1987; *AS11-40-5886*, by Eric M. Jones, Nasa.gov (1995).

AS11-40-5896 (his legs again), AS11-40-5903 (his reflection in Aldrin's visor) and AS11-40-5916 (partial, from the back). Armstrong is also clearly visible in the Apollo 11 television and film footage.

The tale of this error prompts a question for Moon hoax believers: if the photographs of the first Moon landing were faked for propaganda reasons, then how come NASA didn't fake at least one iconic shot of the first man on the Moon that it could feed to the media?

Figure 3-3. Neil Armstrong on the Moon. Detail from photo AS11-40-5886.

The photographs

Many people believe that the Moon landings, especially the early ones, took only a handful of grainy, washed-out photographs, because that's what the media usually show, often relying on poor transfers of old copies instead of using pristine digital scans taken directly from the originals.

Actually, the first lunar landing mission, Apollo 11, took 340 high-quality photographs while on the surface of the Moon (217 from inside the LM and 123 during the actual moonwalk). The other trips took even more pictures: Apollo 17, for example, brought back 2,237 photographs taken on the Moon.

For many years, books, magazines and newspapers simply used the most dramatic and spectacular photographs of this vast collection and ignored the rest. But today the Internet makes it possible to distribute the entire set of photographs at virtually no cost and reveal the true variety and quality of these historic images.

Their detail is indeed superbly fine. The lunar astronauts used black-and-white and color film in 70 mm format, with three and a half times the area of regular 35 mm film: the same format used by most professional photographers at that time (Figure 3-4).

Figure 3-4. Armstrong, Collins and Aldrin inspect 70 mm film rolls. NASA photograph AP11-69-H-1247.

Their main cameras were custom-built by Hasselblad and mounted Zeiss lenses: the state of the art in mobile photography in the 1960s (Figure 3-5).

All these films are still carefully preserved by NASA and have been painstakingly digitized. The resulting scans are freely available online with resolutions of up to 4400 x 4600 pixels from websites such as Apolloarchive.com and Eol.jsc.nasa.gov.

These high-quality scans restore the original colors and detail to the Apollo photographs, offering us today a far more complete, fresh and spectacular vision of the lunar excursions of four decades ago than was available to most people at the time of the Moon missions.

Figure 3-5. A Hasselblad 500EL lunar camera.

Moreover, these pictures, besides being a beautiful testimony to the endeavor, allow anyone to cross-check the internal consistency of the documentation of the lunar landings.

For example, AS11-40-5903 (the famous "tourist photo" of Buzz Aldrin taken by Neil Armstrong during the Apollo 11 mission) is often published in the format and quality shown in Figure 3-6.

Figure 3-6. The classic photograph of Buzz Aldrin on the Moon, AS11-40-5903, as shown online by the JSC Digital Image Collection.

It also turns out that the original shot is quite tilted. Apollo 11's Moon camera didn't have a viewfinder: the astronauts took their pictures by pointing it roughly in the intended direction and relying on the wide viewing angle of the lens. This method usually worked, but in this case Neil Armstrong almost beheaded Aldrin, in the best tradition of tourist snapshots the world over. Indeed, Aldrin's stick-like radio antenna, located on the top of his backpack, is cropped.

For all these reasons, this photograph is often printed in the media by straightening it and adding a portion of fake black sky at the top.

Figure 3-7. A higher-quality, full-frame scan of the same photograph, AS11-40-5903.
Source: Eol.jsc.nasa.gov.

The high-quality scan reveals many details of the image that had been wiped out by the excessive contrast introduced by repeated analog duplication processes. It also restores the original clarity of the picture all the way to the horizon, with none of the fading caused by atmospheric haze in pictures taken on Earth, suggesting that the photograph was taken in a vacuum.

Also, the direction of the shadows and the inclusion of the footpad and probe of the Lunar Module allow us to locate Aldrin with respect to the vehicle.

Aldrin is standing with the sun behind him and to his left, but the sunlight reflected by the daylit surface all around him and by the metallic film that covers the LM fills in the shadows on his bright white suit.

These higher-resolution scans allow us to explore the Apollo photographs in ways that are entirely impossible with the usual media prints. For example, Aldrin's reflective visor holds the distorted mirror image of his surroundings. With this image quality and with today's digital imaging tools, it becomes possible to analyze the reflection.

The photograph can be flipped to reverse the mirroring effect and then color-corrected to remove the gold hue of the visor, obtaining the detail of Figure 3-8. This reveals the scene from Aldrin's viewpoint: the LM to the left, Neil Armstrong (taking the photograph) at the center, with the camera at chest level, the American flag above Aldrin's shadow and the vertical silver strip of the solar wind experiment to the right. Basically, we get to see what was behind the camera, and therefore we can cross-check.

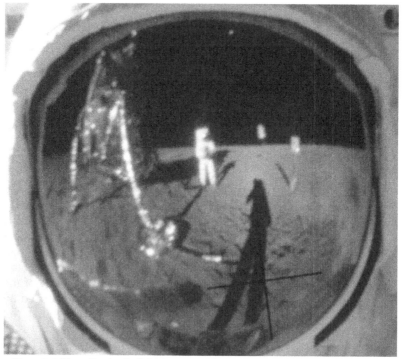

Figure 3-8. The reflection in Aldrin's visor in photo AS11-40-5903, reversed and color-corrected, reveals Aldrin's view. Credit: NASA, Kipp Teague, Apollo 11 Image Library.

For example, the portion of the LM footpad visible in the full picture corresponds exactly to the footpad reflected in the visor, and the positions of the flag and solar wind experiment match exactly the other photos and the TV and movie camera footage of the Apollo 11 landing site.

Faking not one, but *three hundred and forty* photographs at this level of resolution and detail and making them perfectly consistent with the live TV broadcast and the 16 mm movie footage would have been astoundingly difficult with the analog photo retouching techniques that were available in the 1960s. An even greater effort would have been necessary for the lunar missions that followed, with their hours of color footage and thousands of photographs.

But there's more. There's a tiny pale blue dot in the black sky reflected in Aldrin's visor, towards the top edge. That dot is right where the Earth would have been in the lunar sky, reflected by an astronaut's visor, if you had placed him where NASA says that Aldrin was standing for this picture: at the Apollo 11 site in the Sea of Tranquility, on the Moon, on July 20-21, 1969. You can check this with any good astronomy program. From a given point on the Moon, the Earth always has the same position in the sky relative to the lunar horizon (apart from slight changes caused by so-called *libration*), so the exact date isn't too important.[8]

This is just one example of the kind of cross-checking that can be done on the freely available data of the Moon missions. How hard would it have been to fake all this while keeping track of all these minute details? And if somehow someone pulled off such an amazingly detailed hoax, then how come the same people who bothered to get right even such trivial matters as the reflection of the Earth in an astronaut's visor forgot to put the stars in the photographs or didn't notice a suspiciously flapping Moon flag, as many hoax believers claim?

The live TV broadcast

This cross-checking also applies to the television pictures that were sent live from the Moon (Figure 3-9). Most moonwalk photographs were taken while the astronauts were in the viewing field of the lunar TV camera and therefore they can be compared with the television footage. In over forty years, not a single verified mismatch or discrepancy has surfaced.

The TV transmissions covered every minute of all the moonwalks (except for Apollo 12's, whose television camera failed a few minutes after the excursion had begun, and Apollo 14's, for which much of the moonwalk was off-camera).

---

8   Details of the analysis of the blue dot are in the *Apollo 11 Image Library* curated by Eric M. Jones and Ken Glover. The Earth appears tiny in the reflection in the photo because Aldrin's visor is a curved mirror, which reduces the apparent size of objects, especially close to its edge: it's the same effect seen in the passenger-side mirrors of many cars. Seen from the Moon, the Earth actually appears to be about 3.6 times as wide as the Moon is in Earth's sky.

This means that for the longer missions there are dozens of hours of recordings, with long uninterrupted sequences, all in color. All this material is available to anyone in unedited form, for example in the excellent DVDs sold by Spacecraft Films.

Figure 3-9. A frame from the Apollo 11 live television broadcast.

The live TV broadcasts also repeatedly show several phenomena that can only occur in an airless, low-gravity environment and could not have been faked with the special effects technology of the 1960s, as we'll see in detail later.

Film footage

The astronauts also used compact movie cameras loaded with 16 mm color film. Figure 3-10, for example, shows Neil Armstrong as he climbs down the Lunar Module's ladder to take mankind's first step on the Moon, as shot by Buzz Aldrin with the Maurer movie camera through the right window of the LM.

Figure 3-10. Armstrong climbs down to the lunar surface in a frame from the 16 mm film footage (cropped).

The first hour and a half of Armstrong and Aldrin's moonwalk is documented in sharp color on movie film as well as by the still photographs and the television broadcast. This footage, too, allows cross-checks.

For example, Figure 3-11 is a detail of a 16 mm film frame showing Aldrin's salute to the flag: this is the same moment captured from a different viewpoint by Armstrong's famous photograph (Figure 3-12).

Figure 3-11. Apollo 11: Aldrin salutes the flag while Armstrong takes his photograph. Frame from the 16 mm film footage (cropped).

Figure 3-12. Apollo 11: Aldrin salutes the flag. Photo AS11-40-5874.

Like the television broadcasts, this film footage is fully available and shows phenomena that could only occur in low gravity and in a vacuum, documented with the clarity and vivid color of film.

This is important because it adds further layers of complexity to any alleged fakery. Hiding special effects (for example wires to make the astronauts walk in apparent low gravity) in a hazy TV picture might be conceivable; hiding them from the much sharper eye of a movie camera is an entirely different challenge.

Moreover, these hypothetical special effects would have to be accomplished in long, unbroken sequences, without any of the editing and quick scene cuts used by Hollywood to hide the workings of its magic.

Other information sources

The wealth of information on the Moon missions that is publicly available is often greatly underestimated. For example, the complete timeline of all the moonwalks, with the commented transcript of *every single word* uttered on the Moon and every single photograph taken and action performed during the lunar excursions is freely available on the Internet in the *Apollo Lunar Surface Journal*.

Besides countless NASA manuals, handbooks and reports published online, there are many technical books, written by spaceflight experts, that cover the Apollo missions, such as the *Apollo Definitive Sourcebook* by Orloff and Harland, *How Apollo Flew to the Moon* by David Woods, and detailed non-technical accounts such as *Moonfire* by Norman Mailer and *A Man on the Moon* by Andrew Chaikin.

The autobiographies of the lunar astronauts (such as Aldrin's *Return to Earth* and *Magnificent Desolation,* Collins's *Carrying the Fire*, Cernan's *The Last Man on the Moon*) and of the flight directors at Mission Control in Houston (*Failure is not an Option* by Gene Kranz, *Flight* by Christopher Kraft) are also rich in technical details that clarify how we went to the Moon.

Moreover, there is an immense amount of footage covering every aspect of the design, development, evolution, manufacture, testing and launching of the Apollo vehicles. This material is now available both in raw, unedited form from websites such as Archive.org and Footagevault.com and on DVD and as part of many great documentaries, such as *When We Left Earth*, *In the Shadow of the Moon*, *For All Mankind*, *Moonwalk One* and others.

The Internet also provides access to many specialized sites that painstakingly document and catalog the history of spaceflight, such as the vast *Encyclopedia Astronautica*, as well as NASA's own websites. The "Moon hoax" claims are also examined and debunked in detail by experts in sites such as AboveTopSecret.com, Clavius.org and many others.

An extensive list of these resources is provided in the *References* chapter at the end of this book.

3.2 Cross-checking: the radio delay

A very good example of how all this technical material can be examined, verified and checked for consistency, even in unexpected ways, is the research conducted in 2009 by an Italian physicist, Luca Girlanda, and by the students of two high schools in his country. They downloaded from NASA's website the recordings of the radio communications of the Apollo missions from the Moon and noticed that the transmissions included an echo of the voices of Mission Control on Earth.[9]

The echo was caused by the fact that the radio signal from Earth reached the astronauts' headsets and was picked up by their microphones (Figure 3-13), so it was retransmitted back to Earth.

The students timed this round trip, which occurred at the speed of light: about 2.6 seconds for the Apollo 11 transmissions from the Moon. Then they calculated that this delay implied an Earth-Moon distance of approximately 393,000 kilometers (245,000 miles).

However, the Moon's distance from the Earth changes in the course of its monthly orbit around our planet from 363,100 to 405,700 kilometers (225,600 to 252,100 miles). That's quite a large variation, which causes the round-trip radio delay to

Figure 3-13. Neil Armstrong in the LM, tired but clearly pleased after mankind's first moonwalk. Photograph AS11-37-5528.

also vary between 2.4 and 2.7 seconds. So what was the exact Earth-Moon distance on July 20, 1969? Astronomers can compute the answer: 393,300 kilometers (244,400 miles). In other words, the radio delay that has remained dormant for over forty years in NASA's recordings is exactly what it should be.

A Moon hoax believer might object that introducing a fixed delay in the radio recordings would have been fairly easy. But there's more. The same high-school students also checked the radio communications of later missions, such as Apollo 17, which remained on the Moon for longer periods, and found that in NASA's original recordings *the delay is variable and matches exactly the variations of the Earth-Moon distance during that period*. That's the kind of minute detail that any hypothetical fakery would have to take into account and get right.

---

9 *Echoes from the Moon*, Luca Girlanda, INFN Sezione di Pisa, in *American Journal of Physics*, September 2009, vol. 77, Issue 9, p. 854-857. The paper takes into account the variations caused by Earth's rotation and by the fact that the transmitter and the receiver were not located in the geometric center of the respective celestial bodies.

3.3 Airtight conspiracy

Through the decades that have passed since the Moon landings, *not one* of the approximately 400,000 civilian technicians and engineers of the many aerospace companies who worked on the Apollo project has ever spilled the beans, not even by mistake or in a moment of alcohol-fueled exuberance.

No deathbed confessions, no leaked dossiers, no compromising photographs revealing the fakery. Even the Mafia can't achieve that level of airtight silence and secrecy. By contrast, the Soviet Union's top-secret Moon landing project and its humiliating failure, described in Chapter 1, became public within twenty years, despite the fact that they occurred in a closed totalitarian regime with sprawling censorship and secrecy systems.

Figure 3-14. Some of the engineers who built the Lunar Modules. Credit: Lawrence A. Feliu, Northrop Grumman History Center.

Conspiracy theorists occasionally announce that they have uncovered official documents, photographs or film footage that allegedly have been faked or somehow prove their claims. However, it has always turned out that the fakery was actually on the part of the hoax proponents or that these self-proclaimed detectives had cluelessly misinterpreted their findings, as any spaceflight expert would have told them if they'd bothered to ask.

Moreover, the incredibly tight-lipped engineers of the Apollo project aren't nameless faces: they're real people. Their names are public. They're civilians, not military personnel accustomed to secrecy. Many of them are still alive and quite willing to talk and write about their experience and work on the Moon missions. Yet no conspiracy theorist seems to be willing to accuse them individually, to their face, of faking the Moon landings.

Also, the Apollo project didn't just involve Americans. Scientists and engineers from all over the world took part in the science experiments and communications. The solar wind experiment was managed by Swiss researchers. The telemetry, television and radio links with the spacecraft were relayed by Australian and Spanish tracking stations. The knowledge gained from the Moon landings has been shared for forty years with scientists of all countries. Subsequent unmanned Moon missions of many countries relied on Apollo data. European astronauts have been trained by Neil Armstrong and other moonwalkers. Are all these skilled professionals too dumb to realize they've been hoodwinked for four decades?

Figure 3-15. Left to right: Ted Knotts, Richard Holl and Elmer Fredd celebrate in front of the Scan Converter at Sydney Video. The monitor is showing the Apollo 11 live broadcast. Aldrin and Armstrong are safely back inside the LM. Photo courtesy of Colin Mackellar, Honeysucklecreek.net.

3.4 The silence of the Soviets

As detailed in Chapter 1, the Soviets attempted to land a cosmonaut on the Moon ahead of the Americans. The two superpowers' standing in the world was at stake and a show of technological prowess would send a clear message to non-aligned countries that the Soviet Union was a powerful, modern and determined state that it would be wise to have as an ally. But the costly Russian attempt failed catastrophically and was kept secret. The Soviet government pretended that it had never tried to set foot on the Moon.

Therefore, if the Soviet Union had discovered that the American Moon landings had been faked – something which it was well equipped to do, through both radio eavesdropping and espionage – it would have had excellent reasons to reveal any American trickery and thus publicly humiliate its rival and enemy.

But it didn't. On the contrary, in an unprecedented gesture, Soviet state television announced Apollo 11's Moon landing and even broadcast excerpts from the mission's moonwalk. When the crew returned to Earth, Moscow Radio began its evening newscast by reporting that *"the courageous astronauts, Armstrong, Aldrin and Collins are again on our planet".* Soviet head of state Nikolai Podgorny wired US president Nixon after the Apollo 11 splashdown: *"Please convey our congratulations and best wishes to the courageous space pilots."* Many countries of the Soviet bloc issued stamps celebrating the Apollo 11 mission (Figure 3-16).

Figure 3-16. A Romanian stamp series describes Apollo 11 as the "first Moon landing of a human crew".

3.5 Moon rocks

The 382 kilograms (842 pounds) of handpicked samples of Moon rock brought back by the six manned landings are often mentioned as evidence that astronauts walked on the Moon. The nonterrestrial nature of these over 2,000 samples has been confirmed by the studies conducted by geologists from all over the world during the last forty years. Figure 3-17 shows one of these alien samples, known as the *Genesis Rock* because it is approximately four thousand million years old and is one of the most ancient rocks ever found. Dave Scott and James Irwin collected this 269-gram (9.5-ounce), 9-centimeter (3.5-inch) sample during Apollo 15.

A hardcore Moon hoax believer might object, however, that the Soviets, too, brought back rock samples from the Moon by using the Luna 16, 20 and 24 automatic probes, launched between 1970 and 1976 (Figure 3-18). Therefore it would be fair to argue that maybe the US did the same. Indeed, strictly speaking, the lunar rocks prove that the United States sent *vehicles* to the Moon but don't necessarily prove that *astronauts* went to the Moon.

However, there are substantial differences between the Soviet and American sample returns that allow us to include the Moon rocks among the evidence of human lunar landings.

First of all there's quantity. The total weight of all the Moon rock samples collected by the Russian robotic probes is 326 grams (11.5 ounces); the American samples weigh over a thou-

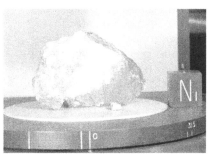

Figure 3-17. The Genesis Rock returned from the Moon by Apollo 15.

sand times more. This difference highlights the huge gap in performance between US and Soviet spacecraft. It shows that NASA was capable of sending to the Moon and returning home a far larger payload per mission than its Russian counterpart. Apollo 17 alone brought back 110 kilograms (242 pounds) of samples.

At the very least, this undermines the conspiracists' claims that the Saturn V booster was an inadequate Moon vehicle. If a single Saturn V rocket and the Apollo spacecraft were capable of returning 110 kilograms (242 pounds) of lunar rocks, it stands to reason that they were capable of carrying at least one astronaut to the Moon and back.

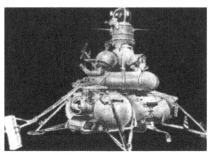

Figure 3-18. A Soviet Luna probe equipped for Moon soil sample return.

Then there's quality. The Soviet "rocks" are actually little more than coarse grains like the one shown in Figure 3-19, which is 2.5 millimeters (one tenth of an inch) long. It's smaller than a grain of rice. Moreover, the Soviet samples were not selected in any way. By contrast, the highly diverse Moon rocks returned by the United States weigh up to *11 kilograms (24 pounds)* each. Some are core samples taken by drilling up to 3 meters (9 feet) into the ground. The best the Soviets managed was a core sample weighing all of 170 grams (six ounces). It was the only sample returned by the Luna 24 mission, and this was achieved in 1976, seven years after Apollo 11.

How could all this have been achieved? Is it more likely that the US somehow, in the 1960s, had incredibly advanced secret robotic technology, or that it sent astronauts to the Moon with the geological knowledge and the right tools to choose the rocks and drill the core samples manually?

Figure 3-19. A sample of the lunar surface returned to Earth by the Soviet Luna 20 unmanned mission in February 1972.

One more thing. Any Moon hoax believer who raises the issue of the Soviet lunar samples paints himself or herself into a corner, because they're geologically identical to the ones returned by the Apollo missions and are different from Earth rocks. In other words, the Soviet rocks authenticate the American ones. Which means that any hoax believer who mentions the Russian Moon samples can't claim that the Apollo rocks are fakes.

3.6 Mirrors on the Moon

The "mirrors" placed on the lunar surface by the astronauts (Figure 3-20) are another frequently cited example of evidence of the manned Moon landings. Actually, they're not mirrors, but arrays of high-precision prisms, known as *retroreflectors*, that reflect light exactly in the direction from which it came, like a bicycle reflector.

Figure 3-20. The Apollo 11 retroreflector. Detail from photo AS11-40-5952.

These passive devices, requiring no onboard power for their operation, were placed by the crews of Apollo 11, 14 and 15. Even today, scientists can fire a high-power laser beam from Earth to the locations of these retroreflectors on the Moon and detect the light that they reflect back. The time it takes for the light to complete the round trip allows researchers to measure the Earth-Moon distance to within a few centimeters (inches) and to conduct many astronomy- and gravity-related studies.

However, they cannot be used as indisputable evidence of manned Moon landings, because the Russians managed to place their own retroreflectors on the Moon by using unmanned probes (Luna 17 and Luna 21, in 1970 and in 1973). They do prove that the United States, in 1969 and in 1971, were actually able to somehow place these devices exactly where they claim to have landed astronauts on the Moon.

3.7 Photographs of the vehicles left on the Moon

Can't we simply point a telescope at the Moon and see if the Apollo vehicles are there? It's one of the most frequent and common-sense questions regarding Moon hoax theories. The answer, unfortunately, is no: even the world's most powerful telescopes are currently unable to resolve such tiny objects at the distance of the Moon, for reasons detailed in Chapter 7. However, if a telescope were placed closer to the Moon, for example on an unmanned space probe, it could take pictures of the sites where NASA claims to have landed.

Actually, this has already been done. In 2009, NASA's Lunar Reconnaissance Orbiter probe (Figure 3-21) began a high-resolution survey of the entire Moon which is still in progress today. The probe's state-of-the-art mapping camera has taken many photographs of the landing or crash sites of many US and Soviet space probes, including the Apollo spacecraft. In 2011 it flew as low as

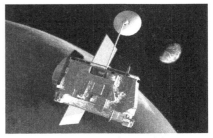

Figure 3-21. Artist's rendering of the Lunar Reconnaissance Orbiter.

22 kilometers (13.6 miles, 72,000 feet) in the vicinity of some of the Apollo sites and imaged details as small as 0.25 meters (about 10 inches).

The LRO images of the Apollo landing sites show that the descent stages of the Lunar Modules and the equipment left on the Moon by the astronauts are still there today, exactly where NASA described and documented them with on-site photographs, TV and movie footage over forty years ago. These images even show the parallel tread marks left by the wheels of the Rover and the lines of footprints produced by the astronauts. On the Moon there's no wind or rain to make them fade, so they're still there right now.

Figures 3-22 and 3-23, for example, are photographs of the Apollo 17 landing site taken by the LRO in 2011. They show the descent stage of the Lunar Module *Challenger*. Its sharp shadow reveals how high it protrudes above the surrounding surface. The ground around the LM is darker because it was disturbed by Cernan and Schmitt's boots.

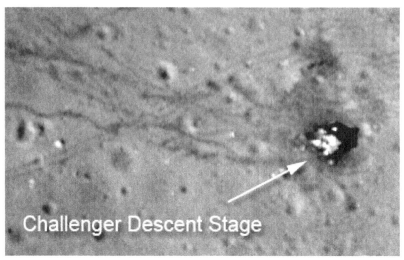

Challenger Descent Stage

Figure 3-22. The descent stage of Apollo 17's Lunar Module, photographed on the Moon by the LRO probe in 2011. Credit: NASA/GSFC/Arizona State University.

The Lunar Reconnaissance Orbiter has imaged the Apollo landing sites repeatedly and is still doing so periodically. For example, the larger white spot in Figure 3-24 is the descent stage of the Apollo 11 Lunar Module and the four dots around it are the LM's footpads, in different lighting conditions (respectively with the sun at a low angle and at a high angle to the local horizon, thus casting long and short shadows).

The arrows indicate the television camera (*TV*), the retroreflector (*LRRR*), the seismograph (*PSE*) and the line of footprints left by Neil Armstrong when he dashed to Little West crater, about 60 meters (200 feet) from the LM, and took a series of photographs, such as AS11-40-5961 (Figure 3-25),

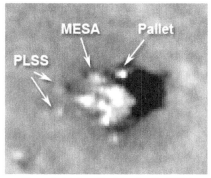

Figure 3-23. Detail of the Apollo 17 LM descent stage imaged by the LRO probe in 2011. PLSS indicates the astronauts' backpacks; MESA is the tilt-down equipment stowage compartment on the descent stage; Pallet is the payload transport pallet. Credit: NASA/GSFC/Arizona State University.

as attested by the radio communications recordings and by the mission reports. The TV recordings show the initial part of Neil's dash.

That's the level of cross-checking allowed by the Moon landing data. And there's more.

The LRO photographs of the Apollo 11 site can be compared with the lunar excursion map published in 1969 by NASA (Figure 3-26), which details the locations of the items left on the Moon and traces the astronauts' movements. It turns out that all the objects, the bootprints and the terrain details we find on the Moon today are almost exactly where NASA said they were over four decades ago. Figures 3-27 and 3-28 are images of other Apollo landing sites taken by the LRO in 2011.

Someone might object that the LRO is a NASA probe and therefore cannot be trusted. Actually, NASA only *launched* the probe: the LRO's camera and the analysis of its images are managed by a separate academic group, the LROC Science Operations Center at the Arizona State University, together with other scientific organizations. The LROC website provides the full list of participants.[10]

All these people, too, would have to be part of the massive cover-up, or someone would have to fake all the pictures

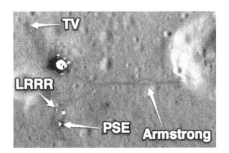

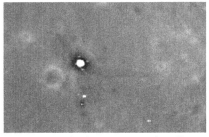

Figure 3-24. The descent stage of Apollo 11, photographed by the LRO with the sun at a low angle to the horizon (top, 2011) and almost overhead (bottom, 2009). Credit: NASA/GSFC/Arizona State University.

Figure 3-25. Neil Armstrong on the rim of Little West crater. The thin shadow on the right is cast by the ALSCC instrument (stereo macro camera for geology imaging). NASA photograph AS11-40-5961.

10   *Lunar Reconnaissance Orbiter Camera - Our Team*, lroc.sese.asu.edu.

that keep coming from the Moon. The fakery would have to be so perfect that the researchers at the Arizona State University and elsewhere wouldn't realize they were being duped. Considering that they're digital imaging analysis experts and that fake images would have to be generated whenever the LRO flies over the six Apollo landing sites and would have to take into account the ever-changing sun angle, that's quite a substantial challenge.

A single slip in any point of this process would reveal the entire decades-old conspiracy to the world, because the Lunar Reconnaissance Orbiter pictures are regularly posted on the probe's website.

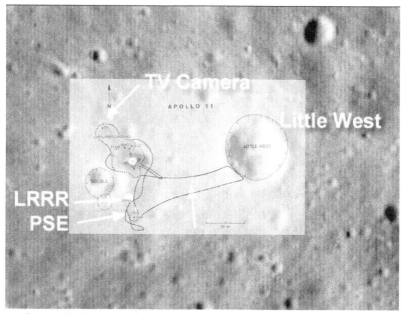

Figure 3-26. Comparison between the Apollo 11 Traverse Map (1969) and a site photograph taken by the LRO probe (2009). Credit: NASA/GSFC/Arizona State University.

It strains credulity to claim that any government agency could attain and maintain this level of absolute secrecy and perfection for over four decades.

Another, perhaps more sensible objection might be that the LRO photographs only show the *vehicles*, but obviously not the astronauts. But if so, how were the bootprints made? Did NASA send a robot with boots to the Moon, to trace the exact patterns faked on the movie set? *Six times?*

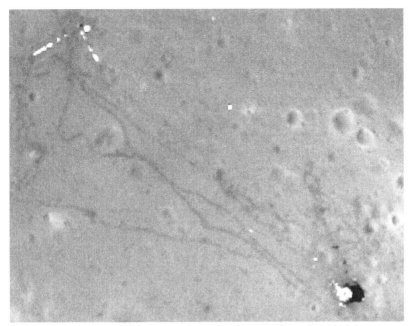

Figure 3-27. The Apollo 12 landing site, imaged by the LRO probe in 2011. Credit: NASA/GSFC/Arizona State University.

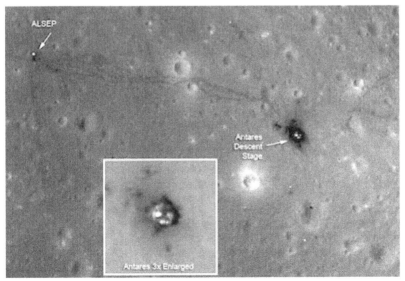

Figure 3-28. Detail of the Apollo 14 landing site, taken by the LRO in 2011. Credit: NASA/GSFC/Arizona State University.

3.8 Evidence, but not proof

So far we've seen strong indications of the authenticity of the manned Moon landings, which are quite convincing for anyone who considers the balance of evidence. They show that any attempt at fakery would have been absurdly complicated, but they aren't *proof*, strictly speaking. Certainly they're not definitive proof for a hardcore Moon hoax believer.

If we're looking for proof, what we need is something that demonstrates beyond doubt that in 1969 there were no bizarre robots in boots hopping around on the Moon, but that *human beings* were actually there. Something that documents an event that could have occurred only on the Moon four decades ago and in the presence of astronauts. Something preferably provided by an independent source, not by NASA.

Surprisingly enough, such proof exists.

3.9 Kaguya's 3D Moon maps

The Kaguya/Selene automatic Moon probe, launched by the Japanese space agency JAXA, spent 20 months orbiting the Moon, ending its mission in 2009 (Figure 3-29). Its laser altimeter had a vertical precision of 5 meters (about 16 feet), which allowed JAXA's scientists to generate highly accurate digital 3D maps of the Moon's surface. The map data are available at Kaguya's website.[11]

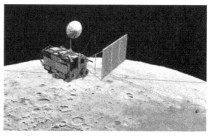

Figure 3-29. Artist's rendering of the Japanese Kaguya probe. Credit: JAXA.

The highly detailed pictures from Kaguya's camera can be combined with the altimeter's 3D terrain measurements to generate virtual views of the moonscape as seen from any point on or above the lunar surface.

The Japanese space agency's engineers tested Kaguya's systems by comparing their results with NASA's, using only their own data to generate a digitally rendered view of the lunar surface as it would appear if the observer stood at the site where the Apollo 15 astronauts took a series of photographs in July 1971 and looked in the same direction as they did. The comparison is shown in Figure 3-30 and speaks for itself.

---

11   *https://www.soac.selene.isas.jaxa.jp/archive/index.html.en.*

 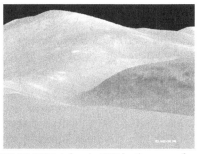

Figure 3-30. Left: a detail of NASA photo AS15-82-11122, taken in 1971 by the crew of Apollo 15. Right: the digitally rendered view from the same spot on the Moon, based on the 3D maps and photographs generated from the data of Japan's Kaguya probe in 2009.

The object on the far left in the NASA photograph is a portion of the Lunar Rover, the electric car used by the astronauts. Indeed, the other photographs of the NASA sequence include astronaut David Scott, who is working on the Rover, as can be seen in the composite picture shown in Figure 3-31.

Figure 3-31. Composite image of NASA photos AS15-82-11120, AS15-82-11121, AS15-82-11122 from the Apollo 15 mission (1971). The astronaut leaning over the Rover is David R. Scott.

In other words, in 1971 NASA published photographs that showed a lunar mountain range seen from a specific point on the surface of the Moon and included an astronaut and his vehicle. Thirty-eight years later, a Japanese probe went to the Moon, scanned that same mountain range and found that the view from that specific location matches exactly what NASA had shown nearly four decades earlier in the Moon landing pictures. How did NASA know in 1971 what that ground view looked like? How did it get a Rover and an astronaut in the picture?

Perhaps NASA secretly carried to the Moon a Rover, a dummy dressed in a spacesuit, and a robot that set them in position, took their photograph and returned the high-resolution film to Earth. But that would imply that in 1971 the US space agency was already capable of performing extremely complex Moon missions with substantial payloads. But if it had such an advanced capability, then it would have been able to put real astronauts on the Moon. Or maybe the US sent an automatic probe to the Moon in 1971 or earlier and gathered high-precision altimetric data of the contour of the lunar surface, or took photographs from ground level, and then built movie sets that replicated exactly the actual appearance of each Moon landing site.

It would be ludicrous to think that a government organization could carry out successfully such a complex operation in absolute secrecy, and do so six times, involving inevitably a very large amount of people to create the fakery, without anyone ever making mistakes or revealing too much, and with the risk of catastrophic humiliation in case of a slip-up. It would have been far easier to actually go to the Moon, and it would have been politically safer: even in case of failure, at least there would have been no danger of being caught faking it.

3.10 Telltale dust

There's another apparently trivial aspect of the visual record of the Moon missions that hoax proponents have great trouble explaining: the dust.

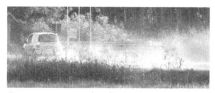

Figure 3-32. Dust cloud on a dirt road. Credit: PA.

On Earth, the dust kicked up by the wheels of a car, for example, stays in the air for a long time, producing a long billowing cloud that dissipates slowly, such as the one shown in Figure 3-32.

However, in the color film footage of the astronauts' electric car ride on the Moon the fine dust that it kicks up falls immediately to the ground in a parabolic arc (Figure 3-33). That's because on the Moon there's no air to brake its fall and keep it floating. This footage, therefore, must have been shot in a vacuum.

This unusual behavior of the lunar dust also occurs on a smaller scale when the astronauts walk. At every step, the dust they strike with their boots fans out and falls sharply to the ground. This is an especially conspicuous effect in backlit TV and film footage of the Moon missions* and can be glimpsed even in the footage of Apollo 11, the first lunar landing, as shown in Figure 3-34.[12]

Figure 3-33. Apollo 16's Rover kicks up dust, which exhibits an unusual behavior. Detail from a 16 mm movie film frame.

Figure 3-34. Detail from three successive frames of the 16 mm color film footage of Apollo 11's moonwalk: Aldrin demonstrates the fanning and sharp fall of moondust.

How could this have been achieved with the special effects technology of the 1960s?

Some hoax proponents have suggested the use of heavy, coarse sand, but nobody so far has been able to show that such sand actually behaves like the dust in the Apollo footage. It's not just a matter of falling sharply without forming clouds: it also has to change the way it reflects the light when it is kicked up, becoming very dark in some lighting conditions and extremely bright in others, as occurs in the Moon mission television recordings and movies.

Placing an entire soundstage in vacuum, including the fake astronauts, movie cameras, TV cameras, lights and stagehands, would have been a technical nightmare. Moreover, it would have required a truly immense vacuum chamber, since some Apollo footage shows the astronauts and their electric car walking or driving uninterruptedly for hundreds of meters (yards). Even today, the world's largest vacuum chamber, located at Plum Brook Station in Ohio, is only 30 meters (100 feet) in dia-

---

12 Samples of footage showing this behavior of the lunar dust are available in *The behavior of moondust kicked up by Apollo astronauts*, Moonhoaxdebunked.com.

meter. The Lunar Module alone would have filled one third of this chamber, leaving little room to walk around it. Again, it would have been easier and safer to actually go to the Moon.

The behavior of the dust is also eloquent in the Moon landing footage. When the Lunar Module is about to touch the ground, the dust scatters horizontally in straight lines, propelled by the LM's rocket exhaust, forming a thin, shallow mist that hides the details of the surface (Figure 3-35). As soon as the rocket motor shuts down, the dust settles suddenly, without billowing at all, and the ground becomes visible again.

Figure 3-35. The Apollo 11 landing in a frame from the 16 mm color movie footage.

It's interesting to compare the Apollo lunar landing footage with the Moon landing shown in *2001: A Space Odyssey*, a movie that at that time of its release in 1968 was the peerless state of the art in visual effects. The movie was directed by Stanley Kubrick, who is often mentioned by hoax proponents as the visual effects master who faked Apollo's photographs, television broadcasts and film footage.

It turns out that the behavior of the dust in *2001* is hopelessly wrong: it floats and forms swirling eddies (Figure 3-36). This means that the scene was shot in an atmosphere, not in a vacuum. If this is the absolute best that could be achieved with the special effects technology of the 1960s, how did NASA fake the Moon footage?

Figure 3-36. A Moon landing as depicted in 2001: A Space Odyssey (1968). Credit: MGM.

3.11 The size of the soundstage

People who claim that the Moon mission footage was produced on a movie set often fail to consider that many Apollo photos were taken in sequences while the astronaut-photographer slowly turned around. Therefore, these pictures can be assembled into huge panoramic images, as in Figure 3-37 from the Apollo 11 mission.

Figure 3-37. Composite image based on a sequence of photographs taken by Neil Armstrong during Apollo 11 (AS11-40-5930/31/32/33/34/39/40). Credit: Moonpans.com).

Achieving the same result with special effects would have required a colossal soundstage. The movie set, moreover, would have had to be lit entirely by a single, high-power light source, because multiple lights would have produced multiple shadows.

There's more. The Apollo missions that carried the Rover Moon car brought back footage from the onboard movie camera that shows the Rover traversing the lunar surface in uninterrupted sequences that last tens of minutes. For example, the color film footage known as *Traverse to Station 4* from the Apollo 16 mission lasts 25 minutes without breaks (these long durations were achieved by using low frame rates). This footage shows the changing surroundings and terrain under the Rover's wheels, which kick up dust that falls sharply to the ground.

Achieving this effect by using Hollywood-style tricks would have required a colossal movie set, and since the Rover is seen kicking up dust that falls sharply to the ground as it travels, that giant movie set would have to be entirely in a vacuum. All this would have to be lit by a single light source.

Hoax proponents might suggest a highly sophisticated scale model of the Rover and of the lunar surface, placed in a manageably smaller vacuum chamber. But that would not explain uninterrupted video sequences such as the one shown in Figure 3-38, which can be viewed on YouTube[13] and is taken from the live television broadcast of the Apollo 16 mission: it shows astronauts (impossible to simulate with models) walking continuously away from the camera until they almost disappear from sight, despite the camera zooming in, without ever reaching the far end of the alleged movie set.

---

13   *http://www.youtube.com/watch?v=4BDWVIbnJ3s.*

It is important to bear in mind that on the Moon there's no atmospheric haze that blurs the details of distant objects and provides a visual hint of distance and size. There are no familiar references, such as trees or houses, that can provide a sense of scale. Indeed, the rock that appears to be just behind the astronauts as they walk towards it turns out to be as tall as a four-story building (hence the name *House Rock*): as detailed in NASA's *Apollo 16 Preliminary Science Report*, it is 12 meters (40 feet) tall, measures 16 meters by 20 (50 by 65 feet) at its base, and lies 220 meters (720 feet) from the television camera, which is mounted on the Rover.[14]

It is really hard to imagine a secret movie set, placed entirely in a vacuum and lit perfectly by a single light source, of such gigantic size as to allow such a long, uninterrupted walk.

Figure 3-38. John Young and Charlie Duke (Apollo 16) walk from the Rover towards the boulder nicknamed House Rock, 220 meters (720 feet) away. On the left, House Rock can be glimpsed behind the leading astronaut. In the center, the camera zooms in to follow the astronauts. On the right, Young and Duke almost vanish behind the massive boulder (the arrow indicates one of their helmets).

For those who speculate that the Moon pictures were faked using painted backdrops to simulate the distant horizon, it should be noted that many photographs were taken as stereo pairs, which can be assembled digitally to produce 3D images that clearly reveal the actual depth of the scene. Several collections of these 3D photographs are available in NASA's *Apollo Anaglyph Albums* and can be viewed with red-blue glasses. The original picture pairs can also be edited by anyone to create a stereogram for glasses-free 3D viewing in color.[15]

3.12 The Moon walk proves the moonwalks

People who allege that the visual record of the Apollo missions was faked frequently claim that the astronauts' gait on the Moon was simulated by using wires or slow motion or both.

---

14 *http://www.hq.nasa.gov/alsj/a16/as16psr.pdf.*

15 *http://www.hq.nasa.gov/alsj/alsj-AnaglyphAlbums.html.*

In 2008, Discovery Channel's *Mythbusters* show put this claim to the test. Adam Savage, one of the show's hosts, donned a spacesuit replica and tried to simulate the lunar walk by slowing down the recording of his strides and by using a special harness that supported five sixths of his weight, simulating the Moon's low gravity, which is one sixth of the Earth's (Figure 3-39).

Both methods failed miserably. Direct comparison between the Apollo footage and the effect of wires and slow motion reveals glaring differences. The harness and wires reduce the effect of gravity on the fake astronaut's *body*, but not on the items he is wearing or carrying, which dangle and swing under full Earth gravity, giving away the trick.

Slow motion instead slows *all* of the simulated astronaut's movements, whereas the Apollo footage shows that the astronauts made quick arm and hand motions as they walked

Figure 3-39. Mythbusters *tries to simulate the astronauts' gait by using wires and slow motion. Credit: Discovery Channel.*

on the Moon. Achieving this effect through slow motion would have required the fake astronauts to move impossibly fast, so that their gestures would appear normal when slowed down.

There's only one way to achieve on Earth the fluid motions of the astronauts and the slow oscillation of the items they carry that we see in the Apollo footage: flying in a special aircraft which traces rollercoaster-like parabolic arcs (Figure 3-40).

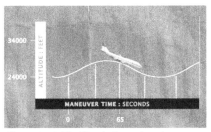

By adjusting the aircraft's speed and inclination appropriately, these arcs create brief periods during which the cabin conditions are equivalent to lunar gravity, just like a car driving at speed over a hill makes its occupants "float" for an instant. The effect is the best approximation of the zero- or low-gravity conditions of spaceflight. In-

Figure 3-40. The Vomit Comet's trajectory as described by Mythbusters. *Credit: Discovery Channel.*

deed, this is how Apollo astronauts trained for their spacewalks and moonwalks. The same technique was used for some of the zero-gravity shots in Ron Howard's great movie *Apollo 13* and is still used today to train current astronauts. Not unsurprisingly, the aircraft is known as *Vomit Comet*.

Mythbusters performed flights that used this method and obtained footage showing a very smooth gait that matches exactly the Apollo moonwalk footage without resorting to wires or slow motion (Figure 3-41).

One might wonder whether this method could have been used to shoot fake moonwalks in the 1960s, but there's a catch: the low-gravity effect produced in this way only lasts a few seconds at a time. Moreover, it occurs within the cramped

Figure 3-41. Mythbusters' *Adam Savage moonwalks in simulated one-sixth gravity in the padded cabin of the Vomit Comet. Credit: Discovery Channel.*

space of an aircraft cabin. The Apollo footage instead includes uninterrupted hour-long shots taken in very large spaces.

Also, we've seen that the visual record of the Moon missions shows phenomena that can only occur in a vacuum, such as the behavior of the dust. The cabin, therefore, would have to be a colossal top-secret flying vacuum chamber capable of hour-long parabolic arcs. Once again, flying to the Moon would have been easier.

Shooting fake Moon footage underwater might also be considered. Carefully adjusting the buoyancy of every single item carried and worn by the astronauts could provide a credible visual appearance of low gravity. However, this technique would require an immense and very deep tank filled with crystal-clear water, and a single stray bubble would reveal the fakery. Besides, in an underwater environment the simulated moondust would not fall back suddenly as it does in the Apollo footage: it would tend to float and swirl about, once again giving away the trick.

Indeed, the key problem of faking the Apollo moonwalk footage isn't achieving a single visual effect, but *achieving them all simultaneously* and for long, unbroken sequences, which must all be perfectly consistent, because the TV footage must match the film footage and both must match the photos.

In a nutshell: in the 1960s, the only way to obtain footage of astronauts walking on the Moon as shown by the Apollo visual record was to actually go to the Moon, and if the Apollo footage is authentic, so are the Moon landings.

3.13 Attempted simulations in movies

Even the best visual effects of today often fail to recreate authentically and simultaneously all the physical phenomena observed in the original Apollo lunar footage.

For example, Michael Bay's blockbuster *Transformers – Dark of the Moon* (2011), in which the Apollo 11 mission plays a key part and is reconstructed extensively, gets the lunar dust wrong: Neil Armstrong's first step kicks up a cloud of dust, revealing that the scene was not shot in vacuum (Figure 3-42).

Figure 3-42. A still from Transformers 3 *reveals a mistake in the special effects: the moondust billows instead of falling in arcs, as it should in a vacuum. Credit: Paramount Pictures.*

The TV series *From the Earth to the Moon* (1998), produced by Tom Hanks, Ron Howard and Brian Grazer, is considered one of the most accurate reconstructions of the moonwalks, which were simulated in a huge soundstage by attaching large helium-filled balloons to a harness inside the spacesuits, so as to give the astronaut-actors a visual buoyancy similar to lunar gravity.

The sharply outlined shadows of the original Apollo images were obtained by lighting the entire set with a single light source: a 2-meter (6-foot) convex mirror onto which twenty of the most powerful spotlights available in the film business projected their beams. The production even featured an original lunar module, a leftover of the canceled

Apollo 18, 19 and 20 missions. Yet despite these amazing efforts, the beautiful visual effects sequences of the show lack other phenomena, such as the correct behavior of lunar dust as the astronauts walk.

The IMAX documentary *Magnificent Desolation: Walking on the Moon 3D* (2005), also featuring Tom Hanks among its producers, finally got the moondust right (Figure 3-43) and also solved the challenge of camera and set reflections in the mirror-finished spacesuit helmet visors. However, these feats were achieved by resorting to digital visual effects, which were not available in 1969.

Figure 3-43. Digitally generated moondust being kicked up by an astronaut in Magnificent Desolation: Walking on the Moon 3D. *Credit: IMAX Corporation.*

3.14 An impossible feat

In summary, here's the best evidence that the Moon missions were authentic:

- vast amounts of publicly available documentation, which can be cross-checked and has been validated by experts from all over the world for more than forty years

- highly complex and perfectly realistic radio and television signals

- not a single confession or leak in over four decades

- no objections by the rival Soviet regime

- no objections by any expert in spaceflight, astronomy, astrophysics, radio communications or any other relevant field

- carefully selected Moon rocks returned to Earth

- reflectors placed on the Moon, which can be checked even today

- recent photographs of the Apollo vehicles and instruments left on the Moon, which are consistent with the forty-year-old NASA documents of the lunar missions

- pictures that could only be taken in the presence of an astronaut on the Moon and have been confirmed independently by non-US space missions

- dust that behaves in the Apollo footage in a way that is possible only in a vacuum

- astronauts walking in a way that is possible only in one-sixth gravity.

In view of all these facts, the inescapable conclusion is that the Moon hoax theorists are right about the Moon landings in one respect: it's true, as they often say, that the technology of the 1960s was not up to the challenge.

The challenge of faking them.

4. Moon hoax proponents and popularity

You might wonder whether the many Moon hoax conspiracy theories are really worth debunking in detail, especially after reading the previous chapter. It's easy to think of these theories as the delusions of a small bunch of oddballs or as the concoctions of peddlers of ultimate truths seeking followers who are easily parted from their money.

But Moon hoax theories and doubts about the Moon landings are widespread in public opinion. Try an informal poll among your friends and relatives and you'll notice this, especially in younger people. Modern cynicism and distrust of government, the passage of time and the gradual passing of the living witnesses of the Apollo missions will increase the appeal of conspiracy theories if nothing is done to expose their fallacies. These are the same processes that, on a very different level, feed Holocaust denial.

Besides, dealing with these claims is an excellent opportunity to retell the fascinating story of the Moon missions in a way that's not pedantic but often lively and sometimes truly amusing.

4.1 How many people believe these theories?

Between 1995 and 2013, the percentage of American adults who believe that the Moon landings were faked in some way has remained stable around 6%.

In 1995, a Time/CNN/Yankelovich Partners, Inc. poll found that 6% of Americans believed that *"the government staged or faked the Apollo Moon landing"*, whereas 83% disagreed and 11% said they had no opinion. A similar Gallup poll taken in 1999 indicated the same 6% figure, but with 89% disagreeing and 5% having no opinion.[16]

A 2001 Zogby poll yielded essentially similar results: 7% hoax believers, 87% convinced that the Moon landings were real and 4% not sure.[17]

---

16 *Landing a Man on the Moon: The Public's View,* by Frank Newport, Gallup.com (1999).

17 *As Seen on This Morning's NBC Today Show: Truth or conspiracy: Lunar landing – Did the mission to the Moon really get off the ground?*, Zogby.com (2001).

Public Policy Polling found similar results in a 2013 US voter poll: 7% supported the claims of fakery, 9% were not sure and 84% said they believed the Moon landings were real.[18]

Six or seven percent might seem a small figure, and Gallup explains that the margin of error in its poll was 3%, adding that *"it is not unusual to find about that many people in the typical poll agreeing with almost any question that is asked of them",* but even so it means that several million Americans believe Moon hoax theories.

Moreover, the figure is considerably higher in a specific age group: young people. A poll taken in 2006 by Dittmar Associates among young American adults indicated that 27% expressed some doubt that NASA went to the Moon, with 10% of the overall sample indicating that it was *"highly unlikely"* that a manned Moon landing had ever taken place.[19] The Zogby poll mentioned earlier concurs, noting that *"fewer 18-29 year olds than any other age group believe the Moon landing occurred".*

Informal polls in other countries suggest highly variable percentages of hoax believers. In the United Kingdom, a 2008 Internet poll on a sample of 1000 people, arranged by 20th Century Fox for the launch of the movie *X-Files: I Want to Believe,* indicated that 35% of the participants thought the Moon landings were faked. A 2009 survey yielded an estimate of 25%.[20]

In Germany, an ongoing Internet poll launched in 2001 by *Der Spiegel* magazine reported that 47% of the participants agree with hoax theories. Other similar surveys suggest hoax theory support at 44-62% of participants in France, 40% in Sweden, and 49% in Russia.[21] However, these polls are not based on a statistically representative sampling of the population, but rely on volunteer participation, and since hoax theory supporters tend to be rather active in spreading their beliefs these percentages should be considered with a degree of caution.

Moon hoax belief also has significant political overtones. Admitting that Americans landed on the Moon entails acknowledging their technological superiority, and some ideologically-driven people and regimes aren't very keen to do so.

---

18 *Democrats and Republicans differ on conspiracy theory beliefs,* PublicPolicyPolling.com, 2 April 2013.

19 *Engaging the 18-25 Generation: Educational Outreach, Interactive Technologies, and Space,* Mary Lynne Dittmar, in *AIAA 2006-7303* (American Institute of Aeronautics and Astronautics).

20 *US Base Leads Poll's Top Conspiracy Theories,* in *The Guardian,* July 31, 2008; *Britons Question Apollo 11 Moon Landings, Survey Reveals,* in *E&T Magazine,* 2009.

21 *Ein kosmischer Streit,* Spiegel.de; *L'Homme a-t-il marché sur la Lune?,* 20min.ch; *Pensez-vous que l'homme a marché sur la lune?,* Pourourcontre.com; *Tror du att den första månlandningen var en bluff?,* Aftonbladet.se; Cnews.ru. Polls surveyed in June 2013.

For example, space historian and journalist James Oberg noted in 2003 that *"many Cuban schools, both in Cuba and where Cuban schoolteachers were loaned, such as Sandinista Nicaragua, taught their students that Apollo was a fraud".*[22]

When British documentary film maker Sean Langan was kidnapped by the Taliban in the Afghanistan-Pakistan border region in 2008, *"during his three-month ordeal he was interrogated by his captors many times and he was often surprised by what they wanted him to confess to. One subject they kept returning to were the Moon landings. They refused to believe that America had put men on the Moon and, again and again, they tried to browbeat him into admitting that NASA's programme of manned space flight had been an elaborate hoax."*[23]

Anti-Americanism is a significant driving force behind lunar conspiracy claims, like it is for theories regarding the 9/11 attacks and UFOs, even in some moderate countries where popular resentment against US government policies is widespread. Within the United States, this resentment takes the form of a specific distrust of the federal government and of authorities in general, as clearly shown by the writings of Bill Kaysing, Ralph Rene and many other Moon hoax theorists.

4.2 Healthy doubt versus misinformed paranoia

People who have no doubts that the Moon landings really happened often make the mistake of thinking that hoax theorists are all stupid and paranoid. This misconception is a frequent cause of embarrassment when it turns out that people whom they hold otherwise in high esteem are doubters or conspiracy believers.

Unquestionably, some of the hoax theory supporters are very paranoid: they believe not only in the Moon hoax but also in the many other conspiracy theories that are especially abundant on the Internet, such as "chemtrails", 9/11, the Kennedy assassination, earthquakes controlled by the US military, alternative medical treatments suppressed by multinational pharmaceutical companies, contacts with extraterrestrials covered up by the world's governments and all

---

22 *Lessons of the "Fake Moon Flight" Myth*, in *Skeptical Enquirer*, March/April 2003, Jamesoberg.-com; *Getting Apollo Right*, ABC News, 1999, ABCnews.go.com. It should be noted that Oberg based his claim on just three anecdotal reports and that Moon landing denial does not appear to be the current position of the Cuban government, at least according to the official Ecured.cu encyclopedia.

23 *Obama's cancellation of moon landings is a case of 'No we can't', not 'Yes we can'*, by Toby Young, *The Telegraph*, 2010, Telegraph.co.uk.

sorts of secret power cliques, from "international banking cartels" (a euphemism for Jews) to the Illuminati and the Reptilians.

However, not everyone who leans towards alternative theories regarding the Moon missions is like that. There's nothing wrong in questioning any officially dispensed truth, at least until it is corroborated by reliable independent sources. After all, governments do lie and conspire, as was shown at the time of the Apollo flights by the Watergate scandal and the misinformation about the war in Vietnam.

Many people are simply misinformed or not informed at all: they have only seen some of the many Internet sites and TV programs that support the Moon hoax theories and are unaware of the immense amount of information and evidence that debunks them. Part of the reason is that most of the in-depth evidence is only available in highly technical jargon.

There's also nothing stupid or paranoid in being seduced by the powerful, professionally packaged images of a biased television show designed to grab attention at any cost. We're naturally inclined to assume that what we see in a documentary or a book is true and authoritative because it's backed by a publisher or a national radio or TV network and it's labeled as journalism. Sadly, that's not always true.

The difference between a poorly informed or misinformed person who has doubts and a hardcore conspiracy theorist is very simple. The doubter, after being presented with all the facts, realizes that he or she has been misled and accepts those facts; the conspiracy theorist will deny the evidence, hold on to some trivial unexplained detail as if it were definitive evidence of the hoax, and often accuse those who argue that the Moon landings were real of being "sheeple" or paid shills of America or of the hidden forces that organized the conspiracy.

Basically, a Moon hoax believer is someone who after being shown that two plus two is four, keeps on arguing that it's actually five. Spending time in a debate with such people is therefore pointless. It is instead time well spent with a doubter, who will often be grateful after seeing all the evidence that has dispelled his or her doubts. So if you decide to debate, choose your sparring partner wisely.

Wide but shallow media coverage

One of the reasons why some people have been taken in by Moon hoax theories is that the media coverage during the Apollo missions was vast but nonetheless surprisingly shallow if compared to today's drinking-from-a-fire-hose standards.

In the Sixties and Seventies it was very complicated and prohibitively expensive for an ordinary person, especially outside the United States, to go beyond what was offered by the media and obtain copies of NASA's technical reports or of a complete, high-resolution series of the photographs taken on the Moon, which would have to be printed or microfilmed and mailed.

The only sources of readily available information were the press and the radio and TV networks: most people got only what these sources deemed fit to broadcast or publish, which rarely included technical minutiae. Astronomy and aviation magazines provided more detail, but they were read only by enthusiasts; the general public didn't get that kind of in-depth information. Today, instead, thousands of pages of original, complete technical reports and tens of thousands of Apollo photographs are just a click away on the Internet.

Information regarding the Moon flights was also politically sensitive and therefore subject to control, not necessarily as censorship by government order but as self-censorship of news organizations, which often chose to promote America's image of technical prowess and declined to publish unsavory details that would spoil it and damage the political competition with the Soviets on the world's highly volatile stage.

The end result was a widespread but false impression of magically flawless missions, on which Moon hoax theorists often prey. At the time, only the people who were closely involved in the Moon missions knew otherwise. Today, now that the Cold War is essentially over and many confidential files (such as spy satellite photographs of the Soviet lunar spacecraft and N-1 booster) have been released by the US and Russian governments, everyone can find out how things actually went. It's a fascinating journey of discovery even for non-doubters.

This dearth of material to show and the highly technical nature of the subject sometimes led the media to publish their own little Moon hoaxes. For example, for Apollo 11's first Moon landing, the front page of Italian newspaper *Il Messaggero* of July 21, 1969 was noted by *Time* magazine, and is currently featured in the Kennedy Space Center exhibition, for spectacularly covering three-quarters of its front page with three words: *"Luna – Primo Passo"* (*"Moon – first step"*). But since the now-famous photograph of Buzz Aldrin's bootprint was not available at the time (it was still undeveloped in a Hasselblad film magazine on the Moon), the newspaper nonchalantly faked it by using the print of an ordinary fishing boot (Figure 4-1).

Of the thousands of photographs that were taken, the general public only got to see the small set chosen and published by newspapers and magazines or issued by NASA, and even those images suffered from several analog transfers that eroded the quality and sharp detail of the originals (Figure 4-2).

The color film and television recordings were available only when they were broadcast by the TV networks or shown in movie theaters, often in the form of faded, grainy, low-quality transfers that don't do justice to the actual clarity and definition of the originals.

Figure 4-1. The front page of Italian newspaper Il Messaggero, *July 21, 1969.*

Figure 4-2. Buzz Aldrin on the Moon during the Apollo 11 mission (cropped). Left: scan of an original 1975 NASA print of photo AS11-40-5949. Right: scan taken directly from the original film and now downloadable from NASA's website.

Today, instead, anyone can buy DVDs and Blu-ray discs with direct digital scans and transfers of the entire Apollo visual record and view the original detail and the pictures that the media, at the time of the Moon landings, didn't show due to inevitable space and time constraints. The complete recordings of the radio transmissions of all the missions are also available to download. Even the audio and transcripts of Apollo 11's onboard voice recorders are now online in NASA's archives[24] and at Live365.com.[25] Rather paradoxically, we have a far more complete and detailed coverage of the Moon landings today, over forty years later, than we had while they were taking place.

Media misdirection

There were no live TV transmissions from the Apollo spacecraft during the lunar module's descent to the surface of the Moon, so most newspapers covered the first Moon landing by showing artist's renderings of the event. For Walter Cronkite's famous live TV coverage of the Apollo 11 landing, CBS showed an animation which was timed to match the scheduled timetable of the landing but went confusingly out of sync when Neil Armstrong delayed the actual touchdown to find a safe landing spot (Cronkite, however, correctly announced *"We're home. Man on the Moon!"* and exclaimed his famous *"Oh, boy!"* after Armstrong had radioed that the LM had landed).

These renderings and animations were dramatically effective but often quite inaccurate in their artistic license and created misleading expectations in the public. For example, they almost invariably depicted visible stars and a bright, fiery exhaust plume from the LM's descent engine, although in actual fact the stars would be too faint to see against the glare of the daylit lunar surface, and the LM engine plume was colorless and essentially invisible in the vacuum of space. Aesthetics took precedence over scientific accuracy, and the visible exhaust was also a very convenient visual shorthand to explain how the spidery spacecraft could fly and hover in a vacuum. Moreover, the same inaccuracy occurs in many NASA illustrations.

A truly unbelievable journey

Other extenuating circumstances must also be considered when looking back at the birth of Moon hoax theories. The space age had begun only *twelve years earlier*: Sputnik, the world's first artificial satellite, had

---

24   *http://www.nasa.gov/mission_pages/apollo/40th/apollo11_audio.html.*

25   *http://www.live365.com/stations/apollo_11_oda.*

been launched in 1957. The first human space flight had occurred in 1961, yet just eight years later mankind was walking on the Moon. In a world that had just begun to see the introduction of jet airliners to replace propeller-driven aircraft, this kind of progress was literally beyond belief. Many people simply didn't have the time to get accustomed to the reality of spaceflight.

Moreover, until Apollo 8 flew around the Moon in 1968, no human flight had ever gone beyond low Earth orbit. Going to the Moon meant flying suddenly three hundred times farther than any other manned mission – the previous record belonged to Gemini 11, which had attained an altitude of 1,374 kilometers (854 miles) – and reaching a highly symbolic destination.

In other words, it should not be a surprise that the Moon missions were met with some disbelief. Considering that all subsequent human spaceflights, even Shuttle and Soyuz missions to the International Space Station or to service the Hubble Space Telescope, have never climbed more than 600 kilometers (372 miles) away from the Earth's surface, it's almost understandable that there is still some doubt about the Apollo flights, which forty years ago reached a distance of *four hundred thousand kilometers (nearly a quarter of a million miles)*.

Such vast distances are hard to visualize. Consider that if you shrunk the Earth to a 40-centimeter (16-inch) ball, the Moon would be 10 centimeters (4 inches) in diameter and the Earth-Moon distance would be 11 meters (36 feet). At this scale, a flight to the International Space Station would rise above the Earth by *a single centimeter (less than half an inch)*.

4.3 Origins and history of Moon hoax theories

Hoax claims regarding the manned lunar missions are not a recent phenomenon. In his book *A Man on the Moon*, Andrew Chaikin notes that they circulated even before the landings, questioning Apollo 8's flight around the Moon in December 1968.

There are anecdotal reports of doubters in the newspapers of the time,[26] but it's difficult to find any hard figures. One year after the first Moon landing, an informal US poll by Knight Newspapers reported that over 30% of the 1,721 respondents were suspicious of NASA's claims.[27]

---

26 *A Moon Landing? What Moon Landing?* by John Noble Wilford, *New York Times*, 18 December 1969, p. 30.

27 *The Wrong Stuff*, in *Wired* 2.09, September 1994, Wired.com; *Newsweek*, 20 July 1970; *Many Doubt Man's Landing on Moon*, *Atlanta Constitution*, 15 June 1970.

The figure rose to 54% among African Americans, although space historian Roger D. Launius notes that this *"perhaps said more about the disconnectedness of minority communities from the Apollo effort and the nation's overarching racism than anything else."[28]*

Many sources report that the very first pamphlet dedicated to the subject was *Did Man Land on the Moon?* by mathematician James J. Cranny, who self-published it in Johnson City, Texas, in 1970. Little is known, however, about its content or its author.

Moon hoax claims were soon referenced in popular culture. For example, in the movie *Diamonds are Forever* (1971), secret agent James Bond escapes by driving a stolen "Moon car" through a wall of an elaborate set where a moonwalk is being simulated (Figure 4-3).

Figure 4-3. The "Moon set" in Diamonds are Forever *(1971). Credit: Metro-Goldwyn-Mayer Studios Inc.*

Bill Kaysing, grandfather of Moon hoax proponents

The first widely publicized book promoting Moon hoax claims appeared in 1974, two years after the end of the Apollo lunar missions, when William Charles Kaysing (1922-2005) self-published the book *We Never Went to the Moon: America's Thirty Billion Dollar Swindle* (Figure 4-4), which presented a long list of alleged evidence that the lunar missions had been faked.

In *We Never Went to the Moon*, Kaysing presents a letter from the Rocketdyne Division of Rockwell International, which states that he was hired as senior technical writer in 1956 and subsequently worked there as service analyst, service engineer

By
Bill Kaysing

Figure 4-4. The cover of Bill Kaysing's book as available currently on Amazon.com.

---

28 Roger D. Launius, *American Spaceflight History's Master Narrative and the Meaning of Memory*, in *Remembering the Space Age*, Steven J. Dick (ed.), 2008, p. 373-384.

and publications analyst until he quit for personal reasons in May 1963. Rocketdyne built the Saturn V's rocket engines, so this would appear to qualify Kaysing as a significant authority on the Apollo project.

However, as his online biography acknowledges,[29] Bill Kaysing had no formal technical education: he had a bachelor's degree in English literature. In his book he actually states that his *"knowledge of rockets and technical writing both equalled zero"* (page 30).

Moreover, Kaysing left Rocketdyne in 1963, well before the Moon missions began. It is therefore unlikely that his experience in the aerospace industry allowed him to acquire any special knowledge of the Apollo vehicles and technologies, which were still in the early stages of development when Kaysing quit and in any case were massively redesigned after the fatal fire of Apollo 1 in 1967.

Indeed, Kaysing makes the following remarks about the period after his employment at Rocketdyne:

> *"I had not really given the Apollo program much thought in the years since leaving Rocketdyne. I had followed it in a cursory fashion, becoming aware of it only through the more startling developments: the fire on Pad 34, for example. [...] I watched none of the moon "landings" nor did I pay much attention to print media presentations. [...] I paid even less attention to the follow-on "flights" of Apollo and noticed that many others were equally neglectful."*

> *– We Never Went to the Moon, page 7.*

He also states that his disbelief was not based on the technical documents to which he had access, but on *"a hunch, an intuition; information from some little understood and mysterious channel of communication... a metaphysical message" (ibid.)*. In other words, Kaysing had no hard evidence to support his conviction.

As often happens with supporters of many kinds of conspiracy theory, their alleged authoritativeness vanishes when their credentials are cross-checked. Indeed, so far nobody having any significant qualification in the aerospace industry or at least in special effects technology has ever supported the "Moon hoax" theories.

Capricorn One

A major boost to the popularity of hoax theories came from the movie *Capricorn One*, directed by Peter Hyams in 1978. Its entertaining story of high-level rogues within NASA trying to save their face by faking a

---

29 *billkaysing.com/biography.php.*

manned Mars landing on a secret soundstage is often mentioned in all seriousness by conspiracy theorists as a prime example of how easily the Moon landings could have been staged (Figure 4-5).

Rather amusingly, conspiracists hail *Capricorn One* despite the fact that the attempted fakery depicted in the movie actually *fails*: the fakers forget a crucial technical detail and their deception is spotted by a NASA engineer and disclosed spectacularly by a journalist. Moreover, the movie's technical explanation of the effects used to fake the landing is riddled with implausibilities and absurdities.

Nevertheless, the story played well on the theme of distrust of government, and the allusion to the Moon missions was rendered even more explicit by using Apollo hardware for the faked Mars landing and by the tagline *"Would you be shocked to find out that the greatest moment of our recent history may not have happened at all?"*

Figure 4-5. The poster for Capricorn One (1978).

Ralph Rene

Ralph Rene (1933-2008), a self-taught American writer and inventor with no formal background in spaceflight, self-published several editions of his book *NASA Mooned America!* in the early 1990s (Figure 4-6), which rapidly became popular among conspiracists. His Moon landing fakery claims led to interviews for several television programs produced by The History Channel, National Geographic, Fox TV, Showtime and other networks around the world.

The 2001 Fox TV show *Did We Land on the Moon?* described him as a *"physicist"* and as an *"author/scientist"*, but Rene acknowledged in his own online biography that he *"did not finish college and is, therefore, without 'proper academic credentials.'"*[30]

---

30 ralphrene.com/biography.html.

However, the same biography claims that he was a former *"consultant to NASA and the Rand Corporation"* with *"impeccable"* credentials because he had been contacted by Rand *"pleading for contributions of free inventions or thoughts relating to space for NASA", "at least one of his ideas"* had passed *"three sequential screening committees,"* and his name had been published in a NASA *"propaganda document"* regarding possible manned missions to Mars.

On his website and in his book *The Last Skeptic of Science* (1988), Ralph Rene argued that the official value of pi is wrong, that Einstein's theory of relativity is not valid and that Newton's law of universal gravitation is in error. [31]

Figure 4-6. The cover of Rene's book NASA Mooned America! *(1994 edition).*

Despite Rene's questionable background, his claims regarding the Apollo missions continue to this day to be quoted in traditional media and on the Internet. They will be discussed in detail in the chapters that follow.

Fox TV's *Conspiracy theory: Did We Land on the Moon?*

In February and March 2001, the Fox TV network broadcast *Conspiracy theory: Did We Land on the Moon?*, a one-hour show which gave ample space to the allegations of hoax theorists (Ralph Rene, Bill Kaysing, Paul Lazarus, David Percy, Bart Sibrel and others) without any basic fact-checking and without providing any significant time for a technical rebuttal.

As a professionally-produced show broadcast on a national network, *Did We Land on the Moon?* appeared to be authoritative and consequently had a far greater impact on public opinion than the self-published efforts that had preceded it.

---

31 *ralphrene.com/circle_squared.html.*

The show caused outrage in the aerospace community, yet was picked up and translated into several languages around the world, continuing to circulate despite the fact that each one of its claims has long been debunked by the astronomers and space professionals that Fox chose not to consult.[32]

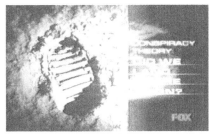

Figure 4-7. Main title of the Fox TV show.

2002, the year Buzz made contact

The advent of the Internet as a popular medium in the early 1990s allowed hoax theory proponents to spread their ideas rapidly. Low-cost camcorders and video editing systems gave them the means to produce many home-brew videos, disseminating them at first on videocassettes for sale and later directly on the Internet and on DVD.

This, together with the Fox show, led to an explosive production of Moon hoax videos and spawned a new generation of conspiracy theorists and theories. One of these theorists is Bart Sibrel (Figure 4-8).

In 2001, Sibrel released a 47-minute video, *A Funny Thing Happened on the Way to the Moon*, in which he claimed to have found a "secret" videotape of the Apollo 11 mission that proved the fakery.

Figure 4-8. Bart Sibrel in 2001.

The footage was actually a test TV transmission performed during the mission and was well-known to space experts and historians, but Sibrel's allegation and his appearance in the Fox TV show propelled him to great popularity in conspiracy theory circles.

Sibrel began following the Moon astronauts (even when they went to the supermarket) and asking them to swear on the Bible that they had really walked on the Moon. Some did; others refused.

On September 9, 2002, Sibrel chased Apollo 11 astronaut Buzz Aldrin with a cameraman and a sound technician in front of a Beverly Hills hotel and accused Aldrin of being *"a coward and a liar"*. Aldrin, who was 72 at the time, replied with a punch to Sibrel's face (Figure 4-9).

---

32 *Conspiracy Theory: Did We Go to the Moon?*, Prof. Steven Dutch, University of Wisconsin, Uwgb.edu; *Fox TV and the Apollo Moon Hoax*, Phil Plait, astronomer, Badastronomy.com.

The incident attracted world-wide media attention and inevitably rekindled the Moon hoax debate. Charges against Aldrin were dropped when *"witnesses came forward to say that Mr Sibrel had aggressively poked Aldrin with the Bible before he was punched".* Moreover, Sibrel *"sustained no visible injury and did not seek medical attention, and Mr Aldrin had no previous criminal record."*[33]

Figure 4-9. Buzz Aldrin (right) initiates a hard docking maneuver with Bart Sibrel (far right).

Sibrel continued to pester Moon astronauts Alan Bean, Gene Cernan, Michael Collins, Al Worden, Bill Anders, John Young, Neil Armstrong and others, sometimes presenting fake credentials (for example to Edgar Mitchell). According to Clavius.org,[34] he trespassed on Neil Armstrong's property while trying to confront him with his hoax allegations (Armstrong called the police). Sibrel was subsequently fired from his job as a cameraman for a Nashville TV station.

Another Sibrel video, *Astronauts Gone Wild* (2004), showed Cernan, Bean and Mitchell swearing on Sibrel's Bible that they did go to the Moon, as the conspiracy theorist demanded. Despite this, Sibrel still claims that the Apollo Moon landings were faked. The video also showed Armstrong politely refusing and saying *"Mr Sibrel, knowing you, that's probably a fake Bible."*

Other notable hoax proponents

Moon hoax theorists and their claims have achieved significant popularity in many other countries besides the United States. British film and TV producer David Percy co-authored a book, *Dark Moon: Apollo and the Whistle-Blowers* (2001), and produced a video, *What Happened on the Moon?* (2000), alleging varying degrees of fakery. French writer Philippe Lheureux argued in his book *Lumières sur la Lune* (*"Lights on the Moon",* 2002) that Americans went to the Moon but published fake photographs to prevent other countries from making use of the scientific information gathered by the flights.

---

33 *Ex-astronaut escapes assault charge,* BBC News, September 21, 2002, News.bbc.co.uk.

34 *http://www.clavius.org/bibsibrel.html.*

German author Gernot Geise published three books, *Der Mond ist ganz anders* (*"The Moon is completely different",* 1985, republished in 2003), *Die dunkle Seite von Apollo* (*"The dark side of Apollo",* 2002, republished in 2006), and *Die Schatten von Apollo* (*"The shadow of Apollo",* 2003), arguing not only that the Moon landings were faked, but that key facts about the Moon itself, such as its true gravity and the presence of vegetation and ancient buildings, have been kept secret by NASA.

Geise's allegations were promoted on German TV in the documentary *Die Akte Apollo* (*"The Apollo File",* 2002) by Gerhard Wisnewski and Willy Brunner. Wisnewski also published the book *Lügen im Weltraum* (*"Lies In Space",* 2005) covering the same themes.

Roberto Giacobbo, anchor and assistant director of Italy's national TV network RAI, brought Moon hoax theories to large television audiences with his *Voyager* series (Figure 4-10).

Several Russian authors, such as journalist and politician Yuri Mukhin and science professionals such as Alexander Popov and Stanislav Pokrovsky, have also voiced their claims of conspiracies in articles, books and websites.

Figure 4-10. Italian TV anchor Roberto Giacobbo talks about Moon hoax theories in an episode of Voyager *(2009), The upper caption says* "Moon, is there another story?".

4.4 The four fundamental hoax scenarios

There are many Moon hoax claims, leading to multiple alternative explanations of what allegedly actually happened. As is often the case in the bizarre world of conspiracy theories regarding many events, for the Moon landings there is a single "official" version, which is self-consistent, extensively documented and widely accepted by the experts, and there are many alternative versions of the hoax scenario, which contradict each other.

Accordingly, it can be highly instructive, and sometimes entertaining, to avoid the usual debate between "believers" and "skeptics" and instead arrange a confrontation among Moon hoax proponents that support different and mutually incompatible versions of the way the events were faked.

Knowing these various aspects of Moon hoax theories is important, because it highlights their inconsistencies and shows that many conspiracy theorists and doubters haven't really thought through the consequences and implications of their pet arguments and therefore end up making self-contradictory statements, as detailed in the chapters that follow.

We never went. Ever

Supporters of this theory allege that NASA lacked the technology for a Moon landing and that even today the radiation of the Van Allen belts that surround the Earth is a lethal barrier to any crew venturing away from our planet. Accordingly, they argue that all manned flights to the Moon, including Apollo 8, 10 and 13, which orbited around the Moon without landing, had to be faked.

Therefore, they claim, all the photographs and film footage, the radio and TV broadcasts and the telemetry from the lunar surface and from lunar orbit had to be faked by using special effects (Figure 4-11). Likewise, the lunar rocks and all the science brought back from the Moon had to be fabricated or acquired through other means.

Figure 4-11. Artist's impression of Moon fakery movie set. Credit: Moise.

This scenario implies the need to fake every detail of *nine* complete lunar missions: six Moon landings and three flights around the Moon.

Supporters of this theory allege that NASA failed in this immensely complicated simulation of so many missions and that the skeptical eye of hoax theorists was sharper than the experts' vision in spotting mistakes and anomalies in the pictures and in noting scientific impossibilities.

We went, but the first landing was faked

Some conspiracy theorists argue that the first Moon landing (Apollo 11) was faked because the vehicles were not ready or were untested, but all the previous and subsequent missions were real (Figure 4-12). This theory seeks to explain, for example, the difference in quality between the grainy, black-and-white television footage of the first landing and the sharper color images of the subsequent Moon missions.

It also appears to justify the difference in quality and quantity between the photographs taken by Apollo 11 and those taken by all the later missions, as well as the use of different spacesuits and the far longer duration of the moonwalks: the Apollo 11 astronauts made a single lunar excursion that lasted two and a half hours, yet Apollo 12 already had two moonwalks that lasted almost four hours each. The fact that the Apollo 11 moonwalkers stayed very close to their landing spot, differently from all the other missions, is explained by the need to stay within the confines of the movie set.

Figure 4-12. Artist's impression of true/fake mission sorting process. Credit: Moise.

The initial fakery, in other words, was meant to fool the Soviet Union into believing that it had lost the race to the Moon and gain time to go there for real later.

We went, but the photos were faked

Another school of thought claims that the Moon missions were all real but their photos were unusable and had to be faked. The films, it is argued, were fogged by cosmic radiation, melted by the excessive heat in the sun, or frozen by the extreme cold of lunar shadows, or the lighting on the Moon was so unearthly that the cam-

Figure 4-13. Artist's impression of film liquefaction issues. Credit: Moise.

era settings were wrong and the resulting photographs were unacceptable in terms of propaganda effectiveness (Figure 4-13).

A variation on this theory suggests that the real photos contained scientific information that the US did not want to share with rival countries and therefore a set of simulated pictures was prepared.

We went, but we found ET

The fourth main scenario of Moon hoax theories argues that perhaps not all the landings were real, but we did go to the Moon sooner or later, only to find that it was already occupied by extraterrestrials (Figure 4-14).

Figure 4-14. Artist's impression of unexpected discoveries on the Moon. Credit: Moise.

Proponents of this theory say that some photos show UFOs in the lunar sky and that clandestine recordings document the astonishment of the astronauts as they discovered that they were not alone on the Moon.

Some claim that mankind has not returned to the Moon since those first landings because the aliens have told us to stay away. Others say that additional secret Moon missions were carried out to recover abandoned alien vehicles, from which NASA extracted the technologies for the Space Shuttle and for many other covert military projects.

That's really what they say

Before you ask: no, these four main scenarios are not fabrications of the supporters of the "official" story, designed to ridicule Moon hoax proponents. Each one of these scenarios is documented in the books, videos and Internet sites of the various conspiracy theorists. There are even more ludicrous ones.

More importantly, the supporters of each one of these four main theories claim that they have incontrovertible evidence of their allegations, which contradict the other competing conspiracy scenarios. Standing aside and watching these people argue among themselves, therefore, can be extremely enlightening.

4.5 None of the experts have doubts

Supporters of Moon hoax theories claim to have found many anomalies in the photographs and footage of the Apollo missions and to have identified several technical and physical impossibilities that prove their hoax claims.

In actual fact, these alleged anomalies and impossibilities exist only in the opinion of people who are not experts in the relevant fields. Anyone who is professionally involved in photography, space technology or astronomy knows very well that what a layman might consider strange or implausible is instead exactly what science expects to occur in the unfamiliar environment of space and on the Moon.

Only incompetent amateurs question the authenticity of the Moon missions. In over forty years, no real expert has ever raised documented doubts.

On the contrary, many of the apparent anomalies actually *authenticate* the visual record of the Apollo missions, as explained by Dennis Muren, winner of six Academy Awards for the visual effects of movies such as *Jurassic Park, Terminator 2, The Abyss, E.T.* and *Star Wars*:

> *"A moon landing simulation* [produced with the special effects of the 1960s] *might have looked pretty real to 99.9 percent of the people. The thing is, though, that it wouldn't have looked the way it did. I've always been acutely aware of what's fake and what's real, and the moon landings were definitely real. Look at* 2001 *or* Destination Moon *or* Capricorn One *or any other space movie: everybody was wrong. That wasn't the way the moon looked at all. There was an unusual sheen to the images from the moon, in the way that the light reflected in the camera, that is literally out of this world. Nobody could have faked that."*[35]

The second part of this book will sort the alleged hoax evidence into categories and debunk each claim systematically by using technical facts.

You probably won't be surprised that the house of cards of the lunar conspiracists' "evidence" ultimately collapses completely; but it's very insightful to explore the nature of the recurring errors and patterns of thought on which these theories are based.

Moreover, disproving some of this evidence requires considerable research, especially because hoax theorists usually present documents, photographs and videos without specifying their source or the mission to which they relate, and also requires familiarity with the errors and

---

35 *The Wrong Stuff*, by Rogier van Bakel, Wired.com (1993).

deceptions often made by hoax theory proponents. This makes it hard even for many experts in astronomy or aerospace technology to find the exact technical explanation of some alleged anomalies and to provide accurate answers to the Moon hoax questions that often come up during their public talks. One of the purposes of this book is to gather the explanations that have already been provided over the years and offer a handy guide to answering these questions.

In particular, the printed version of this book is useful for settling discussions with the most obstinate Moon hoax theorists: it can be used as a highly persuasive blunt instrument.

Just kidding.

5. Alleged photographic anomalies

Many Moon hoax proponents claim that there is evidence of blatant fakery in the photographs that NASA presented to the world over four decades ago.

Most of these claims are based on a lack of understanding of the basic principles of photography. This is not really surprising, especially today, when many people have never used anything other than a fully automatic digital camera and therefore are unfamiliar with the technical issues of film photography and know little or nothing about the use, capabilities and limitations of this medium.

Today the concepts of not seeing a picture as soon as it is taken, of setting exposure and focus manually and of dipping a strip of flexible film into chemicals in darkness to reveal a picture sound rather quaint and arcane. Yet that's how countless masterpieces of photography were taken for over a century and a half, and that's how photographs were taken on the Moon trips.

5.1 Apollo still photography: a quick primer

Approximately 20,000 still pictures were taken during the Apollo missions, all using photographic film: there were no digital cameras at the time.

The cameras taken to the Moon by the Apollo astronauts used mostly Kodak Ektachrome MS and EF color film, with a *speed* (sensitivity to light) of ISO 64 and 160 respectively, and Kodak Panatomic-X black-and-white film, with a speed of ISO 80.

Both films were in the 70 mm format, which means that the film strip was 70 millimeters (2.75 inches) wide. The *resolution* (capacity to record details) of these films was impressive even by today's standards: 80 lines per millimeter for color film and 170 lines per millimeter for black-and-white. In today's digital units, that's roughly equivalent to 40 megapixels for color pictures and to a whopping

160 megapixels for black-and-white ones, according to the Arizona State University's state-of-the-art Apollo image scanning project.[36]

So-called *color reversal* film was used. This kind of film produces *slides* (transparencies) that can be viewed directly instead of *negatives* (images with reversed colors) that need to be printed. This choice might appear unusual, since negative film is more tolerant to difficult lighting and to over- and underexposures, but it was dictated by the awareness that negatives would have entailed color accuracy problems: photographs taken in space or on the Moon often don't include any familiar objects that can be used as a color reference and therefore print lab technicians would not have known how to set their printing equipment correctly to render the true colors. Color reversal film doesn't have this problem.

The Apollo films were derived from the ones used for high-altitude photo reconnaissance, which were designed to withstand temperatures down to -40°C (-40°F). Their special Estar polyester base had a melting point of 254°C (490°F) and was thinner than usual, allowing each film magazine to store enough color film for 160 photographs or black-and-white film for 200 photos.

These magazines were removable and light-tight and constituted the rear portion of the custom-built, motorized Hasselblad 500EL cameras used for nearly all the photographs taken during the Lunar excursions. These cameras had manual exposure and focus setting and a lens with a fixed focal length (i.e., no zoom) (Figure 5-1).

Magazine

Shutter release button

Motor

Figure 5-1. A Hasselblad 500EL lunar excursion camera. Credit: Hasselblad.com.

On the lunar surface, Apollos 11 to 14 only had a single Zeiss Biogon wide-angle (60 mm) lens; later missions added a 500 mm telephoto lens.

The cameras had large adjustment levers to allow handling even with the thick gloves of a lunar spacesuit. The shutter release button was much larger than normal for the same reason. Film advancement was controlled automatically by the electric motor of the camera (the lower block in Figure 5-1).

---

36   *http://apollo.sese.asu.edu/.*

Focusing was guided by distance markings on the lens and simplified by the considerable *depth of field* (range of distances over which objects are in focus) of the wide-angle lens at the settings allowed by the bright sunlight: the recommended *aperture* (also known as *f-stop*) was f/5.6 for photographs in shadow and f/11 for taking pictures of subjects in full sunlight. The standard exposure time was 1/250th of a second. The film magazines carried a sticker which reminded the astronauts of these settings (Figure 5-2).

The Hasselblad cameras had no viewfinder, since the astronauts would have been unable to use one while wearing their helmets, so aiming was done by pointing the camera roughly in the direction of the subject. The moonwalkers were aided in this by their extensive photography training and by the wide field of the lens (approximately 49° width and height, 66° diagonal).

Figure 5-2. A film magazine used for the Apollo 11 mission. Note the sticker that reminded the astronauts of the settings for the various lighting conditions.

A silver-colored coating was applied to the camera bodies used on the lunar surface, in order to reflect the light and heat of the sun and reduce the risk of overheating. Onboard cameras were coated with a more traditional black.

Having established this basic information on the techniques used for the still pictures taken on the Moon by the Apollo astronauts, we can now deal with the alleged anomalies that hoax supporters claim to have found in these images.

5.2 No stars in the photographs

IN A NUTSHELL: *There are no stars in the Moon photographs simply because there shouldn't be any. The surface of the Moon was in daylight, so the cameras were set for daylight. Stars are too faint to be photographed with daylight settings. Only the planet Venus and the Earth shine brightly enough.*

THE DETAILS: This is usually the very first objection raised by doubters: why aren't there any stars in the Apollo photographs? After all, illustrations and movies that depict the Moon often show the stars in the sky.

However, this is an artistic license. Adding stars makes a picture much more interesting, but it's scientifically inaccurate. In actual fact, the sky is starless in all photographs ever taken in space in sunlight with normal daylight settings.

There are no stars in pre-Apollo pictures, such as the one shown in Figure 5-3, which was taken in 1965 in Earth orbit during the Gemini 4 mission. There are also no stars in more recent space photographs, such as the ones taken by Space Shuttle astronauts (Figure 5-4). Only with the advent of highly sensitive digital cameras has it been possible to photograph stars from space in any detail.

Figure 5-3. Ed White during his spacewalk (Gemini 4, 1965). No stars.

The reason is very simple: stars are far too faint to be recorded by a camera set for daylight photography like the Moon cameras were. You can test this easily: take a photograph in daylight with a camera that allows manual settings and make a note of the exposure time and *aperture* (the number after the "*f/*") that yield a good picture. Then try taking a photograph of the night sky with the same settings. The sky will turn out pitch black, except for the Moon and possibly Venus.

Figure 5-4. Swiss astronaut Claude Nicollier against the blackness of space during Shuttle mission STS-103 (1999). No stars.

The astronauts couldn't see any stars while they were on the Moon for the same reason. If you stand in a city street at night, your eyes are dazzled by car headlights and street lighting, so you'll have trouble seeing any stars. Imagine how dazzled the moonwalkers were by the *entire lunar surface* all around them bathed in direct sunlight. If you've noticed how bright a full Moon is and how it blocks out the stars in the night sky, just think how bright it must be when you're actually *standing* on that Moon.

This is a basic concept of photography and optics, so those who question the lack of stars in the Apollo visual record are simply revealing their lack of technical knowledge. That's what prominent Moon hoax theorist Bill Kaysing did when he asked *"Where are the stars in the lunar sky?"* in his book *We Never Went to the Moon* (page 23).

However, it is incorrect to say that there are no stars at all in *any* of the pictures taken on the Moon during the Apollo missions. For example, photograph AS16-123-19657 (Figure 5-5) shows the stars of Capricorn and Aquarius as a backdrop to the Earth. However, it wasn't taken on the Moon with an ordinary camera, but with a telescope loaded with ultraviolet-sensitive film, using night settings (a long exposure time), during the Apollo 16 mission in April 1972.

Figure 5-5. A sample of ultraviolet star photography from Apollo 16.

The Apollo visual record also includes pictures of other heavenly bodies, although strictly speaking they're not stars. For example, NASA photos AS16-117-18815, -18816 and -18817 (Apollo 16) show the planet Venus. During Apollo 14's moonwalk, astronaut Alan Shepard noticed that Venus was shining above him, next to the crescent Earth, and took a series of photographs. A detail of one of his pictures is

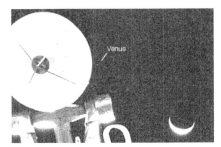

Figure 5-6. Detail of photograph AS14-64-9191. The object on the left is one of the antennas of the lunar module.

shown in Figure 5-6. Venus is far brighter than any true star, so much that it can be seen even in daytime on Earth if you know where to look. Yet in these Apollo photographs it is merely a faint dot.

The Earth and the lunar module antenna are instead greatly overexposed and washed out, confirming that when the camera is set to capture the faint light of stars, the ground and any sunlit objects will be overexposed and show up in featureless white. The lunar astronauts were interested in taking pictures of the moonscape, not of the stars, so they usually set their cameras to take good pictures of the terrain around them.

Incidentally, close examination of the high-resolution scans of the Apollo photographs that are now available online sometimes reveals bright dots in the lunar sky. However, these are not stars, but point-like scratches, blemishes or lunar dust particles on the film: they change position from one photo to the next and also occur on parts of the pictures that show the ground. Real stars would be in the same place in the sky in photographs taken from the same viewpoint, in the same direction and around the same time, and their positions relative to each other wouldn't change.

5.3 The flag is blowing in the wind

IN A NUTSHELL: *No, it's not. It looks like it's blowing because it's hanging from a horizontal rod, but it's actually quite motionless.*

THE DETAILS: Some hoax theorists say that the American flag is fluttering in the wind in the Apollo photographs (Figure 5-7). But there's no air on the Moon. Therefore, they argue, the photographs are fake.

Actually, the flag *seems* to be fluttering because it's hanging from a horizontal rod, which is clearly visible along its top edge if the photographs are examined carefully (Figure 5-8). NASA, not being dumb, realized well before the landings that on the airless Moon there would

Figure 5-7. Apollo 11's flag. Detail of photo AS11-40-5874.

be no wind to make the flag wave, leading to a rather uninspiring droop, so this simple technical workaround was devised.

The flag also looks like it's wind-blown because of its billowed-out shape. But if you look carefully, you'll notice that it's crumpled and creased, rather than wavy as a wind-blown flag should be. It has sharp creases due to the fact that it was carried to the Moon tightly packed and folded in a casing attached to one of the legs of the lunar module.

When the astronauts erected it on the Moon, they chose not to smooth out all of these creases, so that it would look like it was being proudly flown by the wind, like a traditional flag.

In some missions the telescopic horizontal rod didn't extend fully, so the upper edge of the flag remained gathered instead of being stretched straight. This brought out the creases even more and enhanced the remarkable illusion of a billowing flag. Further evidence that the flag isn't fluttering in a draft on a movie set is that pictures taken at different times (Figure 5-9) show that its shape never changes unless the astronauts touch it. The same crease pattern persists for tens of minutes.

Figure 5-8. The horizontal rod that supports the flag. Detail of photo AS11-40-5874.

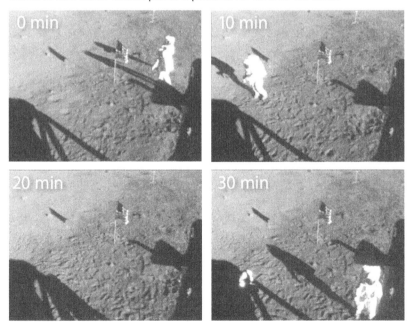

Figure 5-9. The wrinkles in the Apollo 11 flag never change shape after the astronauts have erected it. Frames taken from the 16 mm movie camera footage.

Moon hoax theorists also claim that the flag moves suspiciously in the live television and movie footage of the missions. These claims will be discussed in Chapter 6.

5.4 Objects in shadow are strangely well-lit

IN A NUTSHELL: *That's because shadows on the Moon are not pitch-black as many people imagine them to be. Anything standing in shadow on the dayside of the Moon is still bathed in the glare from all the surrounding sunlit objects: the lunar surface, the Lunar Module, the bright white spacesuits.*

THE DETAILS: Moon hoax proponents argue that since the only source of light on the Moon is the Sun and there's no air to diffuse the light and soften the shadows, any object in shadow should be completely black. But in Apollo photographs such as AS11-40-5869 (Figure 5-10), the astronauts are unexpectedly well-lit even when they're in the large shadow cast by the lunar module. Some conspiracy theorists say that this effect proves that studio lighting was used.

Figure 5-10. Aldrin on the LM footpad. NASA photo AS11-40-5869.

At first glance the picture does indeed seem strange and unnatural. But it's not because NASA used studio lights; it's because the natural lighting on the Moon is very different from our everyday experience. We're not used to a pitch-black sky in daytime; we're used to a bright sky that diffuses light. On the Moon, with no atmosphere to scatter sunlight and illuminate the sky, other lighting effects become more evident.

Aldrin's highly reflective white suit is simply lit by the sunlight reflected off the lunar surface all around him, which is in full daylight. It's quite a glare: although the Moon is only about as reflective as tarmac, the amount of light that it reflects is sufficient to make it shine so brightly in Earth's sky that it can be seen even in daylight. That reflected sunlight is what makes Aldrin visible. Anything rising above the lunar surface will be lit by the glare of the surrounding sunlit surface. The presence of an atmosphere has nothing to do with this effect.

Of course, the light of the Sun reflected by the lunar surface towards anything that rises above it is not as bright as direct sunlight, so the astronauts simply set their cameras for shadow photography (note the reminder on the film magazine in Figure 5-2). This means that in photos for which the camera was set for shadow any object in full daylight should be overexposed and washed out. Indeed, the sunlit lunar surface in Aldrin's photograph is nearly white instead of being its natural gray.

It's easy to demonstrate that the glare of the tarmac-like lunar surface is sufficient to light an astronaut standing in shadow. All it takes is a model of the lunar module and of an astronaut, placed outside at night on a dark gray surface and lit by a single, powerful light source, with no nearby walls or objects that might reflect the light. The result is shown in Figure 5-11.

Figure 5-11. A model of a lunar landing scene, lit outdoors at night by a single light source. The astronaut in the shadow of the LM is visible. Credit: PA.

If you set the camera to take a good picture of the objects in the shadow of the LM, you get the same effect seen in Aldrin's photo: the astronaut on the ladder is well-lit by the light reflected off the simulated lunar surface, but the parts of the surface that are in direct "sunlight" are overexposed and almost white.

5.5 The shadows aren't parallel

IN A NUTSHELL: *The shadows in the Apollo photographs actually are parallel, but perspective makes them appear to diverge. The same effect can be seen easily on Earth, for example in railroad tracks: their spacing only appears to change with distance but it's actually fixed.*

Figure 5-12. An Apollo photograph showing non-parallel shadows, as presented in the Fox TV show Did We Land on the Moon? *(2001).*

THE DETAILS: If you trace the directions of shadows in many Apollo photographs, you'll notice that they're not parallel (Figure 5-12). Moon hoax proponents say that they should instead be parallel, because on the Moon there's only one light source (the Sun), which is very far away and therefore, according to the rules of optics, casts parallel shadows.

Bart Sibrel, in the Fox TV show *Did We Land on the Moon?*, stated that *"Outside in sunlight, shadows always run parallel with one another, so the shadows will never intersect".*

Intersecting shadow directions, it is argued, imply multiple light sources, which are impossible on the Moon and suggest studio lighting. No explanation is given by Moon hoax proponents as to why NASA or the alleged hoax perpetrators would have made such a colossally stupid and glaring mistake.

In actual fact, multiple light sources would cause each object to cast multiple shadows, as occurs with the players in a football or baseball match played at night. But in the photographs taken on the Moon each object casts only one shadow.

Sibrel is correct in stating that in sunlight shadows run parallel to each other, but he seems to have forgotten about *perspective*, which causes shadows that are actually parallel to appear to converge if viewed or photographed from most angles. It's a basic optical principle that occurs on Earth as well: parallel objects, such as railroad tracks, appear to converge in the distance, but they don't actually become closer or intersect. That would make it rather hard for trains to work.

Figure 5-13. My wife Elena patiently stands in for a lunar astronaut. Credit: PA.

This perspective effect is really easy to demonstrate in real life. Figure 5-13 shows shadows cast at sunset by trees and by my very patient wife Elena. The sun is on the right. From this angle, the shadows look essentially parallel, as indeed they were.

But if the same scene is photographed a few seconds later from a different angle, as in Figure 5-14, those very same shadows suddenly appear to converge. However, it's just an optical illusion caused by perspective. The shadows haven't actually moved.

Figure 5-14. The same shadows as in the previous photograph, taken from a different angle, now appear to converge. Credit: PA.

In other words, anyone who claims that intersecting shadows in Apollo photos are evidence of studio fakery merely shows a lack of understanding of the very simple concept of perspective and reveals very limited powers of observation. All it takes to realize that this claim is bogus is to go outside and look around.

5.6 The astronauts cast shadows of different lengths

IN A NUTSHELL: *Of course they do. The Moon's surface isn't perfectly smooth and level. If there's a slope, a bump or a hollow in the ground, the astronaut's shadow will follow its shape and vary its length accordingly. The same happens on Earth.*

THE DETAILS: In some Apollo photos and movies the shadows of the astronauts have different lengths (Figure 5-15). Moon hoax proponents such as David Percy

Figure 5-15. A frame from the Apollo 11 movie camera shows that the shadows of the astronauts have different lengths.

argue (for example on the Aulis.com website)[37] that this is because the fake astronauts stood at different distances from the overhead studio lights.

However, Percy's explanation doesn't hold water, because in Figure 5-15 the astronaut that is closest to the hypothetical spotlights (as indicated by the direction of the shadows) has the longest shadow, whereas in real life objects that are closer to an elevated light source cast *shorter* shadows. This can be demonstrated easily by standing at various distances from a streetlight.

The correct explanation for the different shadow lengths is that the surface of the Moon is uneven and has all sorts of slopes, rises and hollows, which sometimes aren't easily detected in photographs because there are no familiar items for visual reference. These differently sloping portions of the surface alter the length of any shadow that falls onto them. The same thing happens on Earth.

This can be shown by building a model of the lunar surface and lighting it with a single distant spotlight (simulating the Sun). It turns out, per-

37 *www.aulis.com/nasa6.htm.*

haps surprisingly, that a model astronaut placed even in a shallow depression casts a shadow which differs greatly in length from the one cast by another identical astronaut standing on level ground (Figure 5-16).

In the Apollo 11 picture shown in Figure 5-15, taken from the 16 mm film footage, the astronaut on the left is simply standing in a slight hollow of the ground, which shortens his shadow. This hollow isn't detectable in the picture, but it's definitely there: it's revealed by the curved shadow of the flagpole in photo AS11-37-5473 (shown cropped in Figure 5-17).

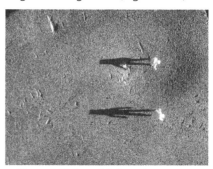

Figure 5-16. A model shows how even a small hollow changes shadow lengths. Credit: PA.

What's certainly surprising is that Percy is a member of the British Royal Photographic Society and has received several awards for his work as cameraman. In theory, therefore, he should be quite knowledgeable about lighting and the behavior of shadows on uneven ground.

Figure 5-17. Detail of photo AS11-37-5473 (Apollo 11).

5.7 The shadow of the LM reaches the horizon

IN A NUTSHELL: *That's not the horizon. It's the raised rim of a nearby crater that hides the actual horizon, which is a lot farther away.*

THE DETAILS: In photograph AS11-40-5931 (Apollo 11), the shadow of the Lunar Module appears to extend all the way to the horizon (Figure 5-18). Moon hoax theorists argue that this makes no sense: the horizon

Figure 5-18. Detail of photograph AS11-40-5931 (Apollo 11).

should be miles away. For them it proves that the picture was taken on a small movie set and that the "horizon" is actually the line where the black backdrop that faked the sky met the edge of the set floor.

However, if we look at another photograph of the same location, taken from a greater distance in roughly the same direction (Figure 5-19), we can see that the shadow of the LM doesn't reach the horizon at all. Moreover, the alleged "movie set" must have been huge.

Figure 5-19. Photo AS11-40-5961 (Apollo 11).

Actually, in Figure 5-18 the tip of the LM shadow is falling on the rim of a crater, known as *Double*, which is about 15 meters (50 feet) in diameter. The actual horizon is hidden by this rim. The crater can be seen in the reconnaissance photographs taken by the Lunar Orbiter unmanned probes in 1967, two years before the Apollo 11 landing (for example in photograph V-76-H3) and in the more recent pictures taken by the Lunar Reconnaissance Orbiter probe in 2009 (Figure 5-20).

In Figure 5-20, the Double crater is located to the left and slightly below the Lunar Module, which is the bright spot at the center. The four tiny dots around this spot are the LM footpads; the other bright dots are the instruments left on the Moon by Neil Armstrong and Buzz Aldrin.

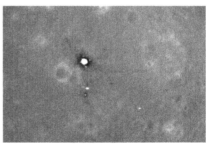

Figure 5-20. A photograph of the Apollo 11 landing site taken by the Lunar Reconnaissance Orbiter (2009).

It should be noted, however, that the horizon on the Moon is much closer to the observer than on Earth because the Moon is a smaller world. Barring any valleys, hills or mountains, the lunar horizon is about 2.43 kilometers (1.5 miles) from an observer whose eyes are 1.7 meters (5 feet 7 inches) above the ground. On Earth, for that same observer the horizon is about 4.7 kilometers (3 miles) away. From the point of view of the cameras mounted on the astronaut's chest bracket, about 1.5 meters (4 feet 11 inches) above the ground, the lunar horizon would be even closer: just 2.28 kilometers (1.41 miles).

5.8 There's no flag shadow in the salute photograph

IN A NUTSHELL: *That's the way it should be. The shadow of the flag fell out of the frame because of the shallow Sun angle, but it can be seen in other photographs. The shadow of the flagpole is visible in high-quality scans of the salute photo.*

THE DETAILS: The famous photograph of Buzz Aldrin's salute to the American flag on the Moon (Figure 5-21) is often alleged to be a fake because the shadow of the flag is missing. The missing shadow, it is claimed, proves that the flag was added later.

Figure 5-21. Photograph AS11-40-5874 (Apollo 11): Buzz Aldrin salutes the Stars and Stripes on the Moon.

Sometimes the claim is boosted by showing another photograph, taken seconds later (AS11-40-5875), in which Aldrin hasn't raised his arm to salute and therefore appears to be simply standing on the lunar surface as if the flag were not there (Figure 5-22).

Actually, the shadow of the flag is missing from the photograph for a very good reason: it lies

Figure 5-22. Detail of photo AS11-40-5875.

outside the viewing field of the camera, beyond the right margin of the picture, because the Sun was low on the horizon and therefore all the shadows were very elongated. Calculations and documents indicate that the elevation of the Sun above the horizon, at the Apollo 11 landing site between July 20 and 21, 1969, ranged from 14° to 15.4°.

The shadow of the flagpole is actually visible in the picture, as it should be, but only in the high-quality scans (Figure 5-23): it's the thin dark line behind the astronaut's legs, roughly at ankle height. The rod was only about 2.5 centimeters (1 inch) thick, so it cast a very thin shadow, especially when viewed sideways as in the photograph in dispute.

The flagpole shadow is rather hard to locate because it's not where you expect it to be, i.e., at the same level as the base of the pole: a shallow depression in the ground bends it, so it's further down. The depression in which the shadow of the flagpole falls is shown in Figure 5-17.

Moreover, other photographs of the same site show that the flag is exactly in the same position (Figure 5-17 itself, for example). There's also a 16 mm film frame (Figure 3-11) that shows the salute from a different angle and clearly reveals the shadow of the flag and of the pole.

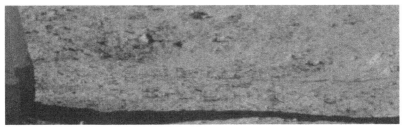

Figure 5-23. Detail of AS11-40-5874 (Apollo 11). The thin shadow of the flagpole is faintly visible above the shadow of Aldrin's legs.

5.9 The spacecraft casts an impossibly huge shadow

IN A NUTSHELL: *It's not the shadow of the Apollo vehicle cast on the lunar surface. It's the close-up silhouette of one of its small maneuvering thrusters.*

THE DETAILS: On page 13 of his book *NASA Mooned America!*, Ralph Rene shows a photograph (Figure 5-24) that he describes as *"the apex of chicanery"*. He claims that it shows, in the lower left corner, *"the shadow [...] from the engine shroud whose diameter is 8.5 feet [2.6 meters]"* or from one of the LM's *"small directional thrusters which are 6 inches [15 centimeters] in diameter"*. Rene wonders sarcastically what kind of a *"wondrous place is*

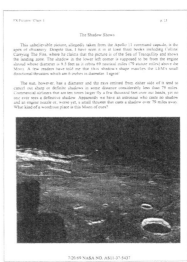

Figure 5-24. The page of Rene's book showing the allegedly fake Apollo photograph.

this Moon of ours" if an engine shroud or thruster can *"cast a shadow over 79 miles [130 km] away"*.

Actually, if we examine the original photograph (AS11-37-5437, Figure 5-25) instead of relying on Rene's very poor duplicate, it becomes clear that what Rene described as a shadow cast on the surface of the Moon isn't a shadow at all. It's the silhouette of one of the thruster quads of the lunar module, shown for example in Figure 2-4. This becomes evident by examining the original photograph (AS11-37-5437, Figure 5-25) instead of Rene's low-quality copy: the alleged giant "shadow" actually has metallic reflections in its upper conical part, and the uncropped picture also includes a portion of another thruster nozzle.

As often occurs, an alleged Moon mystery is spawned simply because the conspiracy theorist failed to perform basic research and inspect the original images.

Figure 5-25. Photograph AS11-37-5437 (Apollo 11).

5.10 All the photographs are perfect

IN A NUTSHELL: *No, they're not. There are many bad pictures, but unsurprisingly NASA and the press prefer to show just the best ones.*

THE DETAILS: Mitch Pileggi, as host of the Fox TV show *Did We Land on the Moon?*, asks dramatically: *"If the cameras were so difficult to manipulate, how were thousands of photos taken with crystal clarity, precise framing?"* Then Bill Kaysing piles on the disbelief: *"The pictures that we see, that allegedly were taken on the Moon, are absolutely perfect!"*

It's a fairly reasonable question, considering that nobody had ever taken photographs on the Moon before, the cameras had fully manual exposure and focus and didn't have a viewfinder to aim them precisely.

The answer is that it's not true that all the Apollo photographs offer *"crystal clarity, precise framing"*: NASA, and consequently the press, simply published the ones that turned out well; the others were disregarded. Indeed, if we examine the full set of Moon pictures, we find dozens of underexposed, blurred, out-of-focus, fogged and badly framed photographs, which are hardly ever shown precisely because they're so bad.

Some of these photographic blunders are heartbreaking from a historical point of view. For example, Figure 5-26 shows NASA photograph AS11-40-5894, taken during the Apollo 11 mission. It's a greatly underexposed picture of the LM. In the bottom left corner there's a barely recognizable silhouette of an astronaut. Had it been exposed correctly, it would be the only frontal portrait of Neil Armstrong, the first man on the Moon. Digital processing allows to recover some of the lost detail, as shown in the inset of Figure 5-26, suggesting that

Figure 5-26. Photograph AS11-40-5894 (Apollo 11) would show Neil Armstrong's face (inset) if it had been exposed correctly.

Armstrong's gold reflective visor was raised and therefore his face would have been visible. So much for *"absolutely perfect".*

There are many more examples of this kind of photographic mishap in the complete Apollo archive, as shown by Figures 5-27 and 5-28. Even Neil Armstrong's world-famous portrait of Buzz Aldrin (Figure 3-7) was almost a fiasco: careful inspection of the original shot reveals that Armstrong almost cropped Aldrin's head (indeed, Aldrin's radio antenna is missing) and tilted the camera so much that a piece of fake sky is often added to this photograph in order to straighten it and make it look better.

Figure 5-27. A series of overexposed photographs from the Apollo 17 mission.

When photographs could be disseminated only through the press, nobody wasted space and money by publishing the bad shots. That's why many people got the impression of absolute perfection. Today, however, the complete photographic record can be shared at no cost on the Internet and therefore all the images are now available for viewing. The full film rolls of all the Apollo missions can be examined at the website of the Lunar and Planetary Institute and contain long sequences of poor shots.[38]

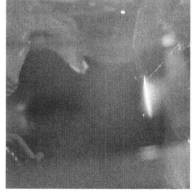

Figure 5-28. Photograph AS12-47-7009 (Apollo 12).

---

38 *www.lpi.usra.edu/resources/apollo/catalog/70mm/.*

Despite these mistakes, the astronauts managed to bring back a good number of correct shots. How could they achieve this result on the first attempt? First of all, theirs were not the first photographs taken on the lunar surface: automatic probes had already sent back pictures of their landing sites. Therefore the lighting conditions of the Moon were known in advance and correct exposure settings were computed before leaving Earth. On the Moon, moreover, there were no clouds or haze that could alter the lighting.

The astronauts had also been trained for photography and were accustomed to composing their pictures simply by sighting along the camera's longitudinal axis, without using a viewfinder. Their cameras had wide-angle lenses that had a broad viewing field and therefore didn't require very precise aiming.

The bright daylight also reduced focus problems by allowing to close the diaphragm of the camera, producing a great *depth of field* (range of distances that are in focus), which reduced the need for exact focusing of every photograph.

5.11 Photos show the landing site without the Lunar Module

IN A NUTSHELL: *It's not the landing site, but a different location nearly a mile away. The hills in the background look identical not because they're shot from the same location, but because they're actually distant mountains, which don't change appearance if the viewpoint moves by a mile or so, just like on Earth.*

THE DETAILS: Some Moon hoax theorists point out that certain pairs of Apollo photographs show the landing sites with and without the Lunar Module. They claim it's the same location because the hills in the background are identical in both pictures.

According to Fox TV's *Did We Land on the Moon?*, this is *"seemingly impossible, since the LM never moved and its base remained even after the mission."* And obviously there was nobody available to take photographs at the landing site before the LM landed, so there was no way to have a photo of the landing site without the LM. The show illustrates this argument with the pictures shown in Figure 5-29.

Hoax proponents often claim that this is evidence of fakery: they argue that the backgrounds were clumsily recycled to simulate different locations.

Figure 5-29. Two photographs with identical backdrops, shown in Fox TV's Did We Land on the Moon? *(2001).*

One might wonder why the alleged perpetrators of one of history's greatest conspiracies would be so dumb as to reuse a movie backdrop and hope to get away with it, but never mind: a little research reveals the technical fallacy in the hoax theorists' argument.

The two photographs shown in Figure 5-29 come from the Apollo 15 mission: they're cropped versions of photos AS15-82-11057 (left) and AS15-82-11082 (right). The mission records at Apolloarchive.com and at the Apollo 15 *Surface Operations Overview*[39] of the Lunar and Planetary Institute report that the first photograph was taken from a point named *Station 8*, approximately 125 meters (400 feet) northwest of the lunar module, while the second one was taken from an-

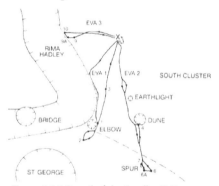

Figure 5-30. Detail of the Apollo 15 Traverse Map. *Station 8 is not visible because it lies too close to the LM (indicated by X).*

other location, known as *Station 9*, 1400 meters (4600 feet) west of the LM (Figure 5-30). In other words, the lunar module is not in the second picture simply because the photograph was taken about a mile away from the spacecraft, not at the landing site.

So why is the background identical? Because what appear to be nearby gentle hills are actually massive and distant mountains that rise to more than 4500 meters (15,000 feet), and there are no familiar references, such as houses or trees, and no atmospheric haze on the Moon to give away the actual distance and size of these features.

---

39 *http://www.lpi.usra.edu/lunar/missions/apollo/apollo_15/surface_opp/.*

Imagine you're taking a picture of a tall mountain from a village located a few miles away. If you move to another place roughly a mile away, you won't be surprised to find that the houses of the village are no longer in the picture, although the mountain will look very much the same. That's exactly what happened in the allegedly fake lunar photographs: they're pictures of distant mountains taken from two different places.

The studio backdrop theory, moreover, is contradicted by the fact that if the original photographs are compared carefully, it becomes apparent that the details of the mountains actually change slightly because of the equally slight change in viewpoint. This means that the mountains in the photos are three-dimensional objects that have depth, not flat backdrops, so much that their perspective changes. Robert Braeunig's *Rocket and Space Technology* website[40] discusses other cases of alleged "recycled backdrops".

5.12 Visors show reflections of studio lights

IN A NUTSHELL: *They're not studio lights. They're reflections of sunlight on the scratches and smudges of the visors. This is made clear by looking at the high-resolution scans of the photographs. Similar reflections are seen in Shuttle and International Space Station images.*

Figure 5-31. An example of the alleged "studio lights", taken from Gernot Geise's appearance on Italian national TV show La Storia siamo noi (RAI, 2006).

THE DETAILS: Some Apollo photos show an unusual row of bright dots on the astronauts' helmet visors (Figure 5-31). Hoax theorists such as German author Gernot Geise have claimed that these are reflections from the rows of studio lights or from the windows of the control rooms used on the movie set where the Moon landing footage was faked.

The allegedly fake photo is a detail of an Apollo 12 picture, AS12-49-7281 (Figure 5-32), taken by Charles "Pete" Conrad during the second moonwalk of that mission. The astronaut in the picture is Alan Bean; Conrad's reflection can be seen in his visor.

---

40 *http://www.braeunig.us/space/hoax-jw.htm.*

If you examine a high-resolution scan of the original photograph, it turns out that the alleged studio lights or windows are neither shaped nor arranged like studio lights or windows. The low-quality version shown by hoax proponents makes them appear to be evenly spaced circular dots, but in actual fact their shape and spacing are very irregular (Figure 5-33).

Figure 5-32. Alan Bean in photo AS12-49-7281 (Apollo 12).

To anyone who uses proper research methods and goes to the original source, the explanation is quite obvious: reflections of sunlight on some of the scratches and smudges of the visor.

These blemishes were produced mainly by the astronaut's dusty gloves when they bumped against the visor in moving their sliding lateral eyeshades, which can be seen pulled down in Figure 5-32 to the sides of the visor. Lunar dust is highly abrasive because it is not smoothed by wind or water as occurs on Earth: it acts like a sort of natural sandpaper. Apollo mission reports often mention scratches and clogging caused by moondust.

Figure 5-33. An enlargement of the "studio lights" from a high-resolution scan of the original photograph.

Similar lines of reflected sunlight can also be seen to the side of the Sun's main reflection in pictures of the Apollo spacesuits taken on Earth during training, such as Figure 5-34. It seems unlikely that there was any need to place a row of spotlights in the sky for this picture.

Figure 5-34. Sunlight reflecting off an Apollo suit visor produces a linear streak during training on Earth. Frame taken from the documentary When We Left Earth.

More recent photographs taken during spacewalks from the Shuttle and the International Space Station, too, show scratched visors: scuffing occurs even in the relatively pristine environment of space. An example is given in Figure 5-35, taken during Luca Parmitano's ISS spacewalk in July 2013.

Figure 5-35. Italian astronaut Luca Parmitano's scratched visor in a self-portrait taken during work outside the International Space Station in July 2013. NASA photo ISS036-E-016853.

One should also take into account the fact that the Apollo helmet used for moonwalks and spacewalks consisted of an inner bubble helmet, a central visor and an outer gold-coated visor. Light striking the outer visor would be reflected back and forth between the three layers, easily forming repeating patterns of light spots.

5.13 Crosshairs covered by objects

IN A NUTSHELL: *The crosshairs aren't covered; they're washed out, as occurs for any thin object photographed against an overexposed bright background, especially after repeated analog duplications of a photo. The apparently covered crosshairs are often visible in the original pictures.*

THE DETAILS: The Hasselblad cameras used for most Moon photographs were fitted with a glass plate on which uniformly spaced crosshairs were etched (Figure 5-36).

These crosshairs, known as *fiducials* or *reseau marks*, were 1 millimeter (0.039 inches) long and 0.02 millimeters (0.00078 inches) wide and were arranged in a 5 x 5 grid. The central crosshair was larger to distinguish it from the others and indicate the center of the original photograph. The crosshairs were used to reveal any warping during the developing, printing and duplication processes and for distance measurements. The glass plate, or reseau plate, was in direct contact with the film when a photograph was taken. This superimposed the crosshairs directly on the original shot.

Figure 5-36. Crosshairs on a glass plate inside a Hasselblad camera. The film magazine has been removed for clarity.

Moon hoax theorists point to the curious fact that in some of the Apollo photographs these crosshairs are *behind* the objects being photographed, as can be seen for example in Figure 5-37.

Figure 5-37. Suspicious crosshairs according to David Percy.

According to David Percy in the TV show *Did We Land on the Moon?* (2001), *"this situation is impossible and has to be the result of technical manipulation and doctoring of the image".* But actually there's a very simple explanation for this allegedly *"impossible"* situation. The main clue is in the pictures chosen by the Fox show: every object that appears to cover the crosshairs is white and strongly lit by sunlight.

It turns out that if you take a photograph of a dark, thin object against a bright, overexposed background, the thin object tends to disappear: it gets washed out by the surrounding glare. This effect is well-known to photographers and can be seen for example in Figure 5-38, where the black thread that crosses the picture becomes invisible when it lies in front of the brightly sunlit model astronaut. The same effect occurs during analog duplication of photographs: fine detail is washed out and gradually lost.

Figure 5-38. A black thread is clearly visible against a correctly exposed background but vanishes when it lies in front of the overexposed model astronaut. Credit: PA.

If you examine high-resolution scans of all of the allegedly doctored photographs, you find exactly the same effect: the apparently missing portion of the crosshairs is always on a very bright, overexposed background, and it turns out that often it's not missing at all but simply very faint.

Figure 5-39, for example, is a high-quality scan of the original photograph from which the detail on the left in Figure 5-37 is taken. It's Apollo 16 photo AS16-107-17446. The detail is indicated by the arrow and is shown magnified on the right in Figure 5-39, revealing that the "missing" crosshair is actually quite present.

Figure 5-39. Photo AS16-107-17446 and detail of the same picture.

Figure 5-40. Photo AS11-40-5931 (cropped) and detail of the same picture.

Figure 5-40 instead shows a better scan of the picture presented in Figure 5-37, which is Apollo 11 photograph AS11-40-5931. The arrow points to the region where the allegedly missing crosshair is located. It is in actual fact quite visible, although somewhat washed out where it lies in front of a white background.

In other words, there's nothing strange about the crosshairs in the lunar photographs. On the contrary, the crosshairs behave exactly as required by the laws of optics that affect photography and therefore are not evidence of doctoring.

5.14 There's a letter C on a rock

IN A NUTSHELL: *No, it's not the set decorator's marking to remember which rock goes where. It's a hair that got into one of the many duplication processes to which the Apollo photographs were subjected for distribution. It's not on the original film.*

THE DETAILS: In a photograph from the Apollo 16 mission record there's a clearly outlined letter C on a rock and another letter C on the ground next to it (Figure 5-41). According to French hoax theorist Philippe Lheureux, this is *"exactly like with some cinema props."* Ralph Rene concurs: *"The large rock in the left foreground is clearly marked with a big capital "C". The bottom right corner has a crease similar to that caused by wetting a folded newspaper. This makes it a showbiz "flap" rock, which the people who work in Hollywood studios throw at visitors. They used to be made from wet newspaper and paste and showed similar flaps. Stage rocks are usually placed by stage hands over similarly lettered markers positioned by the set designer. Did NASA really carry fake boulders and stage hands onto the Moon?"*[41]

---

41   *Moon shots "faked"*, BBC News, 21 June 2001, News.bbc.co.uk; *NASA Mooned America!*, Ralph Rene, page 6.

The photograph is AS16-107-17446 (already seen as Figure 5-39) and shows astronaut Charlie Duke at the Station 4 site of Stone Mountain. The alleged letter C is on a rock toward the bottom left corner of the picture and can be seen in the detail shown in Figure 5-41.

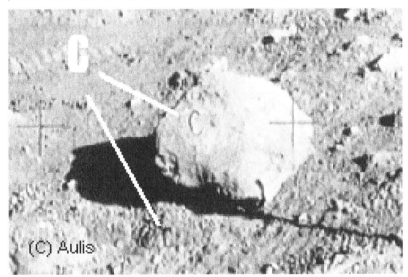

Figure 5-41. The alleged letters C on a rock and on the lunar surface. Image source: Aulis.com.

This alleged piece of evidence is so absurd that it begs the question of how anyone can present it seriously as proof of fakery without realizing that it makes no sense. The official publication of a photograph showing two letters C that shouldn't be there, revealing the top-secret deception that was vital for the destiny and reputation of the United States, would entail a truly unbelievable chain of errors.

First, the set decorator would have to dress the set without realizing that the letters are visible to the cameras. Then the photographer would have to take the picture without noticing the two letters. Then all the people who developed, selected and published the photographs would have to fail to notice the telltale mistake.

The idea that the rocks would be individually labeled to assist in their placement also strains credulity. A single-letter labeling system would allow for only twenty-six rocks, which on a set depicting a rock-littered lunar surface might be somewhat inadequate. Moreover, if the letter C were actually drawn on a sloping face of a rough, irregular rock or on the uneven soil, it wouldn't have such a smooth shape when viewed from an angle as occurs in this photograph.

Yet despite all this, the fact remains that the letters are unquestionably present in the "official version" published by the NASA website of the Johnson Space Center (Figure 5-42).[42]

Figure 5-42. The photograph with the alleged letters C in the low-resolution Internet archive of the Johnson Space Center. The arrows have been added for this book.

42 *http://images.jsc.nasa.gov/luceneweb/fullimage.jsp?photoId=AS16-107-17446.*

The answer to this conundrum, for once, was found by a conspiracy theorist, Steve Troy of Lunaranomalies.com, in 2001.[43] His fellow theorists, however, seem to have ignored his research and continue to peddle this alleged evidence.

In 2001 Troy ordered from various NASA agencies film duplicates of this photograph and analyzed them in search of the letter. It wasn't there. So he contacted the same agencies to inquire why the letter was instead present in one of the "official" NASA websites. One of these agencies, Houston's Lunar and Planetary Institute (LPI), found that one of their reference *prints*, but not their *films* (duplicates of the Apollo originals), had the alleged letter. LPI supplied Troy with a scan of that print at the highest possible resolution. It turned out that the letter was actually a tiny hair (Figure 5-43).

The Johnson Space Center explained that one of these imperfect prints had been scanned in the late 1980s or early 1990s and had remained on the website since then. More recent, higher-quality scans are available online which don't have the hair. These scans also reveal that the other alleged letter, the one on the ground, is just a shadow that looks vaguely like a letter C (Figure 5-44).

Figure 5-43. The "letter" is revealed to be simply a hair.

Figure 5-44. Detail of a more direct scan of the original photograph.

5.15 The backpack antenna appears and disappears

IN A NUTSHELL: *The radio antenna on the astronauts' backpacks only "disappears" if you look at the low-resolution copies of the photographs. It doesn't disappear in the high-quality scans, but it becomes fainter. This is because it was a flat antenna and therefore it became almost invisible when it was edge-on to the camera or to the Sun.*

---

43 The original site no longer exists, but Archive.org has preserved a copy made in 2008 at *http://web.archive.org/web/20080131090910/http://www.lunaranomalies.com/c-rock.htm.*

THE DETAILS: The PLSS radio antenna, located at the top of the astronauts' backpacks, seems to come and go in photographs taken moments apart. This is interpreted by some as evidence that the photographs were not taken in sequence and someone forgot to place the antenna consistently in the various photographs.

Figure 5-45. Detail of photo AS11-40-5942: no antenna.

An example of the disappearing antenna is offered by photos AS11-40-5942 and AS11-40-5943 from the Apollo 11 mission (Figures 5-45 and 5-46), which show Buzz Aldrin as he carries the instruments to be left on the Moon. The numbering of these photographs implies that they were officially taken in sequence. Yet the antenna is missing in the first one and distinctly visible in the second one.

Once again, this apparent inconsistency arises from one of the recurring mistakes of conspiracy theorists: using low-resolution copies instead of high-quality scans of the originals. The first picture comes from the low-resolution online set of the Johnson Space Center and shows no antenna, but inspection of the high-resolution version of the photograph reveals that the antenna is actually present, even though it's very faint (Figure 5-47).

Why does it look so different in the two pictures? Because it's not a traditional rod-like antenna: it's a flat metal strip (Figure 5-48).

Figure 5-46. Detail of photo AS11-40-5943: the antenna is clearly visible.

Seen edge-on, i.e., when the astronaut is directly facing the camera or has his back to it, these VHF antennas are almost invisible against the black lunar sky. Seen from the side, they become clearly visible by reflecting the sunlight from a much wider surface.

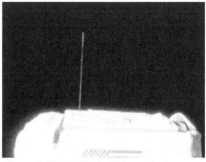

Figure 5-47. Detail of a high-resolution scan of photo AS11-40-5942.

In the first picture (5942), Aldrin is seen squarely from the back and therefore the antenna is edge-on to the camera. In the second picture (5943), the astronaut is turned sideways and so his antenna is showing its flat side to the camera.

In other pictures, such as AS11-40-5874 (the flag salute), the astronaut is seen from the side, but he's facing the sun and therefore the antenna is edge-on with respect to the light source, so only its front edge catches the light, making it hard to see except in the high-resolution scans.

Figure 5-48. Detail of the stowed VHF antenna of Charlie Duke's spacesuit (Apollo 16). Courtesy of K.C. Groneman and D.B. Eppler, NASA Johnson.

5.16 Aldrin's boots shine in shadow, must be spotlit

IN A NUTSHELL: *The sheen on Buzz Aldrin's boots is not caused by a studio spotlight but by sunlight reflected by Armstrong's reflective white spacesuit. The Moon boots in museums have a dull finish because they're worn, but they were initially coated with lubricant which made them quite shiny when brand-new and clean.*

THE DETAILS: In Apollo 11 photographs AS11-40-5866 and 5869, Aldrin's boots have a bright white highlight that looks like a reflection from a flash or a bright spotlight. This is suspicious, it is claimed, because Aldrin is standing in shadow, no flashes or studio lights were taken to the Moon, and Apollo Moon boots had a dull gray finish. Therefore, it is claimed, obtaining this kind of highlight would have required a very powerful local light source. Figure 5-49 shows an example of the controversial reflection.

First of all, the highlight isn't really as bright as it appears in the top part of Figure 5-49, which is a version often used in pro-conspiracy publications and in which contrast and brightness have been exaggerated to the point of losing all shadow detail. The bottom part of Figure 5-49 shows the same detail, but taken (without processing) from the high-resolution scan publicly available at NASA's GAPE site (*eol.jsc.nasa.gov*). The difference is quite remarkable.

Nevertheless, boots with a dull finish shouldn't produce a highlight of any sort. But if we examine the manufacturing process of these boots, it turns out that there's a very good reason for this sheen. The silicone rubber overshoes that formed the heel and sole of the boots were made in a mold. A lubricant was applied to the inside of the mold to prevent the silicone from sticking, so when the overshoe was removed from the mold it was coated with this lubricant.

Figure 5-49. Detail of photo AS11-40-5866 as often circulated in Moon hoax sites (top) and as found in direct scans of the original picture (bottom).

Archival footage of the process shows that brand-new Apollo overshoes were indeed shiny, and in the photographs of Aldrin's descent from the LM these overshoes were being used for the very first time, so they probably still had some lubricant on them.

Finally, there's the question of the light source. Conspiracy theorists jump to the conclusion that a studio spotlight was used, but actually there's another powerful light source: Neil Armstrong's bright white spacesuit. If we look at the TV broadcast, we can see that at this point of the lunar excursion Armstrong is close to Aldrin and is standing in direct sunlight. Apollo spacesuits were designed to reflect as much sunlight as possible to avoid overheating, so Neil's suit is essentially acting as a man-sized reflector. In other words, the highlight is not proof of fakery.

5.17 Aldrin is standing in a spotlight

IN A NUTSHELL: *No, he's standing in a patch of the lunar surface where the lunar module's rocket exhaust swept away the dust, making the surface brighter.*

THE DETAILS: Several Moon hoax theorists observe that in some photographs of the Apollo 11 landing, such as AS11-40-5903 (Buzz Aldrin's "tourist photo", already seen as Figure 3-7), the ground around the astronaut is far brighter than the rest. As the distance from the astronaut increases, the ground becomes unusually darker. That, they claim, is the result of a studio spotlight.

Figure 5-50. Photo AS11-40-5903 as printed in the August 1989 issue of Italian photography magazine Fotografare.

This alleged evidence is often illustrated by copies of these photographs in which the contrast has been pushed, exaggerating the difference in brightness, such as Figure 5-50, which is taken from *Fotografare*, an Italian photography magazine that supported the claims of fakery. Moon hoax literature knows no language barrier.

The common-sense objection to this allegation is that the organizers of the hypothetical fakery on behalf of the US government wouldn't have been short on cash to the point of not having enough spotlights and wouldn't have been so incompetent as to forget to light the background evenly. It would have been a truly amateurish blunder, as any directory of photography will attest. Such a patently obvious blunder, moreover, would somehow have had to get by the inspection of the people in charge of selecting and publishing the alleged fakes, yet be so glaring as to be noticed by the unrelenting gaze of conspiracy theorists.

Another objection is that if Aldrin is standing in a spotlight, his shadow should be washed out in the spotlit patch and then be dark in the foreground, where the "spotlight" effect ceases, but it isn't. Moreover, a spotlight should produce a second shadow of the astronaut, but there isn't one in the pictures.

If the difference in brightness of the ground can't be explained by lighting conditions, then perhaps the ground itself was brighter around Aldrin for some reason. Finding that reason requires a bit of detective work.

First of all we need to locate that part of the ground. In the uncropped version of AS11-40-5903, a leg of the lunar module is visible next to Aldrin. The direction of the shadows allows to determine that it's the LM's right leg (as seen from the crew compartment). So the brighter ground is to the right of the lunar module's right leg. Now we can look for other photographs of the same area. It turns out that AS11-40-5886 (Figure 5-51) is a wider view of that area.

Figure 5-51. Photograph AS11-40-5886 (Apollo 11, cropped).

More importantly, the wider view reveals that the brighter region is actually an elongated streak that crosses the picture diagonally from the upper left to the lower right, and that the LM's shadow is roughly at right angles to the streak. The high-resolution scans of these photographs also suggest that the brighter patch is almost dust-free (astronaut bootprints are shallow or nonexistent in it), as if something had swept away the dust in that particular area and exposed a band of the underlying smoother, more reflective rock.

That *something* could be the LM's descent engine exhaust, if the spacecraft had moved sideways just before touchdown. It did. The radio communications logs and the 16 mm film footage of the landing show that the LM drifted mostly sideways, first to the right (Aldrin: *"4 forward. 4 forward. Drifting to the right a little"*) and then to the left, seconds before landing, with negligible forward velocity. This path is also supported by telemetry data, by the small pits to the sides of the LM footpads and by the orientation of the contact probes that stick out of the ground.

In other words, the explanation that best fits all the available facts is not that a spotlight was secretly and clumsily used, but that Buzz Aldrin was standing in the band of lunar ground that had been swept by the LM's rocket exhaust, which had blown away the surface dust, exposing the brighter rock below.

This is a good example of how it can be challenging, even for a very expert photographer, to explain the apparent anomalies that occur in some Moon photographs without knowing the technical details of the circumstances in which they were taken.

5.18 Backlit photos should show silhouettes in a vacuum

IN A NUTSHELL: *No, they shouldn't. The shadow side of a backlit astronaut is lit by the light reflected off nearby objects. This kind of reflection is perfectly possible in a vacuum and occurs in many other undisputed space photographs.*

THE DETAILS: Many supporters of Moon photo fakery theories have remarked that in some pictures the astronauts have the sun behind them and are therefore brightly backlit, yet they don't show up as dark silhouettes as normally happens in backlit situations. On the contrary, their shadow side is perfectly visible.

An example of this phenomenon is Apollo 15 photograph AS15-85-11514 (Figure 5-52): the direction of astronaut David Scott's shadow indicates that the photographer (James Irwin) is facing the sun and therefore Scott's side facing the camera is in shadow, yet we can see it clearly. It is claimed that this is impossible in the vacuum of the Moon, because there's no atmosphere to diffuse the sunlight and therefore the shadow side of an astronaut should be pitch black. The same claim is applied to Aldrin's "tourist photo", AS11-40-5903 (Figure 3-7).

Figure 5-52. Detail of photograph AS15-85-11514 (Apollo 15).

This argument is based on an incorrect premise. In actual fact, the laws of physics and optics don't say that the shadow side of a backlit object is lit by *diffusion*, which is the scattering of light produced by the gas molecules, suspended dust and water droplets of an atmosphere. They say that shadow lighting is caused mainly by the *reflection* of light from nearby objects, which does not require an atmosphere. So reflection works fine in a near-vacuum such as the Moon.

Indeed, photographers use reflection (not diffusion) all the time to soften the shadows of a portrait by placing the subject close to a brightly lit wall or by using custom-built reflective panels, which are kept out of frame (Figure 5-53).

On the Moon, this reflection is provided by the ground, which is in full sunlight and is all around the astronauts, who are wearing a highly reflective white spacesuit.

The fact that an atmosphere is not needed to obtain a fill light in backlit pictures is demonstrated by Space Shuttle photographs, where the astronaut is in the vacuum of space but the light reflected by the surrounding surfaces and by the daylit Earth below is more than enough to soften the shadows. In Figure 5-54, for example, the

Figure 5-53. Reflection on a bright surface is often used to soften the shadows of a person standing against the sun. Credit: Lisa Attivissimo.

only source of direct light is the sun, but the white surfaces of the Shuttle cargo bay reflect enough of this sunlight to lighten the shadows on astronaut Bruce McCandless.

In other words, the explanation of this alleged anomaly is the same one given for the objection that astronauts in shadow are strangely well-lit. In that case, the conspiracists argued that the counterintuitive lighting was evidence of studio spotlights, whereas here they claim that shadow softening is evidence of an atmosphere. In both instances their claims turn out to be factually incorrect.

Figure 5-54. Astronaut Bruce McCandless works in the vacuum of space outside the Shuttle (1984). Photo GPN-2000-001075.

5.19 Armstrong's boulder field isn't in the photos

IN A NUTSHELL: *Actually, it is. The large boulders that Neil Armstrong says he overflew just before landing are faintly visible in the Apollo 11 photographs, but only in the high-resolution scans, because they're over 400 meters (1,300 feet) away and therefore appear tiny. Moreover, from the landing site they were upsun and therefore impossible to document in detail. However, these boulders are clearly visible in the pictures of the landing site taken in 2009 by the Lunar Reconnaissance Orbiter.*

THE DETAILS: Descriptions of the first Moon landing often mention dramatically that the automatic systems of the lunar module were taking astronauts Armstrong and Aldrin straight into a dangerous crater surrounded by large boulders, but Armstrong took manual control and flew on to find a clear landing spot. This took so much time that the Apollo 11 astronauts landed with less than a minute of fuel to spare. This episode is frequently used to point out the advantages of having a pilot on board to deal with the shortcomings of automatic systems and to stress how difficult and dangerous it was to land on the Moon.

However, the photographs taken by Aldrin and Armstrong show no trace of this alleged boulder field. As far as the eye can see, the landing site is flat and featureless. Perhaps, it is argued, this detail was added to embellish the story and make it more exciting.

That's a doubt that we can dispel by looking at the data. Apollo 11's landing path, or *ground track*, is published in the *Apollo 11 Mission Report* (Figure 5-55).

Armstrong's decision is transcribed in the 1969 *Technical Debrief*; the *Apollo 11 Preliminary Science Report* identifies the boulder-littered crater as *West Crater*. This crater is visible in Figure 5-55, which however shows no boulders due to its low resolution.

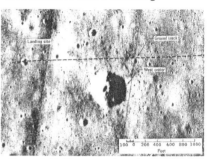

Figure 5-55. The ground track of Apollo 11 ends on the left. The large crater at the center is known as West Crater. Detail from the Apollo 11 Mission Report *(1969).*

Today, however, we have the high-resolution pictures of the Apollo 11 landing site acquired by the Lunar Reconnaissance Orbiter (LRO) probe since 2009. These images show the boulders quite clearly (Figure 5-56).

In particular, image M109080308RE, taken by the LRO probe and shown partially in Figure 5-56, captures West Crater in very fine detail (this image is rotated 90° counterclockwise with respect to Figure 5-55). It shows that the crater is indeed surrounded by boulders, which stand out as white dots. Their size can be grasped by noting that the white dot indicated by the arrow in Figure 5-56 is the central part of Apollo 11's descent stage, which is about four meters (13 feet) wide without the landing legs.

The boulders can't be seen in the photographs taken by the Apollo 11 astronauts for two main reasons. The first one is that they were too far away: the scale of Figure 5-55 indicates that the center of West Crater was over 500 meters (1,600 feet) from the LM.

The second reason is that in order to take any pictures of West Crater, the astronauts would have had to point the camera towards the sun. This would have produced very poor, lens flare-filled photographs, so no photos were taken in that direction. In some pictures, West Crater is at the very edge of the frame and a few boulders can be glimpsed, but only in the high-resolution versions (Figure 5-57).

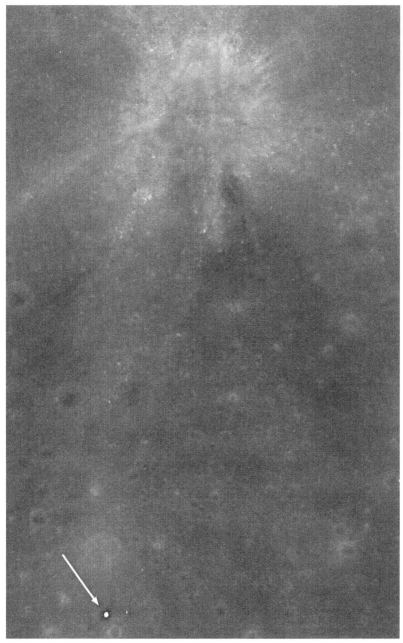

Figure 5-56. The Apollo 11 landing site as imaged by the LRO probe in 2009. West crater is at the top; the image is rotated 90° counterclockwise with respect to Figure 5-55. The arrow indicates the descent stage of the lunar module.

However, there's another source of photographic coverage of the area supplied by the Apollo 11 astronauts: the 16 mm color film shot during descent and landing. Since the lunar module flew past West Crater as it descended to land, the boulder field should be quite visible in this film.

Indeed it is: Figure 5-58 is a frame from that footage, taken from an altitude of about 120 meters (390 feet) with the camera looking down almost vertically. The boulders are large enough to be distinctly visible from that height and cast conspicuous shadows.

Figure 5-57. Detail of photo AS11-40-5873 (Apollo 11), taken almost fully upsun. West Crater is on the horizon, to the left.

As a further cross-check, researchers Rene and Jonathan Cantin produced and published a video[44] that matches the Apollo 11 landing film against a photograph of the same area taken in 1967 by an unmanned Lunar Orbiter probe; the same footage has also been compared by another researcher, GoneToPlaid,[45] with more recent Lunar Reconnaissance Orbiter images of the landing site, included in Google Moon. In both instances, the positions of the craters line up correctly.

Figure 5-58. Boulders near the landing site, seen from approximately 120 meters (390 feet), in a frame of the 16 mm film of the landing.

In other words, instead of being evidence of conspiracy, the issue of the apparently missing boulders is a great opportunity to perform cross-checks on the available documents and verify that they are mutually consistent.

---

44 http://www.hq.nasa.gov/alsj/a11/Apollo11_Version2.wmv.

45 http://www.youtube.com/watch?v=G9Nh5qWzqMY.

5.20 The tracks of the Moon car are missing

IN A NUTSHELL: *They're not missing: they're wiped out by the astronauts' bootprints, or they didn't form at all because the special open-mesh wheels didn't leave deep tracks and because the astronauts often turned the buggy around by lifting it at one end, without leaving wheel tracks.*

THE DETAILS: In some photographs there's no sign of the tracks formed in the lunar dust by the wheels of the electric buggy (the Lunar Rover, Figure 5-59), neither in front of the vehicle nor behind it.

Figure 5-59. Detail of photo AS15-86-11603 (Apollo 15).

Parting Shot!

And here we see an Apollo 17 astronaut making emergency repairs on the buggy' did that with his gloves on is debatable!).

Ok. So far, so good. Now check out the pic where the repair has been done. Then BUT WHAT HAPPENED TO THE BUGGY'S TIRE MARKS? How did it get there? Was t This has nothing to do with gravity or an atmosphere, but shows the hidden side o

Figure 5-60. Alleged evidence of fakery: no wheel tracks. From Davidicke.com.

Yet the same lunar soil clearly registered the astronauts' bootprints. According to some Moon hoax theorists, the studio crew forgot to add tire marks when they placed the Rover on the set, thus revealing the fakery (Figure 5-60).

Actually, there are several reasons why the tracks are sometimes missing. In some photographs the astronauts simply walked over the tracks and wiped them out with their bootprints. To take pictures of the Rover, they had to get off the vehicle and walk away from it, so it makes sense that they sometimes walked over the freshly formed tracks.

Indeed, this is the case in Figure 5-60, which is presented as alleged evidence: a little research reveals it to be a cropped version of photograph AS17-137-20979, which documents the improvised repair of the Rover's fender by the Apollo 17 astronauts. To make this repair (using duct tape, clamps and laminated maps), they obviously had to walk all around the damaged fender, thus erasing any wheel tracks.

If we look at the complete photograph (Figure 5-61), which is in color and far less contrasted and more detailed than the version presented by the Moon hoax proponents, we find that astronaut bootprints are visible at the bottom and on the right. It is interesting to note that the pro-hoax version is conveniently cropped so as to hide almost all the bootprints.

In other photographs, the vehicle was traveling over an area that didn't have a deep layer of dust (like the Earth, the Moon isn't identical every-where) and therefore the wheels of the Rover left faint tracks that can be seen only in the high-resolution versions of the Apollo photographs but are invisible in the poor copies frequently used by hoax theorists.

Figure 5-61. The uncropped version of photo AS17-137-20979 with its original colors and shades.

It should also be noted that the wheels of the Rover didn't have tires or a solid tread. They were made of an open metallic mesh on which spaced titanium laminas were applied in a chevron pattern (Figure 5-62).

The fine lunar dust would pass through the mesh like sand through a sieve and therefore didn't leave the sharply out-lined tracks of a normal solid tire tread, which compacts the ground.

This frequent lack of tracks is due also to another reason, which is rather counterintuitive: the Rover was extremely light, and on the Moon everything weighs one sixth of what it weighs on Earth. The Rover weighed about 210 kilograms (462 pounds) on Earth, so on the Moon it weighed only about 35 kilograms (77 pounds);

Figure 5-62. Detail of photo AS16-108-17620. Note the shallowness of the track and the light that passes through the mesh of the wheel, as revealed by the gaps in the wheel shadow.

therefore the astronauts could easily lift one of its ends. Indeed, that's what they often did when they needed to turn the Rover around: they simply lifted one end and turned it. This was actually a scheduled maneuver during the extraction of the Rover from the LM: the Moon car had to be turned through 180 degrees to point it away from the LM.

This low weight was distributed over the contact area of the four wheels and therefore the Rover applied a very low pressure to the ground even when it was carrying the astronauts, whose weight was likewise reduced by the low lunar gravity. Accordingly, the wheels did not dig deeply into the soil, producing only shallow tracks.

5.21 NASA has published retouched photographs

IN A NUTSHELL: *Yes, some NASA websites contain retouched photos. But the retouching is just to repair scratches or blemishes in old scans of duplicates. The high-resolution master scans available through NASA show no such signs of fixing.*

THE DETAILS: Perhaps surprisingly, it is quite true that some NASA websites have published badly touched-up versions of the Apollo images. For example, image S69-40308 at *Spaceflight.nasa.gov* (Figure 5-63) is crudely retouched by cutting and pasting in its top right part (Figure 5-64). The alteration is revealed by the unusually repeating patterns in the lunar soil.

Figure 5-63. Image S69-40308, a frame from the Apollo 11 16 mm film, as shown at Spaceflight.nasa.gov in February 2010. Note the repeating patterns in the top right corner.

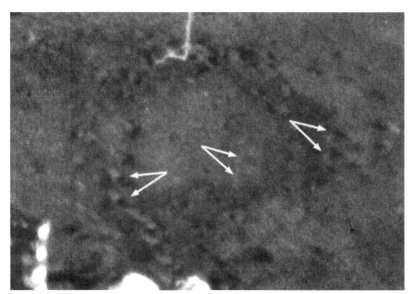

Figure 5-64. Detail of the preceding image. The arrows indicate the duplicated regions.

Copy-pasting is often used in digital retouching to cover unwanted details or a flaw in the picture. Here the touch-up is so blatant that even dust specks that were on the scanned film have been conspicuously duplicated.

However, this doesn't mean that NASA systematically retouches its pictures and is concealing embarrassing or top-secret details: it seems rather unlikely that a high-level cover-up would publish such clumsy and easily detectable fakes. Besides, NASA websites also offer other copies of this image that have not been retouched (for example at the *Apollo Lunar Surface Journal*). These copies reveal that the copy-pasting is merely correcting defects in scans taken from old, damaged copies of the original films. It's just a clean-up, not a deception.

It might seem unusual for NASA to publish such shoddy versions of the Apollo photographs, but contrary to the beliefs of many Moon hoax theorists the US space agency is not a wealthy, monolithic government body. It's a big bureaucracy with many departments that often work in isolation from each other and with limited funds and equipment. The end result is that various NASA departments each published on the Internet their own versions of the Apollo visual record, using the film copies that they had in their archives. In many cases those film copies were duplicates of duplicates made years or decades earlier, faded by time and damaged by handling.

Having no funds allocated for a fresh scan of the Apollo images, the departments used whatever they had. The same process generated the alleged letter C on a rock, debunked earlier in this chapter.

The unretouched, properly scanned originals are available from four main Internet reference sources: the *Apollo Lunar Surface Journal*, the Lunar and Planetary Institute, the *Gateway to Astronaut Photography of Earth* and the Apollo Archive. Details and Internet addresses are in the *References* section of this book.

5.22 The EVA photo of Michael Collins is fake

IN A NUTSHELL: *No, it's not. A conspiracy theorist altered it to make it look fake.*

THE DETAILS: According to Moon hoax theorist Ralph Rene, the autobiography of lunar astronaut Michael Collins, *Carrying the Fire*, contains a faked spacewalk photograph (Figure 5-65).

Rene claims that the autobiography describes this picture as Collins during a spacewalk in the Gemini 10 mission (1966) although it's actually a photo taken during training inside an aircraft and then (says Rene) altered by NASA (Figure 5-66).

According to Rene's book *Nasa Mooned America!*, these pictures *"absolutely prove that NASA began to doctor photos three years before the Apollo missions allegedly landed men on the Moon".* Rene makes the same allegation in Willy Brunner and Gerhard Wisnewski's documentary *Die Akte Apollo*, broadcast by German TV station WDR in 2002 and by Italian national network Rai in 2006.

Figure 5-65. The allegedly faked photograph, as shown by Rene.

Some basic fact-checking shows that the allegedly doctored version of the photograph (Figure 5-65) does not appear in any NASA publication. It only appears in some editions of the Collins autobiography (the 1974 edition by Farrar, Straus & Giroux and the 1975 edition by Ballantine Books) and even there it is not described as being taken during the Gemini 10 spacewalk. The caption clearly states that it was taken during training in an aircraft.

Indeed, Collins himself notes with regret, in his book, that there are no photographs of his Gemini 10 spacewalk (*"One of the great disappointments of the flight was that there were no photos of my spacewalk. [...] I was really feeling sorry for myself, unable to produce graphic documentation for my grandchildren of my brief sally as a human satellite"*).

In 2003, space historian James Oberg offered Rene 10,000 dollars for any edition of the Collins autobiography that described the doctored photograph as a spacewalk snapshot. Rene was unable to provide one, and so far nobody else has either.

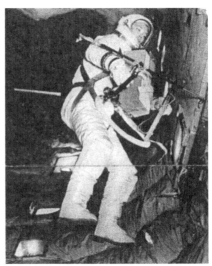

Figure 5-66. The other version of the photograph.

In their documentary, German authors Brunner and Wisnewski resort to misleading editing in order to support Rene's allegation: first they show the cover of *Carrying the Fire* and then they crossfade to a page that contains the allegedly doctored photograph with the caption *"Gemini 10 space walk",* as shown in Figure 5-67.

Figure 5-67. The Brunner and Wisnewski documentary Die Akte Apollo *crossfades the cover of the Collins autobiography with a page from Rene's book (stills from the Italian broadcast of the documentary, 2006).*

However, this page is not taken from *Carrying the Fire*: it's taken from Rene's book *Nasa Mooned America!*, as revealed by the text on the page, which can be read in freeze-frame.

In summary, the entire allegation of fakery against Michael Collins and NASA is made up. Instead of demonstrating *"absolutely"* that the US space agency faked a photo, it demonstrates that some Moon hoax theorists are willing to stoop to falsehoods and editing tricks in order to prop their claims.

5.23 Not enough time to take so many photos

IN A NUTSHELL: *Yes, there was, because many photos were taken in rapid bursts; for example, almost half of the 120 pictures of the Apollo 11 moonwalk were taken with a single camera in quick sets of 8 to 12 shots, as the astronaut turned around on the spot, to form panoramic sequences. The same applies to the other missions.*

THE DETAILS: Conspiracy theorist Jack White claims that the astronauts didn't have enough time to take all the photographs that NASA says were taken on the Moon and also get some work done. Therefore, he argues, some of the pictures must be fake.[46]

White says that the Apollo missions, according to NASA's reports, spent a total of 4,834 minutes on the Moon, taking 5,771 photographs. This is equivalent to an average of 1.19 photographs per minute (one photograph every 50 seconds) throughout the duration of all the moonwalks. White says that the Apollo 11 crew reached an even higher average, with one photo every 15 seconds (121 shots in 151 minutes).

The Apollo 11 figures given by White are almost correct: the film magazine used during mankind's first moonwalk contains 123 photographs (not 121) taken outside the lunar module (catalog numbers AS11-40-5850 to 5970, plus AS11-40-5882A and 5966A), and Armstrong and Aldrin's excursion lasted two hours and 31 minutes according to the *Apollo Definitive Sourcebook*.

Taking 123 photographs in 151 minutes, however, doesn't yield an average of one picture every fifteen seconds. The actual average is less than one picture per minute. How does White get to 15 seconds? He introduces *"arbitrarily"* (as he puts it) a value of two hours to take into account the other activities of the astronauts:

> *Let's arbitrarily calculate a MINIMUM time for these tasks and subtract from available photo time.*

Why two hours and not two and a quarter, or one and a half? White doesn't explain the reason for his choice. It's obviously quite easy to get impossible results if you alter the data by introducing arbitrary values.

White also fails to specify that the astronauts took many sets of photographs from a same point, without wasting time getting into position and aiming again for each picture, so that the photos could be later assembled into panoramic views.

---

46 *www.aulis.com/skeleton.htm.*

In creating a panoramic sequence it's quite easy to take a dozen photographs in a few seconds (try this yourself). This alters considerably the average time required. Here are a few examples.

Photos AS11-40-5881 to AS11-40-5891 (11 frames, almost 10% of all of the Apollo 11 moonwalk photographs) were shot by Buzz Aldrin as he turned around on the spot to form the panoramic view of Figure 5-68.

Figure 5-68. Panoramic view assembled by Dave Byrne for the Apollo Lunar Surface Journal *with photos AS11-40-5881 to 5891.*

Photographs AS11-40-5905 to AS11-40-5916 (12 frames, 10% of the total) compose another panoramic view, again taken by Aldrin and shown assembled in Figure 5-69.

Figure 5-69. Panoramic view assembled by Brian McInall for the Apollo Lunar Surface Journal *with photos AS11-40-5905 to 5916.*

Frames AS11-40-5930 to AS11-40-5941 (twelve shots) were taken by Neil Armstrong to form the panoramic view shown in Figure 5-70.

Figure 5-70. Panoramic view assembled by Brian McInall for the Apollo Lunar Surface Journal *using photos AS11-40-5930 to 5941.*

Figure 3.15 of NASA's *Apollo 11 Preliminary Science Report* shows the location and direction of every photograph taken during the Apollo 11 excursion (Figure 5-71). The number of photographs taken in rapid sequence from the same location is quite considerable.

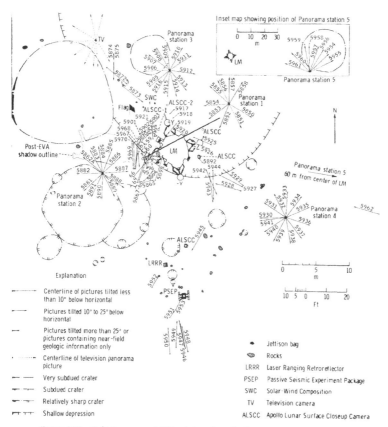

FIGURE 3-15. — Preliminary map of EVA photographs and television pictures taken at the landing site.

Figure 5-71. Map of the locations and directions of every photograph taken during the Apollo 11 moonwalk.

This map indicates that photographs 5850 to 5858 (9 shots) and 5954 to 5961 (8 shots) form two more panoramic views in addition to the ones shown above.

In summary, therefore, during the Apollo 11 moonwalk 52 photographs out of 123 belong to panoramic sequences that were taken in quick bursts, without moving and refocusing between shots.

The same applies to the other moonwalks, in which the astronauts took many panoramic sets (Figure 5-72 is an example of a moonscape from Apollo 16) and also took several *stereo pairs*, i.e., two photographs taken almost simultaneously from two slightly different viewpoints, which can be combined to produce 3D images.

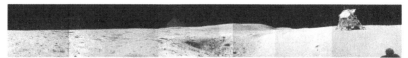

Figure 5-72. Panoramic view assembled using photos AS16-113-18313 to 18330 by Lennie Waugh for the Apollo Lunar Surface Journal.

Once all the facts are on the table, it's no longer surprising that the astronauts took so many photographs. What is surprising, instead, is that Jack White, who claims to have researched the Apollo missions thoroughly before making his allegations of fraud, has failed to consider this simple explanation, which is extensively documented and is self-evident from the photographs themselves.

5.24 The astronaut's shadow is missing

IN A NUTSHELL: *Yes, in the photograph of John Young's salute to the US flag on the Moon, the astronaut appears to cast no shadow. But this isn't evidence of fakery: Young was simply jumping when the snapshot was taken and so his shadow is displaced sideways and isn't visible in cropped versions of the picture; full versions show it clearly.*

THE DETAILS: The photograph shown in Figure 5-73 is often claimed by hoax theorists to be fake because the astronaut quite conspicuously lacks a shadow.

A patient search through the Apollo image archives reveals that it's a cropped version of photo AS16-113-18339, taken during the Apollo 16 mission by Charlie Duke. It portrays his commander, John Young, as he salutes the flag.

Figure 5-73. The allegedly faked shadowless saluting astronaut.

Knowing the context in which the picture was taken provides the answer to the missing shadow. As noted in the mission reports and transcripts, and as recorded by the video footage of the mission, Young jumped vertically during the salute and Duke caught him in midair in the photograph. That's why there's no shadow at Young's feet: the shadow is displaced downwards and to the viewer's right, as occurs normally when someone is photographed during a vertical leap with a low sun angle.

The uncropped scans of the photograph show that the astronaut does indeed cast a shadow in the lower right corner of the picture (Figure 5-74).

Figure 5-74. Detail of photo AS16-113-18339. John Young's shadow is displaced towards the bottom right corner because the picture was taken while he was jumping vertically.

5.25 The United States marking on the LM is too bright

IN A NUTSHELL: *The "United States" marking on the lunar module is surprisingly readable in the photographs even when it lies on the shadow side of the LM not because of a spotlight placed for propaganda reasons, but because it's reflective and is lit by the glare from the daylit lunar surface. In fact it's equally readable in the pictures taken during LM testing in Earth orbit.*

THE DETAILS: There are claims that the *"United States"* lettering on the descent stage of the lunar module has been brightened and made more visible by retouching it in the photographs or by training a studio spotlight on it when the pictures were taken. This was done, presumably, for propaganda purposes, in order to point out that the Moon landing was an American accomplishment (Figure 5-75). With the Sun behind the LM, it is said, the logo in shadow should not be so clearly visible.

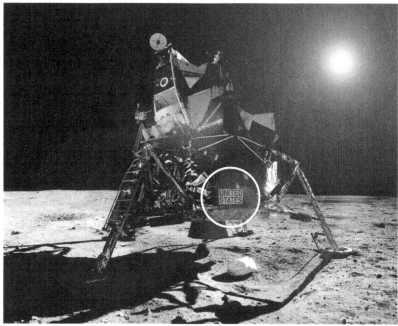

Figure 5-75. The "United States" marking (circled) is allegedly too bright in this picture, which incidentally is not an original Apollo photograph: it's a composite made by Ed Hengeveld (Apollo Lunar Surface Journal).

The logo is indeed lit despite being on the shadow side of the spacecraft. But the lighting doesn't come from an artificial spotlight. It comes from the sunlight reflected off the surrounding lunar surface, which is in daylight. The logo was brighter, flatter and more reflective than the surrounding skin of the vehicle and so reflected more light towards the photographer.

For example, the "United States" lettering stands out also in the photographs of the Apollo 9 mission, during which the lunar module was tested in Earth orbit, because it reflects the glare from the surface of the Earth (Figure 5-76).

Moreover, the picture that is often presented as evidence of this alleged fakery (Figure 5-75) is not a real Apollo photograph. It's a composite image, created by Ed Hengeveld and published in the *Apollo Lunar Surface Journal*, where it is clearly labeled as a montage. It was made by joining various photographs from the Apollo 11 mission and by adding fake portions of sky and an equally fake Sun.

This is revealed not only by the fact that its author openly presents it as a whimsical fabrication, but by the mismatched perspective and by the reflections of the Sun, which are not oriented consistently. The digital compositing also distorts the perception of contrast, which is pushed far more in this montage than it is in the original pictures, enhancing the visual appearance of a strangely bright logo. The logo is not as bright in the original photographs used to create this montage.

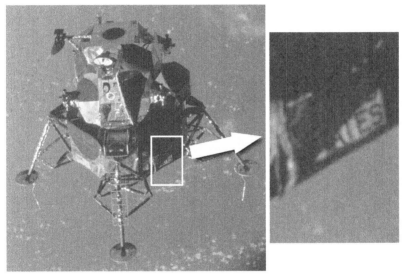

Figure 5-76. Photo AS09-21-3183 (Apollo 9, detail). Here, too, the logo is visible.

6. Alleged anomalies in videos and film footage

Supporters of Moon fakery theories believe that they have found evidence to back up their allegations not only in the photographic record, as discussed in the previous chapter, but also in alleged anomalies in the live TV broadcasts from space and from the Moon and in the film footage of the Apollo missions. Understanding the real reasons for these purported anomalies requires a little knowledge of 1960s television and film technology.

6.1 Apollo video and movie technology: a quick primer

The Apollo visual record includes both video recordings, made using TV cameras that transmitted their pictures to Earth, where they were rebroadcast and recorded on magnetic tape, and film footage, shot using movie cameras that recorded the pictures onboard on 16 mm film.

Today it's quite commonplace to use the term *video* for any kind of moving picture, lumping together TV and film, but in the Sixties there was a huge quality and portability gap between television and movie technology.

The miniaturization afforded by modern electronics was in its infancy. Studio TV cameras for color broadcasts were bulky, inefficient monsters that weighed over 125 kilograms (280 pounds), like the ones shown in Figure 6-1. Early "portable" color TV cameras, such as the Ikegami HL-33, made their debut only in the Seventies. Black-and-white

Figure 6-1. RCA TK-43 color TV cameras in the 1960s. Credit: Oldradio.com.

models were slightly less unwieldy, but they were still massive, power-hungry, heavy devices that could not be used in low light and depended on an external electric power supply and on even bulkier recording equipment. Moreover, they provided rather poor picture quality: nothing even comparable to today's tiny high-definition video cameras and recorders that we carry in our pockets as part of our cellphones.

Movie cameras, instead, were already a mature technology. They were compact, lightweight, sturdy and fully independent of mains power thanks to batteries or wind-up mechanisms. Movie cameras for amateur use were just a little bit bigger than a still camera. For example, a professional Arriflex movie camera using 16 mm film weighed about six kilograms (13 pounds) and required no extra equipment, apart from an optional sound recorder and a good supply of film, to shoot anywhere in the world, taking moving color pictures with a quality that far surpassed that of television. A professional movie camera was, in a way, the 1960s equivalent of today's portable high-definition video gear.

Movie cameras were used for virtually all news footage, for war zone reporting and for detailing science experiments, missile launches and aircraft tests, thanks also to the in-depth analysis offered by *slow motion*, which was easy to achieve with film but technically unattainable with the TV cameras of the day.

The key drawbacks of movie cameras were of course the recording time, which was limited by the amount of film available, and the impossibility of live broadcasts, since film had to be developed by a chemical process. But if live transmission was not indispensable and a deferred viewing was acceptable, in the Sixties film was king. It's important to bear this in mind to understand the technical choices made by NASA in documenting the Apollo missions.

The Apollo movie cameras

The Apollo lunar missions carried so-called *Data Acquisition Cameras* (DAC), movie cameras that used 16 mm color film magazines (Figure 6-2). They were extremely compact and lightweight: including the side-mounted magazine, they measured approximately 22 x 13 x 6.5 centimeters (8 3/4 x 5 x 2 1/2 inches) and weighed 1300 grams (2.9 pounds).

One of these movie cameras was mounted in the Lunar Module so as to look downward out the right side window of the spacecraft, as shown in photograph AS11-36-5389 (Figure 6-3). This simple but effective technology is what gave us color pictures of the lunar module's descent to the Moon and of Neil Armstrong's first footstep on the lunar surface.

Most of mankind's first moon-walk (86 minutes out of 131) was filmed in color with this system. The first few minutes used a rate of 12 frames per second, half that of a normal movie; the remainder of the excursion was shot at one frame per second in order to save film, since each film magazine only contained 39.6 meters (130 feet) of color film, which at a normal frame rate would have been enough to shoot a little more than three and a half minutes.

Figure 6-2. The Maurer 16 mm movie camera used in the command module of Apollo 11. Credit: Smithsonian National Air and Space Museum.

Reducing the frame rate increases the recording time but produces jerkier moving pictures. At one frame per second, the film footage is more like a series of still photographs than an actual moving picture record. Examples of the pictures taken by this movie camera are shown in Figures 3-11, 5-9 and 5-63.

Figure 6-3. The Maurer movie camera in position before Apollo 11's Moon landing. Detail from photo AS11-36-5389.

In later missions, the movie camera was taken outside, on the lunar surface. For Apollo 12 it was placed on the Lunar Hand Tool Carrier (a frame with legs); on Apollo 14 it was installed on the Modularized Equipment Transporter, a sort of wheeled cart; for Apollo 15, 16 and 17 it was mounted on the Lunar Rover (Figure 6-4, which shows how truly small the camera was).

Figure 6-4. Top left: the movie camera mounted on the Rover, next to Charlie Duke, during training for Apollo 16.

All this footage is now available at medium resolution on the Internet and in high resolution on the DVDs and Blu-Rays published by specialist firms such as Spacecraft Films.

The Apollo TV cameras

Transmitting television pictures from space and from the Moon entailed two technological challenges that had never been met before.

The first one was to build a TV camera that could work in a vacuum, withstand great brightness and temperature variations between shadow and sunlight and survive the intense vibration and acceleration of liftoff, yet be compact and lightweight enough to allow an astronaut to carry it and operate it in the confined space of the interior of a spacecraft and on the lunar surface.

The other challenge was to find a way to send back to Earth a live television signal from a distance of almost 400,000 kilometers (250,000 miles) using only the electric power available on board the Apollo craft and the vehicle's radio transmission equipment, which had been designed for entirely different purposes. Live TV from the Moon was, in a way, an afterthought.

Apollo 7 and Apollo 8 carried a single black-and-white slow-scan TV camera made by RCA. With Apollo 9, NASA tested and used a black-and-white TV camera built by Westinghouse intended for later use on the Moon. Apollo 10 introduced a Westinghouse color TV camera, qualified only for inflight use. Apollo 11 carried a color camera for onboard use and a black-and-white camera for use on the Moon.

The Westinghouse Lunar Camera used on Apollo 11 (shown on the left in Figure 6-5) used only 6.5 watts, measured 28 x 15 x 7.6 centimeters (11 by 6 x 3 inches) and weighed 3.3 kilograms (7.25 pounds), yet was capable of working in the harsh environment of the Moon, with its vacuum and its temperature extremes. This remarkable performance, miniaturization and weight reduction were achieved by using 43 integrated circuits, which were very rare in

Figure 6-5. Stan Lebar, head of Westinghouse's Apollo TV camera project, shows the onboard camera (left) and the lunar camera (right) for Apollo 11.

those days, and a special component, an *SEC* (*Secondary Electron Conduction*) tube, which at the time was a military secret.

This achievement, however, came initially at the cost of color. That's why the TV pictures of the first Moon landing are in black and white. As technology progressed and NASA's confidence in being able to receive a complex TV signal from the Moon improved, subsequent missions were provided with a slightly larger color lunar camera, which produced color by using the same method used by the onboard camera: a *color wheel* (a disk with colored filters) spun in front of the camera sensor, generating a set of three color-filtered pictures, which were reassembled by the ground stations on Earth to recreate the original colors. This was a very compact and reliable system, although it caused multicolor halos around rapidly moving objects.

Having solved the issues of weight and size, there was still the question of sending the camera's signal to Earth. The limitations of the Lunar Module's onboard transmission equipment allowed a bandwidth of only 700 kHz, but a standard TV signal required 6,000. This meant that the standard TV format (NTSC) had to be abandoned and a custom one had to be used. For Apollo 11, this format had 320 progressive lines and 10 frames per second, compared with 525 interlaced lines and 30 frames per second of an ordinary TV broadcast. The lunar TV camera also had a "high definition" mode that generated a 1,280-line picture every second and a half, but it was never used.

These nonstandard solutions required special equipment on Earth to convert the signal to the normal television format. Since there was no digital technology capable of real-time video processing in the 1960s, a rather drastic approach was taken: a standard broadcast television camera was pointed at a special high-persistence monitor that displayed the images from the Moon.

The loss of detail and quality caused by this conversion was partly compensated by electronic devices, but nevertheless the difference between the signal that was received from the Moon and the converted signal was great (Figures 6-6 and 6-7).

The Apollo 12 and 14 moonwalks used a color TV camera that had a lower resolution (262 lines) but a higher frame rate (30 filtered frames per second, which became 20 frames after combining them to recreate the colors). The Apollo 15, 16 and 17 missions were provided with a different, bigger TV camera, the *Ground Commanded Television Assembly* (GCTA) manufactured by RCA, which was mounted on the Lunar Rover electric car and was controlled directly from Earth. This TV camera had a 6x zoom lens and a resolution of approximately 200 lines. Like the previous model, it generated 30 frames per second, which became 20 after conversion.

The two final lunar flights, Apollo 16 and 17, also introduced more advanced image processing systems that reduced background noise and improved considerably the quality of the color transmissions.

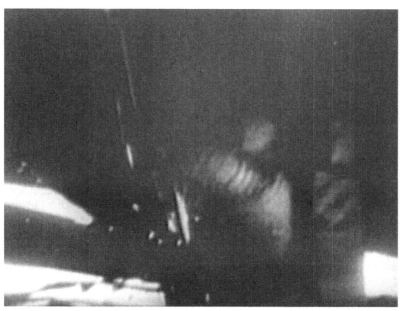

Figure 6-6. The converted image as broadcast by world television networks.

Figure 6-7. The original image as received from the Moon, photographed from the monitor prior to conversion.

This processing was handled by a private company, Image Transform of North Hollywood, California, which received the pictures from the Moon for on-the-fly processing before sending them to the world's TV networks for live broadcast (in a way, therefore, it's true that some lunar live TV footage was created with help from Hollywood). Incidentally, Image Transform was founded by John Lowry, who later also created the Lowry Digital company that restored the Apollo 11 lunar TV broadcast in 2009.

During Apollo 11's moonwalk, the TV signal was received by huge 64-meter (210-ft) dish antennas at Goldstone, California (Figure 6-8) and at Parkes, Australia and by a 26-meter (85-ft) dish at Honeysuckle Creek, Australia. Apollo 11's liftoff from the Moon was tracked by the 26-meter (85-ft) dish at Fresnedillas, near Madrid, in Spain.

All the television broadcasts, including the restored Apollo 11 moonwalk, are now available on the Internet and on DVD, and so is the movie camera footage of the missions.

Figure 6-8. The Goldstone dish antenna in the 1960s.

Now that the key aspects of the video and film technology available to lunar astronauts in the 1960s have been outlined, we're ready to examine the various anomalies allegedly present in the television and movie camera records of the Apollo missions.

6.2 The flag flutters on the airless Moon

IN A NUTSHELL: *It's not fluttering: it's swinging, and it only does so when the astronauts handle it or touch it. Moreover, the way it swings is different from how a flag swings on Earth and actually proves that the footage was shot in a vacuum..*

THE DETAILS: In the TV and film footage of the lunar landings, the American flag sometimes moves as if it had been blown by a sudden gust of air. That, of course, is impossible on the airless Moon. Therefore, according to conspiracy theorists, this proves that the moonwalk footage was faked in a movie studio.

One might ask why the movie set used for the most important and complex fakery of the twentieth century would be so ridiculously shoddy as to have drafts, or why the people in charge of the hoax would be so pathetically dumb as to leave such glaring and revealing mistakes in the final product, but never mind. There's a simple explanation for the apparently strange behavior of the flag.

If you examine the Apollo footage, you find that the flag "flutters" only when an astronaut is shaking it, for example to drive its pole into the ground (Figure 6-9). After the flag has been erected and left to settle, it doesn't move. Even its creases and wrinkles remain unchanged throughout the excursion, as shown by Figure 5-9 for Apollo 11. The alleged flutter is actually caused by the astronaut's handling of the flagpole, not by drafts.

Figure 6-9. Flag oscillation in an Apollo TV transmission while an astronaut drives its pole into the soil.

Just after the astronauts let go of the pole, moreover, the flag has a very revealing behavior: it continues to oscillate stiffly and unnaturally for quite a while, differently from a flag on Earth, which comes to a standstill almost immediately. This happens because in the Apollo footage the flag is swinging in the vacuum of the lunar surface, so there's no air or atmosphere to brake its motion.

In 2008 the TV show *Mythbusters* put this to the test. An accurate replica of an Apollo flag was placed in a large vacuum chamber and its pole was turned, just like the astronauts did on the Moon.

The same turning motion was applied while the chamber was filled with air and after the air had been extracted to produce a vacuum (Figure 6-10). The difference was quite evident: when the flag was in vacuum, it

Figure 6-10. A flag is swung in a vacuum for Mythbusters (2008).

swung for much longer and in the drag-free way seen in the Apollo television record.

In other words, the anomalous motion of the lunar flags doesn't confirm the hoax theories: on the contrary, it confirms that the footage of the moonwalks was shot in a vacuum.

However, there's a moment in the Apollo 15 footage, at 148:57:15 in mission elapsed time, in which the flag moves without (apparently) being touched by astronaut Dave Scott as he passes close to it. At first glance, it does indeed look as if Scott's movement displaced some air which impinged on the flag. But before arguing that this is unquestionable evidence of fakery, other non-conspiratorial explanations should be considered.

For example, the apparently mysterious motion may have been due to actual contact between Scott's left arm and the flag. Due to the wide-angle setting of the camera lens, which exaggerates depth, Scott appears to be farther away from the flag than he actually is.

Another possible explanation is an electrostatic effect. As Scott walked on the lunar surface (which has a significant electrical charge of its own due to the ionizing effect of ultraviolet radiation and particles from the Sun), he may have accumulated a charge which attracted or repelled the flag in the same way that a plastic rod rubbed on a wool sweater attracts or repels hair or pieces of paper.

Since the almost-perfect vacuum close to the lunar surface is highly *dielectric* (i.e., essentially incapable of conducting electric currents), charge accumulation is easier than on Earth. Moreover, any attraction or repulsion of the flag is more conspicuous on the Moon than on Earth because on the Moon there's no air to slow the flag.

Another conceivable scenario is that the discharge from the astronaut's backpack sublimator might have created a momentary puff of gas that impinged on the flag. This would explain the fact that only the bottom corner of the flag moves.

Whatever the actual cause is, it can't be an air displacement on a movie set, because the same video sequence shows that the dust kicked by the astronaut's boots doesn't swirl, but falls sharply and neatly in an arc. This is typical of a vacuum and is not possible in air. The flag's slow and long-lasting oscillation is also consistent with a low-gravity vacuum environment.

6.3 Who was already outside to televise Armstrong's first steps?

IN A NUTSHELL: *Nobody. The TV broadcast of mankind's first steps on the Moon appears to be shot by someone standing on the lunar surface before Neil Armstrong sets foot on the Moon simply because there was an automatic TV camera on the outside of the lunar module.*

THE DETAILS: The technical documentation of the Apollo missions shows that the video camera used to televise the first steps of Neil Armstrong on the Moon was located on a bracket (Figure 6-11) inside a container known as *Modular Equipment Storage Assembly* or *MESA*, located on one of the sides of the octagonal base of the descent stage of the lunar module.

The first astronaut to exit from the LM, while he was still at the top of the ladder, pulled a cable which released this container and allowed it to open by tilt-

Figure 6-11. Apollo 11's lunar TV camera, upside down on its bracket inside the MESA.

ing downward. This positioned automatically the camera (Figure 6-12), which was already switched on and connected to the transmission equipment of the Lunar Module.

The wide-angle lens of this TV camera allowed it to view the ladder and the astronaut as he descended to the surface. The placement of the camera had been preplanned and rehearsed for the very purpose of documenting this historic moment. No external TV operator was required. The same camera was then removed from its receptacle, installed on a tripod and placed at a certain distance from the LM, to which it was connected by means of a cable, so as to televise the entire moonwalk.

During Apollo 12, however, the TV camera was pointed at the Sun by mistake shortly after the beginning of the first moonwalk. The intense sunlight damaged its sensor, putting an abrupt end to live television from the Moon for the remainder of that mission.

The camera was installed upside down in its MESA receptacle and therefore the pictures of the astronauts' descents along the ladder were transmitted from the Moon upside down. Technicians on Earth

Figure 6-12. The astronaut training simulator shows the tilt-down MESA and its receptacle for the TV camera (indicated by the arrow), in position to broadcast the descent along the ladder.

would flip the image to broadcast it right way up, but at the very beginning of the Apollo 11 lunar TV transmission they momentarily forgot this task and so the first seconds of the broadcast are upside down.

6.4 Who stayed behind to shoot the liftoff from the Moon?

IN A NUTSHELL: *Nobody. The footage of the liftoff of the Lunar Module from the Moon was shot using an independently powered TV camera that was radio controlled from Earth.*

THE DETAILS: The visual record of the Apollo missions includes footage of the liftoff of the Lunar Module from the Moon. Some conspiracy theorists and doubters argue that this video must be fake, since there was nobody left on the Moon to take the pictures and even move the camera to follow the ascent stage of the Lunar Module as it climbed into the sky.

Figure 6-13. Apollo 17: a still from the live TV broadcast of the liftoff of the LM ascent stage from the Moon.

The answer is simple: the liftoff was shot only during Apollo 15, 16 and 17, when the TV camera was installed on the Rover (the astronauts' electric car), which at the end of the excursion was parked approximately 90 meters (300 feet) east of the Lunar Module for the very purpose of recording the liftoff of the LM. The camera was controlled remotely by an operator on Earth. Indeed, its technical name was GCTA, which stands for *Ground Controlled Television Assembly*.

The signal from the TV camera left on the Moon was transmitted directly to Earth through the parabolic antenna installed on the Rover, using the same method used to transmit the astronauts' moonwalks.

The entire system was powered independently by batteries and therefore was able to transmit even after the astronauts had

Figure 6-14. Animation of how the LM liftoff videos were shot. From the documentary Live from the Moon (Spacecraft Films).

left the Moon, sending back lonely images of the moonscape, once again devoid of life and motion after humankind's brief visit.

6.5 Wires lift the astronauts when they fall

IN A NUTSHELL: *The astronauts appear to get back up with incredible ease when they fall, as if they were assisted by invisible wires, but this ease is due to the fact that the astronauts on the Moon weighed less than 30 kilograms (66 pounds), and their movements seem odd because their heavy spacesuit and backpack displaced their center of gravity considerably upwards and backwards.*

THE DETAILS: On the Moon, the Apollo astronauts weighed one sixth of their Earth weight due to the lower lunar gravity. Their backpack and spacesuit weighed a total of approximately 81 kilograms (180 pounds) on Earth, which became a mere 13.5 kilograms (30 pounds) on the Moon. Their body weight was likewise reduced.

In other words, on the Moon a fully suited astronaut weighed a total of about 30 kilograms (66 pounds). Getting up after a fall, therefore, was trivial in terms of effort. Doing it without toppling over again, however, was challenging.

The way the astronauts regained their footing looks unusual be-cause in addition to being in one-sixth gravity they were car-rying a backpack (known as PLSS) which was quite heavy in proportion to their body weight (more precisely, its *mass* was considerable if compared to the mass of their body). Their PLSS weighed 26 kilograms (57 pounds) on Earth and 4.3 kilo-grams (9.5 pounds) on the Moon

Figure 6-15. An astronaut picks himself up by pushing with this arms after falling forwards.

– one third of their body weight – and therefore displaced their center of gravity upwards and backwards. That's why they were always leaning forwards: to compensate for the heavy load on their backs.

Moreover, the wire theory fails because the Apollo TV footage includes unbroken sequences that last tens of minutes, during which the astro-nauts change direction and position repeatedly. How would the wires not get tangled up? There's also the problem that the TV coverage in-cludes many wide shots, which would require extremely long wires to keep the control rig and winch out of frame.

6.6 The astronauts' wires catch the light

IN A NUTSHELL: *Occasional colored glows can be seen above the astro-nauts' heads in the video footage, but they're not glimpses of the wires that supported the astronauts to fake lunar gravity. They're simply reflec-tions off the spacesuits' radio antennas, which take on unusual colors due to the process used to generate the color TV picture. Sometimes the glow is a visual artifact produced by repeated digital compression and conversion of the original videos.*

THE DETAILS: The momentary glow that appears above the heads of the astronauts in some TV pictures isn't a studio light reflected by the hypothetical wires used to simulate low lunar gravity. It's usually a reflection off the radio antenna located at the top of the astronauts' backpack. The antenna was flat and shiny, so it was hard to see it when its edges faced the camera but it became suddenly visible, reflecting the sunlight, when the astronaut turned (Figure 6-16).

Figure 6-16. A strange glow above an astronaut's head.

This glow is often brightly colored because the color TV camera used on the Moon was actually a black-and-white camera fitted with a color wheel (Figure 6-17). The colored filters on this wheel rotated rapidly in front of the camera's sensor so as to generate a sequence of monochrome images filtered in red, green and yellow. These filtered images were then blended and processed electronically on Earth to reconstitute the original colors of the scene.

Figure 6-17. The rotating color filters of a lunar TV camera.

This system was sturdy and lightweight, but it had the drawback that if an object flashed rapidly in front of the camera it was caught by only one of the colored filters, acquiring a false coloring in the electronic processing.

In other instances, the apparent reflection of light on wires is a *compression artifact*: a false image detail generated by repeated conversion and compression of a video, for example for posting on the Internet. This sort of effect occurs in any digital video or photograph that is compressed and converted several times. The original video footage of the lunar missions, which is the only valid reference for proper research, doesn't have these artifacts.

6.7 The astronauts only make miserly jumps

IN A NUTSHELL: *They might look miserly until you consider that the astronauts are wearing a suit and backpack that doubles their weight and has very limited flexibility, and that a fall on the airless Moon can kill.*

THE DETAILS: One of the best-known lunar jumps is the one performed by John Young as he saluted the American flag during one of the Apollo 16 moonwalks. Figure 6-18 is a still from the video recording of this event, which was also photographed by Charlie Duke (Figure 5-74).

Figure 6-18. Apollo 16: John Young jumps as he salutes the flag and Charlie Duke takes his photograph.

Moon hoax proponents say that Young's jump is strangely short, and so are all the other lunar leaps. Yet on the Moon, with one-sixth of Earth's gravity, astronauts should be able to perform amazing jumps, maybe six times as high as on Earth. Perhaps the hidden wires couldn't lift them up enough?

Actually, there are very practical reasons for these short hops. First of all, every lunar astronaut was wearing a spacesuit and a backpack that weighed, on Earth, about 80 kilograms (176 pounds): as much as the astronaut himself. It's true that on the Moon this gear weighs one sixth of its Earth weight, i.e., about 13 kilograms (28 pounds), but it is still a substantial extra ballast that the astronaut has to lift in order to jump.

Secondly, John Young performed a standing jump, with no run-up (Figure 6-19), and was wearing a very bulky and rigid suit, limiting his freedom of motion and the energy he could put into his leap. More importantly, the astronaut is on the Moon, surrounded by a deadly vacuum. He is well aware that if he falls and cracks his helmet, damages the backpack that supplies him with air and cooling or plies him with air and cooling or

Figure 6-19. John Young just before his allegedly controversial standing jump.

tears his pressurized inner suit, he'll die by decompression or suffocation. In such conditions, it is rather wise not to try and set high-jump records.

Many hoax theorists also make the mistake of considering Young's jump as the highest ever made on the Moon. Actually, it was just a hop intended to take an unusual salute photograph. Other jumps were much higher and correspondingly more dangerous.

For example, Young himself and his crewmate Charlie Duke engaged in a high-jump contest at the end Apollo 16's third moonwalk; Duke estimated that Young had jumped *"about four feet* [120 centimeters]". Duke made an equally high jump, but fell backwards onto his backpack. In his book *Moonwalker*, he reported that it was *"the only time in our whole lunar stay that I had a real moment of panic and thought I had killed myself. The suit and backpack weren't designed to support a four-foot fall. Had the backpack broken or the suit split open, I would have lost my air. A rapid decompression, or as one friend calls it, a high-altitude hiss-out, and I would have been dead instantly. Fortunately, everything held together."*

Neil Armstrong reported that he jumped up to the third rung of Apollo 11's LM ladder, which was *"easily five or six feet* [150-180 centimeters] *above the ground"*. His leaps are visible in the recordings of the TV transmission of his moonwalk. However, Armstrong refrained from further experimentation, because he noted that *"there was a tendency to tip over backward on a high jump. One time I came close to falling and decided that was enough of that."*[47]

6.8 There's an outtake from the fake TV broadcast

IN A NUTSHELL: *Black-and-white TV footage circulating on the Internet purportedly shows Neil Armstrong climbing down the ladder of the Lunar Module and pronouncing his famous* "One small step..." *remark when an overhead bank of studio lights comes crashing down and a film crew comes into view. No, it's not a failed take from NASA's faking of the first Moon landing that was somehow leaked online: it's a prank, specifically a viral video shot in 2002 by a British advertising company.*

THE DETAILS: A video widely available on the Internet is often presented as a leaked outtake from the faking of the Apollo 11 moonwalk. It can be recognized by the *Moontruth.com* caption (Figure 6-20) and is actually an Internet prank created in 2002 by The Viral Factory, an advertising agency based in London, United Kingdom, to promote itself through word of mouth and create buzz (pun intended) about its work.

Today Moontruth.com is an empty shell, but in 2002 it was owned by the British ad company (as documented by a Whois ownership query

---

47   *Apollo 11 Technical Crew Debriefing*, July 31, 1969, Section 10, pages 61 and 28.

conducted at the time) and it contained text that claimed that the video was an *"Apollo 11 Moon Landing Footage Out-take."* However, easily revealed hidden pages explained the prank:

The clip is FAKED. It is not an out-take leaked from a NASA top secret reel. It was done in a studio, for fun, and to entertain webheads like us. Yes, the clip is fake. It was shot in a studio in London in spring 2002. It was based on an idea by director Adam Stewart, who was a space exploration nut. He had read the conspiracy theory sites and decided he

Figure 6-20. A still from the Moontruth viral advert (2002).

wanted to make a spoof based on the idea that the Apollo 11 moonlanding was faked. [...]

We shot on original 1960's Ikegami Tube Camera in Mount Pleasant Studios in London. The guy in the suit is an actor. The rest of the 'cast' were basically the crew, who thought the idea was very funny and wanted to be in it.

The landing craft and 'moonscape' were a set built by our art director, Richard Selway. The ladder that 'Neil' descends was made according to original blueprints that were downloaded off the Net. The rest of the set was built to match the original as closely as possible. The moon surface was cement dust. It was disgusting. Even with the studio ventilation on full it got everywhere, and at one point there was so much of it floating round, the lights were flaring really badly.

The footage was treated in post-production to give 'Neil' his weightlessness and the ghosting effect of the original. We re-recorded and processed the soundtrack to recreate the effect of sound traveling all the way from the moon.

We think it's pretty convincing, and one thing's for damn sure – it was a lot cheaper than really going to the moon.

This explanation is currently preserved at Archive.org and the true origins of this video are recorded in detail by the well-known Snopes.com hoax debunking site.

6.9 Kubrick's widow, Aldrin and others have confessed on film

IN A NUTSHELL: *A series of videos available on the Internet unmistakably shows astronaut Buzz Aldrin, former US Secretary of State Henry Kissinger, former US Secretary of Defense Donald Rumsfeld, director Stanley Kubrick's widow and other authoritative figures openly admitting that the Moon landings were faked. However, in a final video the confessions are revealed to be part of a French "mockumentary", Opération Lune.*

THE DETAILS: The astonishing confessions are indeed made by Aldrin, Kissinger, Rumsfeld and Christiane Kubrick, among others, not by lookalikes or by lip-synching voice impersonators. But they're all part of a cleverly orchestrated prank, directed in 2002 by William Karel and broadcast by European network Arte as *Opération Lune* (also known as *Dark Side of the Moon*).

Figure 6-21. A still from William Karel's Opération Lune (Dark Side of the Moon) (Arte TV, 2002).

Karel's *Dark Side of the Moon* was originally a single, 52-minute fake documentary intended to test the gullibility of viewers and play with their sense of reality until the end, when the trick is revealed, but it soon found its way onto the Internet, where it was cut into shorter segments, which were presented out of context and often without including the explanation at the end. Accordingly, it is often cited as evidence by Moon hoax theorists, thus proving Karel's point about gullibility, albeit in an unintended way.

The "mockumentary" actually contains several hints to its true nature: for example, if one listens carefully to what Aldrin, Kissinger and Rumsfeld say, it becomes evident that their words are being taken out of context; many of the historical events mentioned are blatantly wrong or false; and several of the names of the interviewees are lifted from famous movies, such as Jack Torrance (from *Shining*), David Bowman (from *2001: A Space Odyssey*, Figure 6-21), Ambrose Chapel from Hitchcock's *The Man Who Knew Too Much*, Eve Kendall and George Kaplan (both from *North by Northwest*). The end credits also include the bloopers made by the famous people interviewed and turned into improvised actors by Karel.

6.10 NASA conveniently "lost" the tapes of the first Moon landing

IN A NUTSHELL: *No, it didn't: it lost the* direct, raw *recording of the first landing, which would have offered a higher image quality than the recordings made from the live TV transmission, degraded considerably by the electronic conversion required to adapt the signal from the Moon to the standards used by terrestrial television. The lower-quality* converted *recordings have not been lost. The loss of the raw recording is due to the fact that it was made in a special video format on expensive telemetry tapes, which were later deleted for reuse because it was believed at the time (before the advent of digital image processing and restoration techniques) that no better conversion was possible. The lost tapes did not contain extra footage or different views.*

THE DETAILS: As described in the technical primer at the beginning of this book, achieving a fuzzy, black-and-white live broadcast from the Moon for the first landing required a substantial technological effort. At the time, television was fully analog and could not benefit from pristine digital transmission and processing. Due to technical constraints, a non-standard TV camera and signal had to be used on the Moon and the pictures had to be converted on Earth, on the fly, for worldwide live broadcast. This caused considerable loss of quality.

NASA recorded this converted television signal on standard videotape reels of the best quality available at the time. These tapes have not been lost (Figure 6-22).

Figure 6-22. One of the converted videotape reels of the Apollo 11 flight. Credit: DC Video.

The non-standard direct signal from the Moon could not be recorded with ordinary video recording equipment, so NASA stored it on a track of the telemetry tapes of the flight. However, these tapes were labeled as ordinary mission telemetry and were placed in storage with all the other technical records at the end of each mission. Several years after the end of the Apollo project, the stored telemetry was deemed of no further interest and its expensive tapes were sent to be wiped for reuse. The best-quality recordings of the Apollo 11 lunar excursion were thus deleted unintentionally.

These are the so-called "lost tapes": they included no extra footage or different shots compared to the recordings that we've seen for over forty years. However, they would have offered a far better view, in terms of detail and clarity, of that unique moment of history (Figure 6-23).

Figure 6-23. Neil Armstrong in the live TV signal as broadcast from Houston (left) compared to the original signal received from the Moon at Goldstone (right, NASA image S69-42583) as recorded by taking a Polaroid photograph of the TV screen of the receiver on Earth.

It should be noted that at the time it was widely believed that nothing better could be extracted from the master tapes. The digital image processing that we now take for granted was still in its infancy, the existing footage was considered good enough, and it was assumed that the master tapes would be preserved anyway.

All is not lost, however. There are photographs and film recordings of parts of the direct, unprocessed transmission from the Moon, taken by Bill Wood and Ed von Renouard, who worked at the receiving stations in the United States and Australia, which offer tantalizing glimpses of what could have been preserved, including the only existing recording (made by von Renouard on a Super 8 movie camera) of the jettison of the astronauts' backpacks after they reentered the Lunar Module. Other unofficial copies of the raw transmission might still surface from various sources.

In 2009, NASA published a detailed report on the extensive international search for the missing master tapes[48] and hired Lowry Digital, a film restoration company, to enhance the best available converted recordings with assistance from many of the engineers who had worked on the original transmission. The restored Apollo 11 moonwalk is now available commercially.

6.11 The astronauts faked footage of Earth seen from deep space

IN A NUTSHELL: *No. Had the footage been faked by shooting it from Earth orbit through a circular window to make the Earth look small and*

---

48 *The Apollo 11 Telemetry Data Recordings: A Final Report* (2009) (*www.nasa.gov/pdf/398311-main_Apollo_11_Report.pdf*).

distant, as some conspiracy theorists claim, the clouds would have changed continuously as the spacecraft flew over different parts of the planet. But in the footage the clouds remain unchanged.

THE DETAILS: Moon hoax theorist Bart Sibrel, in his video *A Funny Thing Happened on the Way to the Moon* (2001), shows an Apollo 11 video recording that he claims to be *"never before seen or heard footage"* in which the astronauts allegedly faked being far from Earth when they were actually still in low orbit around it.

According to Sibrel, they *"placed the camera at the back of the spacecraft and centered the lens on a circular window in the foreground, outside of which it is completely filled with the Earth in low orbit. The circumference of the window then appears to be the diameter of the Earth at a distance, with the darkened walls of the spacecraft appearing to be the blackness of space around it."* (Figure 6-24).

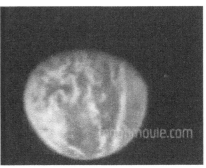

Figure 6-24. A frame from the allegedly faked Apollo 11 video.

In other words, according to Sibrel's theory, the astronauts used the circular window to mask the bulk of the Earth and only show a circular portion of its surface, thus creating the illusion of a distant floating sphere.

In actual fact, the footage is not *"never before seen or heard"* as Sibrel alleges. It is part of a series of color TV transmissions made by the Apollo 11 astronauts on their way to the Moon, 10.5 hours and 34 hours after liftoff, when they were respectively 94,500 and 240,000 kilometers (51,000 and 130,000 nautical miles) from Earth. The full recording has been available for a long time, for example on the Apollo 11 DVDs published by Spacecraft Films. Sibrel's version is recut out of sequence: the unedited footage simply shows the astronauts preparing for TV transmissions and testing the camera settings. This is evident by listening to their communications in full, as available in the *Apollo Flight Journal*, instead of taking selected quotes out of context.

Moreover, the camera trick alleged by Sibrel wouldn't have worked even if the astronauts had tried it. If the Apollo spacecraft had been in low orbit around the Earth, with its TV camera peeking at a small portion of the planet below through a circular mask, the footage would have shown ever-changing clouds and parts of the planet rolling by as the spacecraft rapidly circled the globe. The uncut, less grainy version of the video presented by Sibrel instead shows exactly the same unchanging cloud patterns for as much as fifteen minutes.

The original footage reveals that the frame shown in Figure 6-24 includes the outline of all of the western coast of North America and of Baja California in the upper left region (north is down and to the left). This is confirmed by photograph AS11-36-5337, which was taken approximately at the same time as the TV transmissions and shows the same cloud patterns, allowing to determine that the TV picture actually shows the entire North American continent and most of the Pacific Ocean. This would be impossible from low Earth orbit.

6.12 No exhaust from the LM's ascent rocket engine

IN A NUTSHELL: *That's the way it should be. The propellant of the Lunar Module didn't generate a visible plume. The same occurs in other vehicles that use the same propellant type, such as the Titan launchers used for the Gemini program and as military ballistic missiles.*

THE DETAILS: Bill Kaysing, in Fox TV's *Did We Land on the Moon?* (2001), objects that *"In the footage of the ascent stage going up, what you don't see is an exhaust plume coming out of the rocket engine nozzle... What do we see? We see the ascent stage suddenly pop up without any exhaust plume whatsoever as though it were jerked up by a cable".*

Actually, there's no visible exhaust plume for a very simple reason: there shouldn't be one. Not all rocket propellants produce a bright plume, especially in a near-vacuum such as the Moon's surface. In particular, the Apollo LM used a mix of Aerozine 50 (50% hydrazine, 50% unsymmetrical dimethyl hydrazine) and dinitrogen tetroxide, which are *hypergolic*, i.e., they react spontaneously as soon as they come into mutual contact. This allows a simple and highly reliable engine design. The product of the reaction of these substances is colorless and transparent: that's why there's no visible plume under the LM. A layperson might expect a plume and flames because that's what is usually seen during rocket liftoffs. But most large rockets use different, cheaper and less toxic propellants, which generate a bright, fiery exhaust.

The same type of propellant used in the LM was also used in the massive Titan launchers used in the Gemini manned spaceflight program and as nuclear warhead delivery missiles, and their liftoffs produced a surprisingly small and colorless plume, with no flames (Figure 6-25). The Space Shuttle's maneuvering thrusters also used hypergolic propellants and likewise produced no significant plume.

It's true, however, that NASA is partly to blame for this widespread misconception, because many artist's illustrations published by the space agency actually show a plume both for the ascent stage and for the descent stage of the LM. However, there was no other self-explanatory way to illustrate the fact that the spacecraft was being propelled by its rocket motor.

Figure 6-25. Liftoff of a Titan rocket carrying the Gemini 12 spacecraft on November 11, 1966. Note the almost colorless engine exhaust and the lack of flames.

6.13 Color TV from space but not from the Moon

IN A NUTSHELL: *Yes, Apollo 11 sent color TV pictures during its flight to the Moon, yet the TV transmission from the Moon itself was in black and white because the main spacecraft, the Command Module, had better and more powerful transmission equipment than the Lunar Module and could send a good color TV signal to Earth. Also, Apollo 11's color TV camera was used only inside the spacecraft and therefore didn't have to withstand the vacuum and temperature extremes of the lunar surface; the first moonwalk camera had to be more rugged and simple. Later missions carried improved cameras and equipment that allowed color TV from the Moon as well.*

THE DETAILS: It may seem rather suspicious that Apollo 11 sent color TV pictures during the flight to the Moon (Figure 6-26) but then switched to black and white for the all-important moonwalk.

Indeed, Bart Sibrel, in *A Funny Thing Happened on the Way to the Moon*, notes this discrepancy and suggests that the perpetrators of the hoax decided it would be *"better to open their debut mission with fuzzy pictures and numerous blackouts rather than show too much revealing detail of a false scene that was yet unproven".*

The actual reason for the switch was that the color transmissions were made using the Command Module's TV camera and onboard transmission equipment, which was far more sophisticated and powerful than the Lunar Module's and also had a better antenna. The Command Module was powered by fuel cells, while the LM only had batteries, and this allowed the CM to spend more power on the TV signal.

Moreover, the transmission gear of Apollo 11's LM lacked the bandwidth needed to send a color signal, while the CM had no such limitation, and the ad-dition of color doesn't necessar-

Figure 6-26. Buzz Aldrin in the LM, in a frame from the color TV transmissions sent by Apollo 11. NASA image S69-39532.

ily provide significant detail. However, the CM could not be used as a relay because it orbited around the Moon every two hours and there-fore was often out of contact with the LM or Earth or both.

6.14 Recycled Moon sets

IN A NUTSHELL: *NASA says that two video clips of Apollo 16's lunar excur-sion were shot in different places on different days, but the landscape and the terrain around the astronauts are identical. However, this is not evidence of a recycled movie set: it's an editing error in a NASA documentary. In the original raw footage, the two clips are only seven minutes apart and belong to a long, unbroken sequence that occurs in a single location.*

THE DETAILS: Bart Sibrel's video *The Rocks Cry Out: Apollo 16 An-omaly* and the Fox TV show *Did We Land on the Moon?* accuse NASA of using the same location or movie set for two different sites of the Apollo 16 mission, which according to other NASA documents were located four kilometers (over 2.5 miles) apart and were visited on two differ-ent days (Figures 6-27 and 6-28).

Figure 6-27. A frame of the first clip disputed by Fox TV and Sibrel.

The first clip (Figure 6-27) shows a single astronaut and is captioned *"Day One"* by Fox, while the second one (Figure 6-28) features two astronauts and is labeled *"Day Two",* but the location is unquestionably the same. Even the camera angle is identical. According to the Fox show, *"NASA claims the second location was two and a half miles away, but when one video was superimposed over the other, the locations appear identical."*

Figure 6-28. A frame from the second clip in dispute.

However, reviewing the full set of TV transmissions from Apollo 16 (as published for example by Spacecraft Films) reveals another story. In the original transmissions, the images in the two video clips are not referred to two separate days: they're just *seven minutes* apart and belong to a single, unbroken sequence recorded during Apollo 16's second day on the Moon, at 144 hours and 48 minutes and 144 hours and 55 minutes in mission elapsed time. They also refer to the same location. In other words, the accusations of fakery are bogus.

Moreover, the audio in the clips presented by Fox TV and Sibrel doesn't match the recordings of reference. For example, according to NASA's *Technical Air-to-Ground Voice Transcripts* the phrase *"Well, I couldn't pick a better spot"* in the first clip actually comes from the first day of Apollo 16 on the Moon, at 123 hours and 58 minutes, and the words *"That is the most beautiful sight"* and *"It's absolutely unreal!"* occur at 124 hours and 3 minutes and 144 hours and 16 minutes respectively.

The most likely source of this mismatch is a documentary commissioned by NASA to A-V Corporation in 1972 and rather ironically entitled *"Nothing So Hidden...",* in which the clips have the same, incorrect audio presented by Sibrel and Fox TV and are shown as if they had been taken on different days.

In other words, the entire accusation stems from an editing error that occurs only in a NASA-sponsored documentary but not in the full, original video recordings, which are the only true reference material and which the conspiracy theorists apparently failed to examine.

Editing mistakes in documentaries are not evidence of NASA fakery; they're merely evidence of inaccurate editing. Unfortunately, such mistakes or artistic licenses are frequent in supposedly faithful documentaries and often alter the understanding of an event. For example, as space historian James Oberg notes,

A far more serious distortion appears in most — but not all — television documentaries of the mission. Since the "small step" was really so small and his body movement so subtle, the video of this event is not dramatic enough for some programs. Instead, the audio track of the first words is transferred forward about a minute to coincide with Armstrong's first jump down the ladder to the footpad. This turns the poetic "small step" into an awkward big hop. That may satisfy action-oriented entertainment values but it is false history. It is untrue to the significance of Armstrong's words.[49]

---

49 *Getting Apollo 11 Right - Commemorating What Really Happened,* by James Oberg, ABCNews.com (1999).

7. Alleged technological anomalies

It's fairly easy to refute the accusations of Moon hoax believers when they relate to alleged anomalies in the visual record of the Apollo missions, as shown in the preceding chapters: it just takes time, common sense and a little knowledge of photography.

Things get harder when the debate moves to alleged technological absurdities or anomalies regarding the Apollo missions: many objections can't be debunked without in-depth technical and historical knowledge.

7.1 Nobody ever went to the Moon again

IN A NUTSHELL: *True, but that doesn't mean that we can't or that we didn't. It just means that going to the Moon is very difficult, very expensive and very dangerous, and today nobody wants to go there because there's no longer a political imperative that justifies risking lives and devoting massive manpower and resources to the challenge. The Cold War is essentially over; the Soviet Union, once the rival to beat in the space race, no longer exists. Also, we've already been to the Moon and we've found no viable reason to go back with manned missions.*

THE DETAILS: If we really were able to go to the Moon with 1960s technology, why don't we go again? Some conspiracy theorists suggest, with this question, that we don't go back because if we did it would become evident that we never went with Apollo. Others claim that even today it would be technically impossible and therefore it was equally impossible in the 1960s. But there are also honest doubters who simply ask themselves why we don't repeat the fantastic voyage with today's far more modern technology.

The answer is disarmingly simple: putting astronauts on the Moon is very difficult, hugely expensive (at least for NASA's rather measly budget) and extremely dangerous, and today there's no political motivation for spending massive amounts of public money and for risking human lives in the world's spotlight in this way. The disasters of Apollo 1, Soyuz 1 and 11, and of Shuttles *Challenger* and *Columbia* have shown all too clearly that the loss of a spacecraft crew is seen as a national tragedy and can be justified only if the stakes are tremendously high.

At the time of the Apollo flights, it was a national imperative to beat the Soviet regime and to rebuild the political and technological prestige of the United States. There's no such imperative today; there's no totalitarian enemy to beat. In the 1960s, politicians funded the Moon landings with approximately 170 billion dollars (in current terms) and the lives of the astronauts were considered expendable for the sake of the nation. Thus many technical compromises were made which increased the chances of failure.

For example, Apollo 12 was launched *during a storm* and was struck twice by lightning, almost killing the crew (Figure 7-1). The lunar module had a single descent engine and a single engine for return from the Moon; likewise, the command and service module had to rely on a single engine. If any of these failed, the astronauts would die.

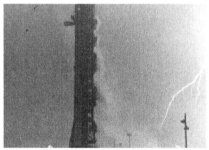

Figure 7-1. Lightning strikes the Apollo 12 launch pad at liftoff. NASA photo S69-60068.

Crucial and delicate rendezvous maneuvers had to be performed in orbit around the Moon, instead of close to Earth, to reduce the weight of the spacecraft. In this way, if the lunar module failed to meet the command module after landing on the Moon, no rescue was possible.

Every mission had its share of malfunctions and near failures. Apollo 13 even suffered a crippling oxygen tank explosion that forced to abort its lunar landing. If the explosion had occurred during return from the Moon instead of on the way out, when onboard reserves were still high and the lunar module was still available as a lifeboat, the outcome would have been fatal.

Today, NASA's budget is almost halved compared to the Apollo era,[50] the safety requirements are far more stringent and the loss of a crew is politically far less acceptable.

The race to beat the Soviets ended four decades ago, so space missions are carried out for science rather than for national pride, taking lower risks and using unmanned spacecraft, which have achieved amazing scientific successes throughout the Solar System; manned spaceflights

---

50 In 2010 dollars, the total sum of NASA budgets in the period from 1963 to 1969 was 209.2 billion; from 2003 to 2009 it was 113.1 billion.

have been confined to Earth orbit, for example to assemble and visit the International Space Station. Right now there is no political, technical or scientific reason that justifies the cost and risk of a manned return to the Moon. Moreover, for the United States it would be a repeat.

It may seem absurd and implausible that forty years ago we could do something that we can't do today, but there are other cases of journeys to remote places that were made once and not repeated for decades. For example, mankind first reached the South Pole in 1911, with Roald Amundsen's team, followed a few weeks later by Robert Scott's men (who died on the return trip). After that, nobody set foot on the South Pole for all of 45 years, until US Rear Admiral George J. Dufek and his multinational crew landed there with an aircraft in October 1956.

The Marianas Trench, the deepest point of all of the world's oceans, almost 11 kilometers (6.8 miles) below the surface, was reached for the first time in 1960 by Don Walsh and Jacques Piccard on board the bathyscaphe *Trieste*. Fifty-two years passed before anyone returned: director James Cameron went there solo in 2012 with the *Deepsea Challenger*.

The apparent contradiction of past technology being superior to today's is explained by similar cases in other fields. In the 1970s we had supersonic airliners (the Anglo-French Concorde and the Russian Tupolev Tu-144). Today, for a wide range of reasons, we don't. Until July 2011, there was a spacecraft capable of taking seven astronauts and twenty tons of payload into Earth orbit and landing on a runway like a glider: the Space Shuttle (Russia had Buran, a very similar spacecraft, but it flew only once, unmanned and without a payload, before the project was canceled). Not anymore: the Shuttle fleet has been retired after thirty years of service, and its current replacements are capsules that land under a parachute, like Apollo did. The Space Shuttles turned out to be too costly and unacceptably dangerous.

7.2 The Russians didn't even try: they knew it was impossible

IN A NUTSHELL: *Actually, they tried, and tried hard, too. But their giant N1 rockets, designed and built specifically for lunar missions, kept exploding during test launches. The Soviet Moon landing project was abandoned and kept secret to avoid international humiliation, as detailed in Chapter 1, but the cover-up was revealed when the Soviet Union collapsed.*

THE DETAILS: There actually *was* a Moon hoax, but not the one most space conspiracy theorists talk about: the Soviet one, meant to hide all evidence of their failed attempts to be the first to fly a manned mission around the Moon and then achieve a manned lunar landing.

The secret Russian L1 fly-around project was based on two scenarios. In the first one, a Proton rocket would launch an L1 spacecraft (a stripped-down Soyuz) equipped with an additional Block D booster stage, flying directly to the Moon.

In the second scenario, the same type of Proton launcher would place an unmanned L1 spacecraft and Block D stage in Earth orbit; a three-man crew would climb to Earth orbit using a second Soyuz on another rocket. Two of the three cosmonauts would then transfer to the L1 spacecraft and accelerate to fly around the Moon, while the third crewmember returned to Earth.

This project was approved and funded by the Soviet authorities and spacecraft manufacturing was started, with the goal of a lunar fly-around by 1967, one year before the Americans. However, the fatal accident of Soyuz 1, which cost the life of cosmonaut Vladimir Komarov,

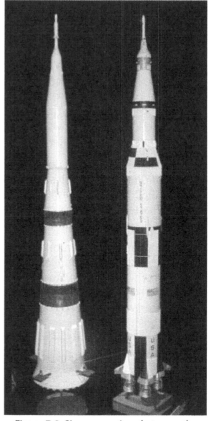

Figure 7-2. Size comparison between the Soviet N1-L3 system (left) and the Saturn V-Apollo stack (right).

and the reliability problems of the Proton launcher caused delays that allowed the American space program to achieve the first manned flight around the Moon with Apollo 8 in 1968.

The Russians also had another secret project, the N1-L3, for landing a single cosmonaut on the Moon, as described in Chapter 1. However, the unreliability of the massive N1 launcher (Figure 7-2) once again caused delays that gave the United States the time to perfect their technology and be the first to land a crew on the Moon.

Russia's last attempt at a lunar fly-around took place a few days before the Apollo 11 landing and failed when the N1 rocket that carried the unmanned L1 spacecraft exploded catastrophically on the launch pad.

The Soviet conspiracy to hide all traces of these attempts and failures was quite successful, so much that even today many Moon hoax believers are blissfully unaware of this aspect of the space race. At the time, the Russian authorities declared that they had never taken part in a race for the Moon, that they had no intention of taking a Russian to the Moon and that they would never risk a Soviet citizen's life on such a dangerous endeavor, which could be accomplished just as effectively with unmanned vehicles. That was the official party line.

Many in the Western media fell for the Soviet hoax. Even celebrated newsman Walter Cronkite stated on TV in 1974 that *"it turned out there never had been a race to the Moon".[51]* However, the reality of the Russian attempts to land a man on the Moon, long suspected by Western experts and partly known to US intelligence, became very public with the collapse of the Soviet Union in the 1990s. Today we even have insider's reports, such as Russian rocket designer Boris Chertok's four-volume *Rockets and People* (1994-1999), detailing the Soviet lunar plans.

7.3 Computers were too primitive

IN A NUTSHELL: *No. The Apollo spacecraft's computer technology was primitive compared to today's, but it was still adequate, also thanks to the presence of three very powerful additional "computers": the astronauts, who were all trained to control the spacecraft and calculate trajectories, orbits and rendezvous by hand if necessary. Moreover, most of the computing power wasn't on board: it was in NASA's much larger computers on Earth.*

THE DETAILS: Moon hoax theorists often point to the fact that a modern cellphone has more computing power and memory than the onboard computer of the Apollo spacecraft and argue, therefore, that it's unthinkable that anyone could have flown to the Moon with such limited equipment.

But first of all, the Saturn-Apollo spacecraft had *five* main onboard computers, not one: two Raytheon AGCs (*Apollo Guidance Computers*), one in the lunar module and one in the command module; one IBM-built LVDC (*Launch Vehicle Digital Computer*) in the Saturn's Instrument Unit; a Honeywell SCS (*Stabilization and Control System*) in the com-

---

51 *Fifth Anniversary – Apollo in Retrospect*, CBS, July 1974, as quoted in *Cronkite on Space: Inspiration, not Information*, by James Oberg, in *Space Review*, 6 March 2006.

mand module; and a TRW-designed AGS (*Abort Guidance System*) in the lunar module.

It's true that the computer hardware of the spacecraft was puny compared to today's standards. For example, the AGCs (Figure 7-3) had about 8,000 bytes of memory each (a laptop computer currently has at least four billion, i.e., five hundred times more RAM) and a 2.048 MHz clock (yes, that's a decimal point, not a thousands separator). But these computers could focus all their power on a small set of core tasks and didn't have to waste power on fancy graphical interfaces or

Figure 7-3. The display and keyboard of an Apollo Guidance Computer (AGC).

other embellishments, so they were adequate for the tasks they had to perform. Moreover, the onboard systems had the backup of Mission Control's mainframe computers. In other words, the available computing power wasn't as small as is often thought.

The astronauts were also trained extensively to control all the spacecraft's systems, to calculate trajectories, rendezvous and orbits using slide rules and precomputed charts, and to navigate using the stars. They acted, in a way, as additional computers, making up for the limitations of the automatic systems available at the time: consider, for example, the manual override decided on the spot by Neil Armstrong during Apollo 11 to avoid landing in an unexpected boulder field that the onboard and ground computers couldn't detect, or the manual realignment performed by James Lovell during Apollo 13 after the automatic navigation system had been shut down to conserve power after an oxygen tank failure crippled their ship.

7.4 Everything went too smoothly

IN A NUTSHELL: *NASA went out of its way to give this impression, but the truth was quite different. Three astronauts died on the launch pad (Apollo 1). Apollo 13 suffered an explosion that scrubbed its lunar landing and almost killed the crew. Apollo 12 was struck by lightning at liftoff. Apollo 11 had a computer overload as it was landing on the Moon. Every mission* *had its significant malfunctions and equipment failures, and many crews were struck by nausea, vomiting and diarrhea, but all this wasn't widely publicized.*

THE DETAILS: Moon hoax theorists often express their sarcastic amazement at the perfection of the Apollo flights to the Moon. How is it possible that such incredibly complex and powerful machines, which pushed the envelope of 1960s technology, could work so flawlessly? And how could astronauts be so impeccably cool and professional on such life-threatening journeys?

Actually, this perfection is only an impression driven by superficial knowledge of the events and by the fact that the political importance of the lunar missions prompted NASA and the media to gloss over the errors and failures and the less dignified aspects of the endeavor. National prestige was at stake, so problems were played down in public. Some failures, however, were too big to be brushed under the carpet.

As a matter of fact, out of seven Moon landing missions, one failed (Apollo 13). Three astronauts died on the launch pad (White, Grissom and Chaffee, Apollo 1). All the missions had problems that brought the crew close to disaster or abort. Here are a few examples taken from the technical mission reports. A more extensive list of the various critical and non-critical malfunctions that affected the various missions is in the *Discrepancy Summary* section of the *Post-launch Mission Operation Reports*.

Apollo 7

Water from the cooling systems pooled in the cabin, posing a serious danger in an environment crammed with electrical wiring.

The crew was plagued by a cold that blocked their nasal passages: a serious problem in spaceflight, because in weightlessness fluid accumulates instead of draining and blowing one's nose can cause severe ear pain, and because during reentry, with their head enclosed in the helmet, the astronauts would be unable to clear their ears and therefore compensate for cabin pressure changes, with the risk of eardrum damage. Despite NASA's strong disagreement, the crew performed reentry without wearing their helmets and suffered no physical consequences.

The Apollo 7 crew also refused orders from Mission Control, and commander Walter Schirra had no uncertain words about the unprecedented workload of the maiden flight of the Apollo spacecraft, speaking openly of *"tests that were ill prepared and hastily conceived by an idiot"* and declaring that he'd *"had it up to here"* and that his crew was *"not going to accept any new games... or going to do some crazy tests we never heard of before."* This was one of several underreported rebellions of spaceflight crews.[52]

Apollo 8

The first manned flight around the Moon was troubled by bouts of vomiting and diarrhea during the first day of flight, nearly forcing an early return home.

Three of the five spacecraft windows were fogged by sealant leaks, hindering viewing and lunar photography. Water formed dangerous pools in the cabin.

Jim Lovell accidentally erased part of the computer's memory, and the crew was forced to compute and reenter the correct data by hand.

Apollo 9

Astronaut Rusty Schweickart vomited repeatedly due to nausea in-duced by weightlessness, forcing cancellation of the emergency pro-cedure test (a spacewalk from the Lunar Module to the Command Module) that he was scheduled to perform.

One of the maneuvering thruster sets of the command and service module and the tracking lights of the lunar module failed due to a mis-placed switch: these were crucial components, since the two modules had to maneuver and fly separately, 185 kilometers (115 miles) apart, in Earth orbit and then find each other and dock again, otherwise the two crewmembers in the LM would have died in orbit, unable to return to Earth. Rendezvous was achieved despite these failures thanks to the skill of the astronauts.

Apollo 10

When the ascent stage of the LM separated from the descent stage, just 14.45 kilometers (47,400 feet) above the lunar surface, an incorrect switch setting made the spacecraft spin wildly about two axes, coming

---

52 *Apollo: the Epic Journey to the Moon*, by David Reynolds and Wally Schirra.

dangerously to a so-called *gimbal lock* (loss of orientation of the navigation system). Astronaut Gene Cernan let slip a heartfelt *"Son of a bitch!"*, which was picked up by his open radio mike and transmitted live to world audiences back on Earth.

Apollo 11

During the first Moon landing, the lunar module's computer overloaded repeatedly. The preprogrammed flight path would have taken the spacecraft to a boulder-strewn area, where landing and liftoff would have been prohibitive if not impossible. Only Armstrong's manual intervention to change landing site saved the mission.

Radio communications in lunar orbit, after separation of the LM from the command module, were so poor and broken up that Armstrong and Aldrin in the LM didn't hear the *"go"* to initiate descent to the Moon from Mission Control. Fortunately it was picked up by Michael Collins, in the command module, who relayed it to his colleagues.

After landing on the Moon, one of the propellant lines of the descent stage failed to vent correctly due to freezing, leading to a potentially explosive pressure buildup. Mission Control noticed the problem and was discussing it guardedly with the crew when it cleared itself up by thawing.

After the moonwalk, the astronauts realized that the knob of a circuit breaker required for arming the ascent engine was broken, probably because it had been struck by Aldrin's backpack. If that circuit could not be operated, liftoff from the Moon would be impossible. The astronauts improvised by using a felt-tipped pen to operate the failed breaker.

On returning from the lunar surface, when the LM docked with the command and service module, the slightly incorrect alignment of the two spacecraft triggered an uncontrolled rotation that the onboard computers both tried to correct, contrasting each other and worsening the spin. Only Collins and Armstrong's skills allowed to correct manually the chaotic tumbling of the mated vehicles.

Apollo 12

The lightning that struck the Saturn V during liftoff caused widespread instrument malfunctions and a total loss of meaningful telemetry. Only an unusual suggestion by John Aaron in Mission Control (the request to set *"SCE to AUX"*), radioed up to the astronauts, allowed them to restore telemetry and prevented the mission from being aborted immediately.

During the live TV broadcast from the Moon, the TV camera was pointed accidentally at the sun and its delicate sensor burned out, ending TV transmissions for the mission's moonwalk.

At the end of the flight, during atmospheric reentry, the wind caused the command module to swing beneath its parachutes and the astronauts were subjected to 15 g of deceleration on impact; a camera fell from its holder and struck Alan Bean on his temple. Had it fallen slightly differently, it would have caused a potentially fatal head trauma.

Apollo 13

As already mentioned, an oxygen tank in the service module ruptured explosively, depriving the astronauts of air and power reserves. It became necessary to use the LM as a lifeboat and return hurriedly to Earth after looping around the Moon. James Lovell had to align the navigation systems manually by star sighting.

Apollo 14

On the way to the Moon, the docking mechanism between the LM and the command module failed five times before finally working. This meant that it might fail again when the LM returned from the Moon, forcing the astronauts to perform a dangerous spacewalk to transfer from the LM to the command module, but the decision was made to go ahead with the landing nonetheless.

An errant solder ball in the LM caused the onboard computer to receive a false abort signal, which during lunar descent could have triggered an unnecessary emergency climb back to orbit, canceling the Moon landing: in the nick of time, NASA and MIT managed to reprogram the computer to ignore the false signal.

Apollo 15

One of the three splashdown parachutes failed to open fully (Figure 7-4), leading to a violent impact with the ocean. The malfunction was probably caused by venting propellants, which could have caused all three parachutes to fail, with fatal consequences for the crew.

Apollo 16

The command and service module main engine, crucial for returning to Earth, reported a malfunction while the spacecraft was in orbit around the Moon. The Moon landing was almost scrubbed.

Figure 7-4. Apollo 15's splashdown with a malfunctioning parachute. Detail of photo AS15-S71-42217.

7.5 Rendezvous in lunar orbit made no sense

IN A NUTSHELL: *It's true that the Apollo flights to the Moon entailed a high-risk rendezvous in lunar orbit and that it would have been safer to perform this maneuver close to home, in Earth orbit, or avoid it completely by landing directly on the Moon with a single spacecraft instead of using a two-part vehicle. But this would have required a truly gigantic rocket, far bigger than the already massive Saturn V. Lunar rendezvous was chosen despite its dangers because it reduced drastically the fuel and payload requirements.*

THE DETAILS: Some Moon hoax believers find it preposterous that NASA chose to perform intricate undockings, redockings and rendezvous between the command module and the lunar module, and to perform them near the Moon instead of in Earth orbit, which offered better chances of rescue. Better still, why not follow the classic method featured in so many science fiction movies and land directly on the Moon with the main spacecraft, without using a separate lunar module?

Actually, NASA's initial plan was indeed to land on the Moon with a single, large, tall spacecraft: a concept known as *tailsitter*. However, a direct flight to the Moon would have required a colossal rocket, the Nova (Figure 7-5), which didn't exist yet and could not be completed in time for President Kennedy's deadline. The only booster that could be developed in time was the Saturn V, which was relatively smaller.

Figure 7-5. The giant Nova booster (right) compared with the C-5, precursor of the Saturn V (center). Document M-MS-G-36-62, April 1962.

Mission planners also considered using a first Saturn V to launch an unmanned tailsitter spacecraft into Earth orbit, followed by a second Saturn with the fuel. This was known as *Earth Orbit Rendezvous* and was NASA's favored plan for some time. However, it entailed two closely coordinated launches and a dangerous transfer of fuel in space.

An alternative option was to split the tailsitter into two separate vehicles: the main one would remain in orbit around the Moon and the secondary one would be a stripped-down, specialized Moon lander. This approach reduced weight and fuel requirements so much that it allowed to launch the entire mission with a single Saturn V rocket. However, the savings came at the cost of a risky rendezvous in lunar orbit (hence the name *Lunar Orbit Rendezvous* or *LOR*), which entailed certain death for the moonwalkers if it failed. A high-stakes gamble, in other words, but a perfectly logical one.

The lunar orbit rendezvous plan wasn't new: it had been conceived in 1916 by Russian spaceflight theoretician Yuri Vasilievich Kondratyuk. Nevertheless, NASA was very reluctant to take this perilous and untested path. John Houbolt, a relatively low-ranking aerospace engineer in the agency, is often credited with turning Wernher von Braun and NASA management around on this matter in 1962.

7.6 Nobody points a telescope at the landing sites

IN A NUTSHELL: *And with good reason, because even the most powerful telescopes currently available on Earth can't see such small features. Trigonometry and the laws of optics dictate that seeing any detail of the vehicles and equipment left at the Apollo landing sites from Earth would require a telescope with a mirror at least 45 meters (150 feet) in diameter. No current telescope comes even close.*

THE DETAILS: The *resolution* of a telescope, i.e., the detail that it can see, is determined by the laws of optics, specifically by a formula known as *Dawes' limit*, and depends essentially on the diameter of the main lens or mirror. Adding a lens to magnify the image acquired by this main telescope component will not yield more detail – only more blur.

The largest objects left on the Moon by the Apollo astronauts are the descent stages of the lunar modules, which measure approximately 9 meters (30 feet) across diagonally opposite footpads. A little trigonometry shows that at the minimum Earth-Moon distance, which is about 355,000 kilometers (220,600 miles), seeing the descent stage is equivalent to seeing a US one-cent coin from 740 kilometers (460 miles) away.

No current earthbound telescope can do that; not even the Hubble Space Telescope (Figure 7-6), which at the distance of the Moon can resolve nothing smaller than about 80 meters (262 feet).

That's an apparently counterintuitive fact. After all, telescopes can see incredibly distant galaxies, so why can't they get a good

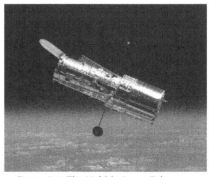

Figure 7-6. The Hubble Space Telescope.

picture of a 9-meter (30-foot) object on the Moon, which is in our back yard, astronomically speaking?

The reason is that galaxies are enormous, while the Apollo objects on the Moon are tiny, and their closeness doesn't compensate for the difference in size.

For example, the Andromeda galaxy is two million light years away (19 million million million kilometers or 12 million million million miles), yet it's bigger than the full Moon in our night sky; it's hard to see with the naked eye because it's very faint. That's why large astronomical telescopes are designed more to collect light from these remote objects than to magnify them.

Dawes' limit dictates that even in ideal conditions, seeing the Apollo lunar module descent stages on the Moon from Earth as nothing more than a bright dot would require a telescope with a primary lens or mirror at least 45 meters (150 feet) wide. Resolving any details of the spacecraft would require even more colossal telescopes.

The largest single-mirror telescopes on Earth are currently just over ten meters (33 feet) in diameter. Even the future record holder, the aptly-named European Extremely Large Telescope, which is scheduled for 2018, will be inadequate, because its composite primary mirror will only span 42 meters (138 feet).

A technique known as *interferometry*, however, allows astronomers to pair two telescopes to obtain a sort of "virtual" instrument that has a resolution equal to a single telescope with a primary mirror as large as the distance between the two telescopes. The Very Large Telescope in Chile, one of the best-equipped observatories for this kind of science, in ideal conditions could achieve a resolution of 0.002 arcseconds: enough to show the LM on the Moon as a handful of pixels (dots forming a digital image).

That sounds promising, but there's a catch. Interferometry doesn't produce directly viewable images, but only *interference patterns*, which require computer processing to extract meaningful information. This means that there's no way to put a Moon hoax theorist in front of a massive telescope and tell him or her to peer into the eyepiece to see the Apollo landing sites in any significant detail.

7.7 Nobody sends probes to take pictures of the landing sites

IN A NUTSHELL: *Actually, several countries, such as India, China, Japan and the United States, have sent science probes to the Moon and have surveyed its entire surface, including the Apollo landing sites. Their images confirm that there are vehicles and science instruments exactly where NASA said it placed them.*

THE DETAILS: Over the course of the four decades since the Apollo manned landings, the Moon has been visited and mapped in progressively greater detail by unmanned probes sent by China, India, Japan and the United States. Some of these spacecraft are currently in operation in orbit around the Moon, sending fresh images and science data.

The 1994 Clementine probe, launched by NASA, was able to image a patch of differently reflective soil exactly where NASA said that Apollo 15's LM had landed. This is compatible with the soil color changes expected as a consequence of the displacement of surface dust and the exposure of differently-colored underlying rock caused by a spacecraft rocket motor.

The same site was photographed in more detail in 2008 by the Japanese Kaguya probe (Figure 7-7), in 2009 by India's Chandrayaan-1 and in 2012 by the Chinese Chang'e-2 spacecraft, confirming the Clementine findings and revealing a dot at the center of the patch: presumably, the descent stage of the Apollo 15 LM or its shadow.

Kaguya also performed altimetric measurements of the Moon, generating a 3D terrain map that matches exactly the terrain shown in the Apollo photographs.

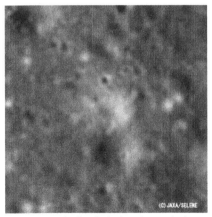

Figure 7-7. The bright halo is located where Apollo 15 landed. Credit: JAXA/Selene.

In 2009 the United States' Lunar Reconnaissance Orbiter (LRO) became the first probe to image directly the Apollo vehicles as well as the science experiments, the lines of footprints of the astronauts and the wheel tracks made by their electric car. Its first pictures were released in July 2009; some are shown in Chapter 3.

7.8 The Moon buggy didn't fit inside the spacecraft

IN A NUTSHELL: *It did. It was folded up inside the Lunar Module's descent stage.*

THE DETAILS: Many people compare the sizes of the Lunar Roving Vehicle or Rover (the electric car used by Apollo 15, 16 and 17) and of the lunar module and wonder how the Rover could fit inside the LM. The Rover was 2.96 meters (116.5 inches) long, 2.06 meters (81 inches) wide and 1.14 meters (44.8 inches) tall and at first glance seems to be incompatible with the dimensions of the lunar module, whose descent stage was about 4.3 meters (14.1 feet) wide and also had to accommodate the descent rocket engine and its fuel.

Figure 7-8. The Apollo 15 Rover, compactly folded into a wedge-like shape with its wheels clustered together, is ready to be stowed in one of the equipment recesses of the LM descent stage. Detail of photo AP15-71-HC-684.

The answer is quite simple: the LRV was designed to fold up for transport so that it would fit in one of the wedge-shaped recesses provided in the descent stage frame, covered only by a thermal protection sheet.

The Rover was simply an aluminum chassis with four small electric motors for driving the wheels and two additional motors for actuating the steering system, a battery pack and two tubular frame seats. On Earth it weighed just 210 kilograms (462 pounds). It required no gearbox, no transmission shafts and no wheel axles (the wheels were coupled directly to the motors) and so it could be folded up into a very compact shape (Figure 7-8).

The TV footage of the moonwalks show very clearly how the Rover was extracted and unfolded into its configuration for use.

7.9 Apollo didn't reach escape velocity

IN A NUTSHELL: *True, but it didn't need to. Getting to the Moon doesn't require escape velocity: a spacecraft only has to achieve a speed that produces a highly elongated orbit around the Earth that reaches a maximum altitude equal to the distance of the Moon, without ever escaping from the Earth's pull.*

THE DETAILS: This pro-conspiracy argument is a fine example of the misuse of science jargon and factual data to give an impression of competence and knowledge. Its premise is that the *escape velocity*, the speed required to escape the Earth's gravity field, is 11.2 kilometers per second (about 7 miles per second), i.e., 40,320 kilometers per hour (about 25,000 mph). This is correct. However, NASA reported that the top speed of Apollo 11 during its climb to the Moon was about 39,000 kilometers per hour (about 24,250 mph). This, too, is factually correct.

In other words, Apollo 11's stated maximum speed was about 1,230 kilometers per hour (765 mph) slower than escape velocity. So, the argument goes, how could the spacecraft escape Earth and reach the Moon?

The answer to this apparent contradiction is that escape velocity is required only if the spacecraft seeks to escape Earth's attraction *permanently*. Anything traveling at this velocity will never fall back to Earth and will continue to climb away from it indefinitely without requiring any additional thrust (more specifically, it will escape from Earth's gravity field yet will still be in the grip of the Sun's gravitational attraction).

A spacecraft doesn't actually need to reach escape velocity to get to the Moon. It just has to achieve a speed that produces an elliptical orbit around the Earth that stretches out to the distance of the Moon and is timed so that the Moon is at the opposite end of the ellipse when the spacecraft gets there. So the Apollo flights didn't have to reach escape velocity to land on the Moon or fly around it.

Actually, staying below escape velocity is a safety bonus, because it allows to use a so-called *free return* trajectory (Figure 7-9): the spacecraft will fall back to Earth spontaneously, without requiring additional maneuvers or thrust from its rocket motors. This is particularly useful in case of major malfunctions, as in the case of Apollo 13.[53]

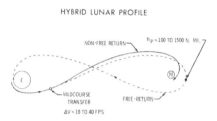

Figure 7-9. The main trajectories used by the Apollo missions. From the Apollo 11 Press Kit.

7.10 The Saturn V wasn't powerful enough

IN A NUTSHELL: *A mathematical analysis of the liftoff footage of the Saturn V, published by Russian scientist Stanislav Pokrovsky, appears to prove that the first stage of the lunar rocket didn't reach the speed stated by NASA and therefore could carry to the Moon far less payload than officially stated. However, the analysis is based on highly inaccurate estimates and on an incorrect premise: the actual work of getting the astronauts to the Moon was performed by the* third *stage, not the first one, which like the second one was only designed to place the spacecraft in Earth orbit and did so correctly, even according to Pokrovsky's analysis.*

THE DETAILS: A highly complex, math-heavy analysis published in Russian[54] by Stanislav Pokrovsky and available in English from pro-hoax site Aulis.com[55] (which describes Pokrovsky as a *"scientist"*) argues that the actual speed of the Saturn V Moon rocket when it exhausted the fuel of its first stage and separated from the rest of the spacecraft was only half of the speed claimed by official documents.

---

53 More specifically, Apollo 13 began its flight on a free return trajectory and then fired its main engine to leave this trajectory and fly towards the Moon. After the onboard explosion, the thrust of the LM's descent engine was used to inject the astronauts into another free return trajectory.

54 *supernovum.ru/public/index.php?doc=62* (in Russian).

55 *http://www.aulis.com/pdf%20folder/Pokrovsky1.pdf.*

Pokrovsky claims that the F-1 engines of the Saturn's first stage were not powerful enough to carry to the Moon the 46-ton payload constituted by the command and service module and lunar module. His calculations suggest that the low speed entailed that the maximum payload that could be delivered to the Moon was approximately 26 tons. Since the CSM weighed over 30,000 kilograms (66,000 pounds) and the LM weighed over 15,000 kilograms (33,000 pounds), Pokrovsky argues that NASA could fly one or the other, but not both, to the Moon, and therefore the best it could achieve was a flight around the Moon, without landing.

However, despite the impressive charts and formulas, the entire analysis is based on an estimate of the progressive apparent distance between the Saturn V and the exhaust plume of the first-stage retrorockets; an estimate made purely by examining blurry footage from one of NASA's tracking cameras (Figure 7-10). It is quite hard to measure the exact point where a rocket plume ends.

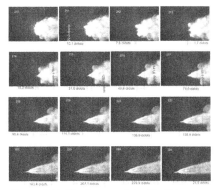

Figure 7-10. The frames of the liftoff footage analyzed by Pokrovsky.

Moreover, Pokrovsky assumes that the retrorocket plume somehow stopped in mid-air, instantaneously losing the tremendous speed of the spacecraft that generated it, and therefore can be used as a fixed reference point to calculate the speed of the Saturn V rocket. But the first stage separated from the rest of the spacecraft (Figure 7-11) at an altitude of over 61,000 meters (200,000 feet), where the atmosphere is approximately 10,000 times thinner that at sea level, so there was no significant air resistance to slow the plume or stop it. By inertia it would continue to climb, chasing the rocket and thus biasing any visual estimate of distance and speed.

Apart from the inaccurate data, Pokrovsky's analysis is invalidated by the fact that the Saturn V's first stage, together with the second stage, only had the task of placing the third stage and the Apollo spacecraft into Earth orbit (with some help from the third stage). The first two stages did not contribute to the actual trip from Earth orbit to the Moon, which was instead powered by the third stage.

Since Pokrovsky acknowledges that Earth orbit was achieved by the Apollo vehicles, all his remarks and calculations regarding the actual speed of the first stage are simply irrelevant in terms of how many tons of payload could be sent to the Moon.

Moreover, in the laws of physics that govern orbital flight what matters is the *final* speed of a spacecraft, which must be sufficient to stay in orbit without falling back to Earth. The speed *during* the climb to altitude is only relevant in terms of fuel consumption and crew comfort: a faster climb uses less fuel, but subjects the astronauts to higher acceleration stresses (up to 4.7 g for the Saturn V; Gemini's Titan launchers reached 7 g). In principle, a slow climb to orbital altitude followed by acceleration to orbital speed would still achieve orbit. Therefore Pokrovsky's issue of first stage speed is irrelevant.

Figure 7-11. Separation of the first stage of the Saturn V during the Apollo 11 flight. Detail from NASA photo S69-39958.

7.11 The LM was too puny to climb back from the Moon

IN A NUTSHELL: *No, it wasn't. It didn't have to fight against air resistance, it only had to cope with one sixth of Earth's gravity, and it only had to reach one quarter of the orbital speed required to orbit the Earth. The fuel demands of a lunar liftoff are far lower than terrestrial ones and the payload was minimal (two astronauts, some Moon rocks and a tiny, ultralight spacecraft). Also, the LM only had to achieve lunar orbit, not lunar escape velocity, since the thrust for the trip back to Earth was provided by the service module's main engine.*

THE DETAILS: The truly minuscule size and fragile appearance of the LM's ascent stage used to return from the Moon (Figure 7-12) are a striking contrast to the colossal size of the Saturn V required to leave Earth. Some people doubt that such a tiny spacecraft could be adequate and wonder, for example, where all the fuel needed to climb and accelerate to orbital speed could be stored.

Actually, the comparison is quite misleading, because it would be harder to find two more dissimilar liftoffs. The Saturn V had to lift its own huge initial mass of approximately 2,900 tons against Earth's gravity and against air resistance (aerodynamic drag) up to a speed of 28,000 kilometers per hour (about 17,400 miles per hour) and inject a 130-ton payload into Earth orbit, at an altitude of 190 kilometers (118 miles).

Figure 7-12. The Apollo 16 ascent stage. Detail from photo AS16-122-19530.

The LM's ascent stage instead had to lift an initial mass of 4.5 tons (of which 2.3 were fuel, leading to a very large loss of mass during the climb as the fuel was used) and accelerate it to approximately 6,600 kilometers per hour (4,100 miles per hour), raising a payload of 2.2 tons to a maximum altitude of 83 kilometers (approximately 51 miles). Moreover, on the airless Moon there was no atmospheric drag and the gravity was one sixth of the Earth's.

The idea of having to reach escape velocity is also wrong: as mentioned in section 7.9, escape velocity is required only to fly away indefinitely from a celestial body without further fuel consumption. But the LM didn't need to do that: it only had to reach a speed that allowed it to enter an elliptical orbit with a minimum altitude of 16.6 kilometers (10.3 miles) and a maximum altitude of 83 kilometers (about 51 miles).

The extra thrust required to leave lunar orbit and fly back to Earth was provided by the rocket engine of the service module, which stayed in lunar orbit indeed to avoid landing and bringing back up additional mass. NASA's choice of a lunar rendezvous was made for this very reason: to achieve great mass and fuel savings.

All these factors drastically reduce the power requirements of a lunar liftoff, so approximately 2,350 kilograms (5,181 pounds) of fuel, constituted by 910 kilograms (2,006 pounds) of Aerozine 50 and 1,440 kilo-

grams (3,175 pounds) of dinitrogen tetroxide, were sufficient to
lift the stripped-down ascent
stage into a low lunar orbit.

That may sound like a lot of fuel
to store in such a small spacecraft, but these substances have
a density of 0.903 g/cm³ and
1.443 g/cm³ (56.372 and 90.083
lb/ft³) respectively, and therefore the quantities reported by
NASA have a volume of approximately 1 cubic meter (35.3 cu-

Figure 7-13. A cutout view of the LM ascent stage published by Grumman.

bic feet) each, which fits quite adequately in the two spherical tanks
located in the bulges at the opposite sides of the cylindrical crew compartment of the ascent stage (Figure 7-13 shows the Aerozine 50 tank).

7.12 The Lunar Module was too unstable to fly

IN A NUTSHELL: *The irregular shape of the LM, with its odd bulges and single central rocket motor, seems strangely top-heavy and as unstable as a football balanced on a finger, ready to tip sideways at the slightest wobble: apparently impossible to fly. But if you look at its internal structure it turns out that it was actually easier to stabilize than a conventional pencil-shaped rocket, because its main masses were located at or below the center of thrust of the motor and therefore its center of mass was quite low.*

THE DETAILS: Moon hoax theorist Bart Sibrel claims that the
Apollo lunar module had a high
center of mass that made it too
unstable to fly. Sibrel is not an
aerospace specialist, yet he appears to believe that he can
judge the stability of a spacecraft just by looking at its picture. Actually, a less superficial
examination based on some
elementary physics reveals that
the LM was easier to stabilize
than a conventional rocket.

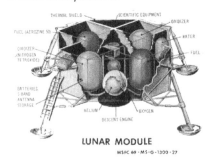

Figure 7-14. Arrangement of the fuel tanks in the LM descent stage.

In the descent stage and in the ascent stage, the fuel tanks, which are the most important masses of the vehicle, were located as low as possible, laterally with respect to the motor (Figure 7-14). This is a far less unstable configuration than a conventional rocket, in which the tanks (and therefore their great masses) are located above the engines. Placing these tanks laterally and at opposite ends actually helped to stabilize the vehicle, somewhat like the pole of a tightrope walker.

Moreover, the main engines were not underneath the spacecraft, as a cursory inspection of the LM might suggest, but were deep inside it, with only the nozzle protruding below. The ascent stage's engine was actually inside the crew compartment (Figure 7-15). This meant that the center of thrust (the imaginary point, located at the top of the nozzle, on which a vehicle "rests" when its engine is on) was close to the center of mass, which was an ideal situation in terms of stability.

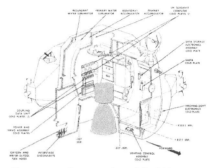

Figure 7-15. Cross-section of the LM ascent stage: the main rocket motor is shaded. Source: Apollo Operations Handbook, volume 1, with added shading.

Finally, the sixteen maneuvering thrusters were placed at the end of outriggers, as far as possible from the thrust axis of the main engine, so as to augment their effectiveness in a lever-like fashion.

7.13 The astronauts would have unbalanced the LM

IN A NUTSHELL: *No, because their movements had a very small effect and were compensated automatically by the onboard computers.*

THE DETAILS: In Fox TV's *Did We Land on the Moon?*, Ralph Rene alleges that the movements of the astronauts in the cabin of the lunar module would have shifted the center of mass continually and therefore would have caused the spacecraft to tip over uncontrollably and crash. Therefore, he argues, the LM could not fly and accordingly the Moon landings are fake.

The facts are quite different. First of all, the LM had not one, but two automatic stabilization systems that controlled the maneuvering thrusters (the ones clustered at the end of the ascent stage's outriggers) to compensate constantly for any imbalance. The astronauts didn't stabilize the spacecraft manually. The computer-controlled stabilization can be noticed in the liftoff footage, which shows a characteristic periodic oscillation induced by the automatic firing of the thrusters as soon as an imbalance was detected.

The concept is not at all unusual: any rocket has the same problem of compensating for shifts in the center of mass (for example due to fuel displacement or depletion). In the atmosphere, fins can be used; in space, gimbaled main engines and small maneuvering thrusters are used. This is a solution shared by all spacecraft of all countries, including the Space Shuttle.

Secondly, the astronauts stood very close to the center of mass of the lunar module and didn't have much room to move anyway (Figure 7-16).

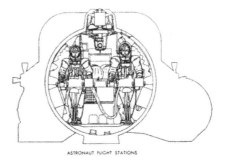

Moreover, the astronauts weighed far less than the fuel tanks, which had a mass of 910 and 1,440 kilograms (2,006 and 3,175 pounds) respectively. The crew's movements, therefore, couldn't affect the balance of the spacecraft to any great extent. The main challenge to stability was the sloshing of the fuel in the tanks as they

Figure 7-16. The position of the astronauts in the LM during flight. The main engine is between them; the fuel tanks are at the opposite sides of the outline. Detail of Figure 1-6 of the Apollo Operations Handbook.

gradually emptied, but this was handled by the computer-based stabilization systems.

7.14 The LM simulator was so unstable that it crashed

IN A NUTSHELL: *Yes, Neil Armstrong narrowly escaped from a crash of the lunar landing simulator. But that doesn't mean that the Lunar Module was unstable. The simulator was a completely different vehicle than the LM, and anyway the crash was caused by a rare malfunction of the vehicle, not by Armstrong's inability to control it. The simulator had flown normally over 790 times without loss of control.*

THE DETAILS: The Apollo astronauts familiarized with the unique characteristics of the lunar module by using two types of flying simulator, known as *Lunar Landing Research Vehicle* (LLRV) and *Lunar Landing Training Vehicle* (LLTV). These were essentially bare frames on which a gimbaled jet engine was mounted vertically, so that its thrust supported five sixths of the weight of the ungainly craft. The remainder (the weight it would have had on the Moon) was supported by two throttleable rocket engines (Figure 7-17).

Figure 7-17. An LLRV in flight in 1964. Detail from NASA photo ECN-506.

Like the LM, these vehicles had sixteen small thrusters for attitude control. An electronic system kept the main jet engine constantly vertical and adjusted its thrust so as to simulate the effects of the reduced vertical acceleration that occurs on the Moon.

Flights lasted only a handful of minutes, but were long enough to practice landing from an altitude of approximately 1,200 meters (4,000 feet).

Two LLRVs were built first, followed by three LLTVs. Armstrong's accident occurred on May 6, 1968, with an LLRV (Figure 7-18): the pressurization system of the attitude thrusters failed, a gust of wind caught the vehicle, and Armstrong had no choice but to eject, landing safely under his parachute while the LLRV crashed and burned.

Figure 7-18. Neil Armstrong parachutes to safety after the malfunction of his LLRV.

During the training flights, these experimental vehicles suffered two more accidents, in December 1968 and in January 1971, leading to their destruction. The pilots were unharmed.

Conspiracy theorists make it sound as if crashing was the normal conclusion of the flights of these vehicles, but in actual fact the five simulators that were built flew a total of 792 flights with successful landings.
Armstrong's LLRV had flown without mishap 281 times before the
crash.[56]

7.15 All the technical problems vanished suddenly

IN A NUTSHELL: *No, they didn't. Problems occurred throughout all the
missions and the first unmanned flights were designed, as usual, to shake
down the vehicles and correct or reduce their defects before the actual
manned missions were flown.*

THE DETAILS: A recurring argument among hoax theorists is that the
early Apollo missions were plagued with problems, leading to very
public delays and cancellations, but all the troubles disappeared just in
time for the flights to the Moon.

For example, Mary Bennett and David Percy claim that *"[the Saturn V]
performed flawlessly throughout the entire Apollo program. But the early
Saturn V F-1 engine tests were absolutely disastrous, with catastrophic explosions on the test stand."* He adds that *"The problem of combustion in-
stability [...] known as the 'pogo effect' (the industry term for those internal
oscillations we mentioned earlier) was in evidence from early testing of the
Saturn rocket right through to the 'Apollo 10' launch – after which
everything worked perfectly!"* And Bill Kaysing asked *"Why was Apollo 6,
a total fiasco, followed by six perfect moon missions which in turn were
followed by the manned orbiting lab debacle?"*[57]

Actually, if you check these claims against the mission reports, it turns
out that the Saturn V's performance wasn't *"flawless"* at all. It always
got the job done, but nearly all flights reported substantial problems.
Far from working *"perfectly"* after Apollo 10, as Bennett and Percy claim,
the Saturn V was troubled by the pogo effect during Apollo 11 and 12
as well, leading to violent vibrations of the central F-1 engine of the
first stage. For Apollo 13, vibrations were so intense that the central J-2
engine of the second stage had to be shut down automatically during
ascent to Earth orbit to prevent it from tearing the spacecraft to pieces.
Changes made for Apollo 14 finally made the problem manageable.

---

56 *Unconventional, Contrary, and Ugly: The Lunar Landing Research Vehicle,* by Gene J. Mat-
    ranga, C. Wayne Ottinger and Calvin R. Jarvis with C. Christian Gelzer. NASA SP-2004-4535
    (2005), p. 142.

57 Mary Bennett and David Percy, *Dark Moon,* p. 127-128; Bill Kaysing, *We Never Went to the
    Moon,* p. 8.

Section 7.4 covers in detail the major malfunctions and problems that affected the Apollo missions.

As regards the *"catastrophic explosions on the test stand,"* that's why rocket designers have tests and use test stands: to iron out the worst kinks before actual flights. Indeed, celebrated Russian designer Boris Chertok noted repeatedly, in his monumental book series *Rockets and People,* that one of the key reasons for the failure of the Soviet moonshot attempts was the unwise decision to avoid building a full-scale test firing rig for the N-1 rocket, opting instead to test the engines directly in a series of unmanned flights. This decision led to four consecutive catastrophic failures of the N-1, after which the project was scrubbed and buried.

The successful performance of the Saturn V was the result of extensive testing not only on the ground, but also in flight. There's a reason why the first actual manned Apollo flight, after the Apollo 1 fire that killed Grissom, White and Chaffee on the pad during a test, was number 7: all the previous ones were unmanned test launches.

Test flights AS-203 and AS-202, launched in 1966, respectively tested the S-IVB, which would become the third stage of the Saturn V (Figure 7-19), and flew the command and service modules, testing the heat shield at reentry speeds similar to those expected for a return from the Moon and also qualifying the Saturn IB for manned flights.

Apollo 4 was the first flight of the giant Saturn V rocket (no flight was ever formally designated Apollo 2 or 3); this unmanned test validated, among other things, the radiation shielding of the crew cabin and was considered very suc-

Figure 7-19. Liftoff of AS-203.

cessful. It was an *"all-up"* flight: a bold gamble to test all the main components at once, rather than one at a time in separate flights.[58]

The next flight, Apollo 5, was likewise unmanned because it was an automatic test of the lunar module in Earth orbit, using a Saturn IB booster. Both of the LM's engines were fired and stage separation

---

58   *Saturn V Launch Vehicle Flight Evaluation Report – AS-501 Apollo 4 Mission.*

was performed. The flight also tested the automatic flight management systems (*Instrument Unit*) in the configuration that would later be used by the Saturn V.

Apollo 6 (Figure 7-20) was the second unmanned *"all-up"* test flight of the Saturn V, also checking the capability of the command module to shield the crew from radiation during their brief transit through the Van Allen belts. It was affected by violent pogo oscillations caused by structural resonances; two of the five engines of the second stage underwent a premature shutdown (one because of the oscillations and one due to incorrect wiring); and the third stage yielded less thrust than expected.

Figure 7-20. Apollo 6: separation of the ring between the first and second stages, filmed by an onboard automatic camera.

These problems were analyzed and addressed in later flights by changing the resonance frequencies of some components, adding dampers and scheduling additional wiring checks. That's what test flights are for. Despite this, the manned flights of Apollo 8 and 10 were troubled by pogo oscillations in the central engine of the second stage.

7.16 There's no engine noise in the Moon landing audio

IN A NUTSHELL: *The powerful engine of the Lunar Module's ascent stage was literally inside the crew cabin, yet there's no engine noise in the recordings of the radio communications. That's because the astronauts kept their microphones very close to their mouths so as to cut out background noise and because the mikes were designed to pick up only sounds at close range, just like aircraft pilot microphones, and in any case in a vacuum the rocket exhaust doesn't interact with an atmosphere, which is what produces most of the familiar roaring noise.*

THE DETAILS: Bill Kaysing, in Fox TV's *Conspiracy Theory: Did We Land on the Moon?*, says that *"the noise level of a rocket engine is up into the 140/150-decibel range. In other words, enormously loud. How would it be* *possible to hear astronauts' voices against the background of a running rocket engine?"*

Indeed, the recordings of the astronauts' communications during landing and liftoff, while the rocket engines are running, contain no engine noise.

This apparently unusual fact is actually quite normal and occurs not only in the Apollo recordings, but also in Shuttle liftoff recordings. Moreover, when we take a plane and the captain makes a passenger announcement, his voice isn't drowned out by the noise of the engines, even though the same noise is audible in the cabin.

The explanation is quite simple: the microphones were designed to cut out background noise and were kept very close to the mouth. Bill Anders (Apollo 8, Figure 7-21) reportedly called them *"tonsil mikes"* because he said that he had to shove them down his throat to make them work. This allowed the voice to drown out the roar of the engines – if there was any to begin with.

Kaysing's claim is in fact incorrect: the noise of a spacecraft engine is not always *"enormously loud".*

When a rocket engine operates in vacuum, its exhaust expands without encountering any obstacle: it doesn't collide at supersonic speed with an atmosphere and therefore it doesn't generate the shockwaves that instead cause the loud noise that is heard on the ground when a large rocket is launched.

Both Apollo astronauts and current spacecraft crews report that when they are in space, sometimes they hear a bang at the moment of ignition, before combustion stabilizes, and they feel occasionally intense vibration; but apart from this, they say that the engines are noiseless. It seems unlikely that they're all lying.

Figure 7-21. Bill Anders prepares for the Apollo 8 mission. Note the microphones on either side of his chin. NASA photo 68-H-1330.

7.17 The fragile LM withstood temperature extremes too well

IN A NUTSHELL: *There's a good reason why the lunar module could stand on the Moon with one side exposed to the sun and the opposite side in shadow, without overheating or freezing: it was insulated by a highly efficient multilayer thermal blanket. This gave it its characteristic "tin foil" appearance, which made it seem fragile while it was actually better protected against temperature variations than the rest of the Apollo spacecraft.*

THE DETAILS: During the voyage to and from the Moon, the great thermal differences between the side of the spacecraft that was in full sunlight and the side in shadow required the astronauts to slowly roll the Apollo vehicle about its longitudinal axis to prevent it from overheating on one side and freezing on the other. This was known formally as *Passive Thermal Control* and less formally as *barbecue mode.*

However, the apparently fragile lunar module, when it landed on the Moon, could no longer roll. It kept the same side exposed to the incessant heat of the sun and the opposite side exposed to the cold darkness of shadow for up to three days, without overheating or freezing.

This apparent technical contradiction actually has a very practical explanation: the service module and the command module were more sensitive to thermal variations than the LM. In the service modules, the fuel tanks for its sixteen thrusters were close to the outer skin and had to remain within very strict temperature and pressure ranges. The command module also had a heat shield that would crack and flake if left to cool off in shadow in space for more than thirteen hours, becoming unusable and leading to crew loss upon atmospheric reentry. The slow roll was introduced to provide a more uniform and less extreme heating and cooling of these components of the Apollo spacecraft.

The LM instead didn't have these limitations: differently from the other modules, it didn't have to cope with the aerodynamic stresses of the liftoff from Earth (during which it was protected by a streamlined fairing), it didn't have a delicate heat shield to protect and it had no fuel tanks in direct contact with the outside skin. Accordingly, it could be equipped with a more effective thermal control system, which included a thermal blanket made of multiple layers of Mylar or Kapton. Spacers formed an insulating gap between the blanket and the pressurized crew compartment. The LM also had a sublimator similar to the one used for the spacesuits.

The apparently fragile, tin foil-like appearance of the LM was produced by this thermal blanket, which concealed the normal underlying metal structure shown in Figure 7-22.

Figure 7-22. A prototype of the Lunar Module, preserved at the Smithsonian National Air and Space Museum, reveals the metallic structure inside the thermal protection covering. Credit: NASM.

8. Alleged physical anomalies

8.1 The camera films would have melted on the Moon

IN A NUTSHELL: *No. The temperature extremes often mentioned by conspiracy theorists refer to the lunar surface, from which the films were insulated by vacuum, like in a thermos flask, and in any case were not reached during the Apollo missions, which landed on the Moon shortly after the beginning of the two-week-long lunar day at the landing sites, when ground temperatures were far lower. The film was also a heat-resistant type used for high-altitude reconnaissance and the cameras were treated to reflect the heat from direct exposure to the Sun, which is comparable with the heat from sunlight on a mountaintop on Earth.*

THE DETAILS: Gerhard Wisnewski is one of the many hoax theorists who claim that the extreme temperatures of the lunar surface would have damaged the camera films irreparably and therefore the photographs must be fake. In his book *One Small Step*, Wisnewski argues thus:

> There was no other protection against temperature extremes of over 100°C plus and under 100°C minus [...] It was to be expected that the sensitivity of the chemical films would be affected by the extreme temperatures – if indeed not rendered useless by temperatures of over 100°C.

However, a little fact-checking shows that Wisnewski's premise is incorrect due to a common misconception about temperatures in space.

First of all, the extreme values mentioned by Wisnewski are reached only after lunar midday (which entails seven consecutive Earth days of uninterrupted exposure to the Sun) and just before sunrise (after fourteen Earth days of continuous darkness). Data from recent lunar probes, such as the Lunar Reconnaissance Orbiter, show maximum temperatures of 110°C (230°F) and minimum temperatures of -180°C (-

292 °F) at the lunar equator; in some polar regions, which are perennially in shadow, the temperature plunges to -238°C (-397°F).

But all the Moon landings took place shortly after local sunrise, when the temperatures were far from these extremes. The maximum elevation of the Sun above the horizon during the Apollo moonwalks was 48.7°, at the end of the third excursion of the Apollo 16 crew. This mission recorded temperatures of 57°C (135°F) in sunlight and -100°C (-140°F) in shadow.

Secondly, all these values refer to the temperature of the lunar *surface*. But on the Moon there's nothing to carry that heat from the ground to the films: there's no significant atmosphere that can be heated by the ground and therefore there is no conduction or convection through air, which is the main heating process on Earth. Vacuum is a very good heat insulator, as thermos flasks demonstrate. On the Moon and in space, heat is transferred between objects that are not in mutual contact only by *radiation*: the same principle by which we are warmed when standing next to a fire. Clearly the heating produced by radiation is nowhere as intense as heating by direct contact: there's a significant difference between warming your hands in front of a fire and putting your hands *in* the fire.

Consequently, on the Moon the temperature of the ground is essentially irrelevant as regards film temperatures and claiming that ground temperatures would overheat the films is a misleading and amateurish scientific error.

Moreover, an object exposed to the Sun on the Moon receives essentially the same amount of heat that it receives on Earth on a mountain top on a clear day, since heat transfer by radiation depends on the distance from the heat source and the Earth and the Moon are essentially at the same distance from the Sun. There's nothing magically incendiary about the sunlight that strikes the Moon: in terms of heat, it's roughly the same that we receive here on Earth.

In other words, a film exposed to sunlight on the Moon is affected by the same level of thermal stresses that affect it on Earth on a bright sunlit day on a high mountain. As we all know, tourists are quite able to take photographs in the mountains and even in the heat of tropical forests or deserts without their film melting or spoiling its colors.

One might object that on the Moon the sunlit side of the camera is heated intensely while the shadow side cools just as dramatically. However, these processes are not instantaneous, because once again there's no air to carry the heat from the camera body to the film or away from the film into space. The camera is in vacuum and therefore the film is like in a thermos flask. Heat transfer between the film and the camera occurs only at their few points of mutual contact.

Besides, if someone argues that it's impossible for film to withstand the vacuum and the temperatures on the Moon, then he or she is implying that *all* the photographs ever taken on film in space during Russian and American spacewalks are fake, because there are no differences, in terms of temperature, vacuum and exposure to sunlight, between the conditions on the Moon and those in Earth orbit.

For example, Figure 8-1 shows US astronaut Ed White during his spacewalk outside the Gemini 4 spacecraft in 1965. He is carrying an ordinary camera (circled) and his picture was taken with another camera, which also was outside in space. Neither of the films in these cameras melted or was spoiled.

Moreover, the Apollo lunar cameras had been treated specifically to have reflective surfaces instead of the traditional black finish, as shown in Figure 3-5. This treatment reflected most of the heat received from the Sun.

Figure 8-1. Ed White used an ordinary camera (shown circled here, in front of the astronaut's chest) during his spacewalk in 1965. NASA photograph S65-30431.

In addition, lunar photography didn't use ordinary film, but a special 70 mm Kodak film engineered specifically for high-altitude reconnaissance applications, in which it had to deal with temperatures as low as -40°C (104°F). This film had a custom-made thin polyester base (Estar), with a melting point of 254°C (490°F), and used an Ektachrome emulsion capable of providing adequate results over a wide temperature range.

Sometimes it is objected that chemical films have a narrow temperature range, so much that professional photographers are very careful to keep their films warm or cool as needed. But this is an *optimum* range, which yields the best possible colors: it doesn't imply that the film will break or melt outside of this interval.

8.2 The Van Allen radiation belts would have killed the astronauts

IN A NUTSHELL: *No. These belts are not as deadly as they're often made out to be. Russian spaceflights have carried animals through them without problems. NASA also conducted sensor-laden unmanned test flights to measure the effectiveness of the shielding of the Apollo command module. In any case, the trajectories of all the moonshots were calculated to fly around the core of these donut-shaped belts and pass rapidly through their less intense outer portions.*

THE DETAILS: Many Moon hoax proponents claim that any manned lunar mission would be impossible due to the lethal barrier of the *Van Allen belts*, two regions of radiation that wrap around the Earth at distances that can vary according to solar activity but are roughly located between 100 and 10,000 kilometers (62 to 6,200 miles) for the more intense inner belt and between 18,000 and 60,000 kilometers (11,100 to 37,000 miles) for the weaker outer belt (Figure 8-2).

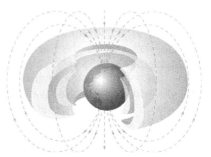

Figure 8-2. A graphical representation of the Van Allen belts.

Vintage technical literature on the subject (for example the papers listed in the *References* chapter of this book) shows that the potential danger posed by the Van Allen belts was well-known when the lunar missions flew (the belts had been discovered in 1958) and was considered perfectly manageable.

In 1968, the Soviet space probe Zond 5 flew through the Van Allen belts to carry around the Moon several living creatures, which returned unharmed from their voyage.

For the Apollo missions, exposure during the crossing of the Van Allen belts was calculated and measured by means of unmanned test flights: specifically, Apollo 6 (April 1968) carried into Earth orbit an empty Apollo capsule equipped with instruments for measuring the capability of the spacecraft to block the radiation from the belts. It was found that the exposure was comparable to the effects of a few medical X-rays and therefore was quite tolerable.

The very first human beings to fly beyond the Van Allen belts were the astronauts of Apollo 8. According to NASA's *Biomedical Results of Apollo* report (1975), over the course of the entire flight Lovell, Borman and Anders accumulated a radiation dose of 1.6 millisieverts. This is the equivalent of about twenty chest X-rays and is therefore far from being immediately lethal as some conspiracy theorists argue.

Moreover, the Apollo 11 *Mission Report* notes that the total radiation dose measured by the dosimeters and received by the astronauts during the trip was between 2.5 and 2.8 millisieverts. The Van Allen-specific dosimeter detected doses of 1.1 millisieverts for the skin and 0.8 millisieverts for the depth reading, well below medically significant values.

For comparison, according to the US National Council on Radiation Protection and Measurement the annual average radiation dose per person in the United States is 6.2 millisieverts; 52% of this is of natural origin.[59]

We don't have to take NASA's word about the Van Allen belts. There is clear consensus in the science community on the matter, as shown for example by the article *The Van Allen Belts and Travel to the Moon* by Bill Wheaton, specialist in gamma ray astronomy at the Jet Propulsion Laboratory (JPL).[60]

Wheaton provides objective data regarding radiation in space and specifically in the most dangerous region of the Van Allen belts. It turns out that the data published by NASA on this subject must be true, otherwise today's automatic satellites would be fried, since they fly through the belts and their equipment, if not shielded adequately against radiation, will malfunction.

James Van Allen, from whom the belts get their name, had already stressed, as early as 1960 in the article *On the Radiation Hazards of Space Flight*, that these belts don't encase the entire planet from pole to pole, but form a sort of donut that fades in intensity from approximately 30° above and below the Earth's equator.

Therefore, to fly around them or pass through their weaker regions it is sufficient to use an adequately inclined trajectory, which is what all the Apollo spacecraft did, both on the way to the Moon and on the way home (Figure 8-3).

Records show that Apollo 11's transit through the Van Allen belts lasted a total of 90 minutes, flying around the region of maximum intensity in about ten minutes.

---

59 *http://www.epa.gov/rpdweb00/understand/perspective.html.*

60 *http://www.wwheaton.com/waw/mad/mad19.html.*

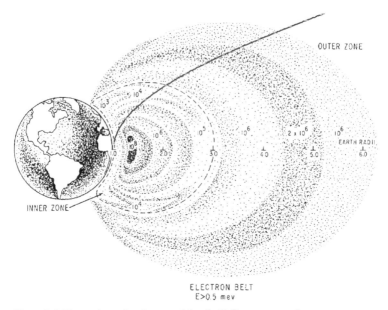

OUTER ZONE

EARTH RADII

INNER ZONE

ELECTRON BELT
E>0.5 mev

Figure 8-3. The outbound trajectory of Apollo 11. The return path was even more inclined. Source: Rocket & Space Technology.

8.3 Deep space radiation would have killed the astronauts

IN A NUTSHELL: *No, it wouldn't have. Radiation normally present in space at lunar distances from Earth is comparable to the radiation received by the astronauts on the International Space Station, who stay in space up to six months at a time. A round trip to the Moon lasted no more than twelve days.*

THE DETAILS: It is often claimed that the lethal radiation of deep space would have killed the Apollo astronauts who went to the Moon, since they spent several days outside of the safety of Earth's protective magnetic field, which provides a shield against this radiation.

However, the claim's premise is factually incorrect: on Earth we're protected against deep space radiation mainly by the atmosphere, not by the planet's magnetic field, which has a small role in shielding us. The dose of cosmic radiation (ions traveling at nearly the speed of light) that reaches anyone who lives at sea level is approximately 0.3 millisieverts/year, which is the equivalent of a couple of chest X-rays. This rises to 0.8-1.2 millisieverts/year for people living at high altitudes, for example on a 3,000-meter (10,000-ft) mountain range. At 12,000 meters (40,000 feet), the usual altitude of airline flights, cosmic radiation rises further to 28 millisieverts/year: nearly a hundred times more than at sea level, even though the aircraft's occupants are still well within the Earth's magnetic field.

Once you leave the atmosphere, this radiation increases considerably right away. In low earth orbit, such as on the International Space Station, it averages 100 millisieverts/year. At this altitude, the protective effect of the Earth's magnetic field becomes significant, but only for astronauts who follow equatorial orbits; the ISS has a highly inclined orbit. In interplanetary space the dose is 130-250 millisieverts/year and by some estimates may be as high as 800 millisieverts/year on a trip to Mars; on the surface of the Moon it drops to 70-120 millisieverts/year.[61]

In other words, the doses of deep space radiation to which the Apollo vehicles were exposed are comparable to those that affect the International Space Station, yet the occupants of the ISS stay in space for up to *six months* without dying of radiation exposure, compared to a maximum of twelve days for the lunar astronauts during Apollo 17.

8.4 X-rays in space would have fogged the films

IN A NUTSHELL: *No, because the X-ray doses received in space would not have been strong enough. The tests performed by conspiracy theorists use flawed methods and vastly exaggerated doses compared to those to which films might be exposed during a trip to the Moon and back.*

THE DETAILS: In the book *Dark Moon*, Mary Bennett and David Percy describe tests conducted by physicist David Groves: films exposed to X-rays became fogged or their pictures were deleted. Therefore, they claim, the same should have happened to the films taken to the Moon.

However, these tests exposed the film to X-rays *directly*, without any protection, whereas the lunar films were kept for almost all of the journey inside shielded canisters, which in turn were protected by the shielding provided by the Apollo spacecraft in the Command Module and in the Lunar Module. Even during the moonwalks, the films were shielded by the metal of their Hasselblad magazine.

Groves' tests also bombarded the test films with an 8-MeV (million electron volts) beam, using a linear accelerator, while astronomers report that X-rays from space have an energy level of less than 5 keV

---

61 *Shielding Space Travelers*, Eugene N. Parker, emeritus physics professor at the University of Chicago and member of the National Academy of Sciences, in *Scientific American*, March 2006.

(thousand electron volts), i.e., approximately 1,600 times weaker than the radiation that fogged films in the Groves experiment.

This difference is crucial not only in terms of numbers, which show how unfair the tests presented by Bennett and Percy are, but also in terms of the shielding required: X-rays with an energy of less than 5 keV are stopped by a few sheets of paper. Under 3 keV, just a few dozen centimeters (inches) of air are all that it takes.

Groves reports that he exposed the test films to 25, 50 and 100 rem of radiation, but this unit is wholly inappropriate, because it refers to radiation absorbed by human tissue. Using it for films suggests an unprofessional approach to the matter: it's like saying that distances are measured in liters (or gallons). However, for X-rays 1 rad is equivalent to 1 rem, so we could assume that Groves meant doses of 25 to 100 rad. Even so, 25 rad (the lowest figure claimed by Groves) are equivalent to *several years* in space.

8.5 Sunlight would have burned or boiled the astronauts' faces

IN A NUTSHELL: *No. If so, then it should also do the same to the faces of astronauts who routinely perform spacewalks outside the International Space Station, since sunlight on the Moon is essentially the same as in Earth orbit. But it doesn't.*

THE DETAILS: Some Moon hoax proponents argue that the fiercely strong sunlight on the Moon, unfiltered by the Earth's protective atmosphere, should have caused intense sunburns or overheating, yet we see photographs and footage of the moonwalkers walking around in full sunlight, sometimes even with their protective visor up (Figure 8-4).

However, the Apollo helmets were designed to protect the moonwalkers adequately both against the ultraviolet solar radiation that causes sunburns and the infrared radiation that causes heating: perhaps not unsurprisingly, these issues had been anticipated and solved during mission planning and suit design and had been tested during spacewalks in the early Apollo flights in Earth orbit, where sunlight is essentially as intense as on the Moon.

There is a common misconception that infrared and ultraviolet protection was provided only by the golden reflective visor and therefore walking around with the visor up would have been impossible or extremely hazardous, as argued for example in Bennett and Percy's book *Dark Moon* (on page 102).

Actually, this protection was provided both by the clear part of the helmet and by the reflective visor and therefore the astronauts could lift the visor when needed, for example in low-light conditions or for a memorable photograph. The visor was mostly intended to reduce the brightness of the sunlight, much like a pair of oversized sunglasses.

This is the same principle that is used today by astronauts working outside the International Space Station and was used in the past by Skylab, Shuttle and Mir spacewalkers. They, too, are exposed to full sunlight without the shielding of the Earth's atmosphere, yet don't get sunburned or overheated; and they, too, often lift their reflective visors with no problems, as shown for example in Figure 8-5.

Figure 8-4. Harrison Schmitt's reflective visor is up in a frame from the Apollo 17 moonwalk TV transmission.

Moreover, temperatures measured on the surface have nothing to do with sunburns, as anyone who's been sunburnt during a cool day in the mountains, with snow or ice on the ground, knows all too well. Sunburns are caused by ultraviolet rays in direct or reflected sunlight, not by heat.

The Apollo technical manuals explain that lunar astronauts

Figure 8-5. Jerry L. Ross working outside the Shuttle Atlantis (1991). NASA photo STS037-18-032.

wore a pressurized helmet (the inner goldfish-bowl transparent enclosure) inside an outer helmet. The inner helmet was made of Lexan, which is very tough and, most importantly, highly opaque to ultraviolet rays. The outer helmet in turn had an inner visor, which filtered ultraviolet and infrared radiation, and an outer visor (the gold mirror-like surface visible in many photographs) that filtered visible light (like mirror shades) to prevent dazzling and provided a further barrier to ultraviolet and infrared rays.[62]

---

62 *Biomedical Results of Apollo*, Section 6, Chapter 6, *Pressure Helmet Assembly*.

Essentially, the moonwalkers didn't get sunburnt for the same reason why you don't get sunburnt if you drive around in your car with the windows up: the transparent material allows visible light to get through but blocks the ultraviolet light that causes sunburns.

Astronauts, both on the Moon and in Earth orbit, often raise their golden visor when they are in shadow and sometimes don't bother to lower it when they move back into sunlight, but in any case the multiple helmet layers still protect them against sunburn. The worst that can happen to them is that they are dazzled by the bright sunlight.

8.6 Meteoroid showers would have killed the astronauts

IN A NUTSHELL: *Unlikely. Meteoroids capable of piercing an astronaut's multilayer spacesuit or a spacecraft are actually incredibly rare. The suits and the vehicles had protective layers designed to absorb the impact of the minute specks that constitute the vast majority of meteoroids. There is no protection against larger meteoroids other than the very low probability of being struck, but this is an acceptable risk, as demonstrated by the fact that satellites, space probes, manned spacecraft and the International Space Station don't get riddled by meteoroids.*

THE DETAILS: The Moon is pock-marked with craters produced by *meteoroids*: rocky or metallic masses of all sizes that travel through space and can strike the Moon at speeds up to 80,000 kilometers per hour (about 50,000 mph). Although the terms *meteor* and *meteorite* are often used, strictly speaking a space rock is a *meteoroid* when it travels through space: it becomes a *meteor* only if it punches into the atmosphere of a planet or moon and forms an incandescent trail and then becomes a *meteorite* if it reaches the surface of the planet or moon instead of disintegrating completely.

Looking at the Moon, it's understandable that someone might wonder how the moonwalkers coped with this constant lethal danger. The answer is actually quite simple: they relied on probability. Meteoroid showers aren't as frequent and dense as often depicted in Hollywood sci-fi productions. If they were, our fleets of satellites that provide us with weather data, TV programs and telephone calls would be destroyed all the time and the International Space Station would be Swiss cheese after over a decade in space. Several automatic probes have been traveling through deep space for three decades or more and have survived essentially unscathed.

Actually, most meteoroids are literally microscopic in size. They have an enormous speed, but an almost negligible mass, so if a micrometeoroid strikes an astronaut it is stopped by the spacesuit's outer layer, which is designed for this purpose. The space suits used by the Apollo moon-walkers and the ones used today for work in space have essentially the same type of multilayer protection against micrometeoroids. That's one of the reasons why they're so bulky.

Non-microscopic meteoroids are quite rare. While the Moon's cratered surface might appear to suggest otherwise, one must bear in mind that those craters are the result of millions of years of exposure. Apollo astronauts and all lunar spacecraft (including the Russian Lunokhod rovers) had a vanishingly small chance of being struck by a significant space pebble.

8.7 Film magazines couldn't be changed outside

IN A NUTSHELL: *Actually, they could. The astronauts had cameras designed to allow film changes even in direct sunlight and while wearing the spacesuit's bulky gloves, as shown in the TV transmissions from the Moon. This wasn't an exceptional technological innovation: the same feature was part of any professional photographer's equipment in the 1960s.*

THE DETAILS: Some Moon hoax theorists argue that astronauts on the Moon couldn't change the film of their cameras while wearing the clumsy, bulky gloves of their spacesuit and while they were in full sunlight, yet the mission records don't report that they ever went back into the lunar modules to reload their cameras. So how were they able to take thousands of photographs?

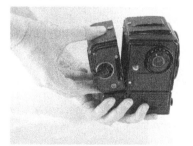

Figure 8-6. Snap-on mounting of a film magazine on a Hasselblad EL/M camera, similar to those used on the Moon. Lunar magazines were larger than the one shown. Credit: PA.

The answer is quite simple but clever: the films used for the Hasselblad cameras taken to the Moon were kept in light-tight magazines that snapped onto the camera body (Figure 8-6) and were designed to be changed even in full sunlight. The same method was used by professional photographers of the time to change films even halfway through a roll.

Not all missions, moreover, changed films during their excursions outside the spacecraft. For example, the Apollo 11 moonwalk made do with a single magazine.

Figure 8-7. Charlie Duke is holding a film magazine and is about to change it outside on the Moon. Frame from the Apollo 16 TV transmission.

Handling the film magazines while wearing the thick gloves of a lunar spacesuit wasn't a problem because the magazines were cubic objects about 10 centimeters (4 inches) wide on each face (Figure 8-7) and had been modified to have larger grip rings, so as to allow easy removal of the so-called *darkslide* (a removable metal lamina designed to protect the film, Figure 8-8) even with gloves.

In standard Hasselblad cameras that used a film magazine, the darkslide was removed after the magazine had been attached to the camera body. This allowed to change film mid-roll, without exposing any frames to the light. Lunar Hasselblads instead required the astronauts to remove the darkslide *before* coupling the magazine to the body of the camera.

Figure 8-8. A standard Hasselblad magazine with its partially extracted darkslide. Credit: Ulli Lotzmann.

This difference was due to the presence of a *reseau plate*, i.e., the glass plate that carried the cross-shaped markings that are visible in most Apollo photographs taken on the Moon, and entailed that the portion of film that was visible during a magazine change would catch the light and become unusable. However, this wasn't a problem in the particular case of the lun-

Figure 8-9. Magazine R of the Apollo 11 flight, currently on display at the National Air and Space Museum of Washington, D.C. Note the larger ring used to pull out the darkslide while wearing spacesuit gloves. Credit: NASM.

ar astronauts, who usually didn't need to change magazine mid-roll. The astronauts, moreover, usually took three or four blank shots when they started and ended a magazine, so as to make the film advance and be sure to use a part of the film that had not been exposed to light inadvertently.

Figure 8-9 shows a film magazine used on the Moon during the Apollo 11 flight. If you compare it with the magazine of Figure 8-8, you'll notice that the darkslide pull ring, on the right, was much larger in the Apollo magazines to allow to use it even while the astronauts were wearing gloves on the surface of the Moon.

8.8 It's impossible to cool an astronaut in a vacuum

IN A NUTSHELL: *No, it isn't: you just have to transfer the astronaut's heat to the water reserve in their backpack and then discard the heated water. Exposing the water to the vacuum of space freezes it, removing even more heat from the astronaut's suit.*

THE DETAILS: People who are not familiar with spacesuit technology are sometimes puzzled by the idea of maintaining a comfortable temperature inside a thick, bulky insulating suit that is in the vacuum of space and goes from being exposed to full sunlight to standing in total shadow, with consequent extreme temperature variations. A vacuum would seem to be an almost perfect insulation into which it might appear impossible to dump excess heat. It obviously rules out the use of a compressor like those used in air-conditioning units.

Yet Russian and American astronauts have been performing spacewalks since the 1960s and have since been joined by astronauts of many other countries, so clearly there must be a technology that allows to keep an astronaut cool in a vacuum, otherwise one would have to claim that every spacewalk ever made was faked (and still is, since spacewalks are routine events on the International Space Station). Many of these spacewalks didn't rely on *umbilicals* (long hoses that supplied air, power and temperature control to the suit) but use self-contained equipment located in the spacesuit backpack, so they were (and still are) very similar to moonwalks.

During lunar excursions, the heat generated by the astronaut's body was captured by a tight-fitting undergarment, known as *Liquid Cooling Garment*, in which water was circulated inside a web of fine tubing. This method is still used today for modern spacesuits. The heated water then entered a heat exchanger, located inside the suit's backpack (Figure 8-10), where it released its heat to a water reserve of approximately four liters (8.5 pounds), which was increased to 5.2 liters (11.5 pounds) in later moonwalks.

This water then reached a *sublimator*, where it was slowly and gradually exposed to the vacuum of space. The consequent pressure drop, in accordance with the laws of physics, made its temperature fall: the water would freeze on the outer surface of the sublimator and turn directly from ice to water vapor, which was discharged through an appropriately provided duct.

This system allowed to dissipate up to 2,000 BTU/hour (approximately 580 W): enough to air-condition a small room and therefore more than adequate

Figure 8-10. The inside of an Apollo spacesuit backpack or PLSS. Credit: Ulli Lotzmann/NASM.

for cooling the inside of an astronaut's suit, so much that John Young, for example, remarked that even the intermediate setting made him feel freezing cold if he was resting.

8.9 There's no blast crater under the LM's engine

IN A NUTSHELL: *True. That's because there's not supposed to be one. The idea that the lunar module's engine should have formed a crater upon landing was suggested by some artist's illustrations published by NASA ahead of the Moon landings. But the crater is merely an artistic license: the engineers already knew that no crater would form because the Surveyor unmanned probes had already landed and sent back pictures of their landing sites, which showed no crater under their engines.*

THE DETAILS: Bill Kaysing argues that the Lunar Module mysteriously failed to blast a crater in the surface of the Moon with its powerful rocket engine.

NO CRATERS! [...] In all pictures of the LEM on the "moon", there is absolutely no evidence of a crater underneath the engine. If indeed the module had landed on the moon, the engine would have blasted out a substantial hole in the dustlike surface of the moon.

– *We Never Went to the Moon*, page 75.

Kaysing repeats the claim in the FOX TV documentary *Did We Land on the Moon?* (2001): *"The fact that there is no blast crater under the LM is one of the most conclusive pieces of evidence that I find supporting the hoax."*

But if a blast crater was expected, why would the alleged fakers be so clumsy as to forget to sculpt one into their lunar movie set?

Actually, the expectation of a blast crater under the LM was fostered by many artistic depictions of the Moon landing that were circulated by NASA and by the press ahead of the event, as witnessed for example by Figure 8-11. But mission planners didn't really expect the LM engine to gouge a crater in the Moon: that detail, like many others in artists' illustrations, was dramatic license.

Figure 8-11. The Moon landing as depicted by NASA in 1966. Detail from S66-10989.

Artistic depictions are, well, *artistic*: they're not intended to portray an event with absolute fidelity, but to bring the event to life, explain it and communicate its significance, drama and excitement. If accuracy gets in the way of the message, it is often set aside. For example, Figure 8-11 includes stars, despite the fact that stars are not visible from the Moon when the lunar surface is in daylight, and the LM is shown without its characteristic protective "tin foil" (thermal blankets and micrometeoroid shielding).

The presence of a crater under the LM in illustrations doesn't prove that the landings were faked: it proves the talent of the artist who found a way to suggest the dynamic action of the engine's exhaust in a static image. Essentially, Kaysing was mistaking artwork for hard science.

Actually, not all NASA illustrations show a crater under the Lunar Module. Figure 8-12 is an artist's concept created for Grumman (the company that designed and built the LM), in which there's no blast crater and the LM is depicted far more realistically than in Figure 8-11 (note, for example, the MESA equipment rack and the exhaust deflectors under the attitude control thruster quads). However, the stars are still shown in order to give depth to the artwork and the Earth is too low on the horizon for any Apollo landing site.

Figure 8-12. An artist's concept of the LM created for Grumman before the first Moon landing. NASA image S69-38662.

Leaving artistic license and conspiracy theories aside, why didn't the rocket blast of the LM form a crater or visibly disturb the surface? After all, the Lunar Module was a 15-ton spacecraft, so it needed a powerful engine to counter that weight and make it hover. Instinctively, we expect that kind of force to do some damage to the landing site.

But first of all, lunar gravity is one sixth of the Earth's, so the LM's weight on the Moon isn't 15 tons; it's 2.5. Moreover, these figures refer to the *initial* weight of the spacecraft, which decreased dramatically as its rocket fuel was used up. For example, for Apollo 12, which had an initial LM mass of 15,115 kilograms (33,325 lb), telemetry data reported the use of approximately 7,810 kilograms (17,200 lb) of propellant mass,[63] leaving a landing mass of approximately 7,305 kilograms (16,104 lb), not 15,115 kg (33,325 lb). The spacecraft essentially halved its initial mass by burning propellant, and in lunar gravity that residual landing mass is equivalent to a weight of just 1,217 kilograms (2,700 lb).

In other words, keeping a LM in a hover above the landing spot entailed countering a weight of just 1,200 kilograms (2,700 lb), not 15,000 (33,000 lb); far less than assumed initially. Since the surface of the Moon consists of hard rock covered by a layer of dust, the rather modest rocket thrust actually required would merely blow away the dust and expose the underlying rock. That's exactly what we see in the Apollo photographs (Figure 8-13).

The LM rocket exhaust might be expected to melt the lunar rocks at the landing spot, but the estimated temperature of the exhaust was approximately 1,500 °C (2,800 °F)[64] and decreased very rapidly because the hot plume expanded into a vacuum and therefore cooled down, like any other expanding gas.

63   *Apollo 12 - The Nasa Mission Reports*, Apogee Book (1999), p. 44 and p. 137.

64   *The Blast Crater, http://www.clavius.org/techcrater.html.*

Figure 8-13. Apollo 11's LM descent engine bell on the Moon. Note the dust-free, smooth, rocky surface in the foreground and the radial pattern formed on the surface by the engine exhaust. NASA photo AS11-40-5921.

Moreover, it takes several minutes of intense heat to melt the kind of rocks that form the surface of the Moon, whereas the LM's exhaust struck the same surface spot only for a few seconds. There simply wasn't enough heat or time to cause significant melting or cratering. What we do see in the Apollo photographs is a slight discoloration, possibly due to charring or to a chemical reaction of the propellant with the rock, and traces of fluid erosion.

No crater was expected by mission planners due to direct previous experience: the automatic Surveyor probes had landed on the Moon between 1966 and 1968, sending back TV pictures of the landing site and chemical and physical tests of the lunar surface, which showed no cratering and indicated a compact rocky nature that allowed safe touchdown. The Apollo astronauts didn't fly into the absolute unknown; they had a fairly good idea of what to expect.

8.10 The timing of the lunar liftoff footage is impossible

IN A NUTSHELL: *Chasing the ascent of the Lunar Module from the Moon with a TV camera controlled from Earth, despite the inherent 2.6-second feedback delay caused by the fact that the remote control commands and the TV signal traveled at the speed of light to the Moon and back, wasn't impossible. Liftoff time was known to the second and the rate of ascent was precalculated precisely, so the camera operator compensated the delay by tilting the camera up 1.3 seconds early with a predetermined rate of motion.*

THE DETAILS: In his *Wagging the Moondoggie* website,[65] conspiracy theorist David McGowan considers with suspicion the spectacular TV footage of the liftoff of Apollo 15, 16 and 17 from the Moon. This footage was shot with the Rover's TV camera, which was remote-controlled from Earth. Considering that the radio commands to move the camera took about 1.3 seconds to travel from the Earth to the Moon and the resulting TV picture took just as long to be received on Earth, how could the camera operator track the ascending Lunar Module? *"There apparently either wasn't any delay in the signal or NASA had the foresight to hire a remote camera operator who was able to see a few seconds into the future",* argues McGowan.

Actually, the remote camera operator (Ed Fendell) *could* see more than a few seconds into the future, in a way, because the liftoff time of the Lunar Module was known very precisely in advance. Exact timing was critical, otherwise the LM would not be in the right place at the right time to rendezvous with the Command Module once in orbit around the Moon. The delay caused by the Earth-Moon distance was also known very precisely. So Fendell knew exactly when to send the commands: about 1.3 seconds ahead of the scheduled liftoff time. The rate of tilt depended on the distance of the camera from the LM and had to be calculated carefully.

The first attempt at this remarkable shot (during the Apollo 15 liftoff) failed because the tilting mechanism malfunctioned and the camera didn't tilt up. The second attempt (Apollo 16) went better, but the Rover was parked closer than expected to the LM and this threw off the calculations, so the camera lost track of the LM quite early. The third attempt worked out perfectly, and Apollo 17's lunar liftoff was tracked until the LM became a tiny bright speck on the TV screen.

---

65 *davesweb.cnchost.com/Apollo5.html.*

8.11 No dust on Apollo 11's LM footpads

IN A NUTSHELL: *Yes, the footpads of the Apollo 11 lunar module are dust-free despite landing while the rocket engine was blowing moondust everywhere. But dust moved by a rocket exhaust in an airless environment such as the Moon will not billow up around the spacecraft and then settle on it: it will travel in straight lines away from the vehicle, unhindered by any air resistance, and therefore is unlikely to end up on the vehicle's footpads.*

THE DETAILS: Photographs of Apollo 11's lunar module footpads on the Moon show them to be completely dust-free (Figure 8-14). To some this seems suspicious. Shouldn't the engine blast have blown at least some dust onto the footpads? Says Bill Kaysing in the 2001 documentary *Did We Land on the Moon?*: "If they had truly landed on the Moon, this dust

Figure 8-14. A spotless Apollo 11 footpad. NASA photo AS11-40-5920 (cropped).

would have then descended on the lunar lander, on the footpads, and we find not a trace of dust on the footpads."

The Moon is airless, so there's no atmosphere to carry the dust and allow it to form billowing clouds that then settle. The dust simply gets blown sideways and outward, racing roughly parallel to the ground and away from the landing spot, and then falls down at the end of its essentially rectilinear trajectory, without floating around. This effect is visible in the footage of the Apollo lunar landings and liftoffs.

Moreover, in a vacuum only the dust that is struck *directly* by the exhaust gets moved, so the displacement is very localized (on Earth, such a displacement has a broader action because the exhaust displaces the surrounding air, which in turn displaces dust, spreading out the effect). Indeed, the Apollo 11 photographs show pebbles and dust a short distance out from the footpads, as evidenced in Figure 8-14 by the footprints behind the LM's landing gear.

The dust that is moved, however, can travel quite a distance at high speeds, since there's no air resistance to slow it down and the low gravity drags it down more gradually than on Earth. On Apollo 12, dust displaced by the LM exhaust reached the Surveyor probe, roughly 200 meters (650 feet) from the LM, as evidenced by the sandblasting detected on the side of Surveyor that faced the LM.[66]

---

66 *Watch Out for Flying Moondust*, by Trudy Bell and Dr. Tony Phillips (2007), Nasa.gov.

8.12 After Apollo 11, other LM footpads are dusty

IN A NUTSHELL: *Yes, sometimes they are. That's because the other Lunar Modules landed in other regions of the Moon, which were geologically very different (e.g., more dusty), and sometimes landed more roughly than Apollo 11, so their footpads dragged on the ground, scooping up dust. The astronauts also occasionally kicked dust into the footpads as they walked close to the LM landing gear. Lack or presence of dust on the footpads is not evidence of fakery.*

THE DETAILS: While Apollo 11's lunar module landing gear is immaculately dust-free, the footpads of other lunar modules are very dusty. Compare, for example, Figure 8-14 (Apollo 11) with Figure 8-15 (Apollo 16). According to some doubters, this conspicuous difference proves that Apollo 11 was faked badly (forgetting to sprinkle dust on the footpads) but later missions were faked better, correcting this omission.

Figure 8-15. A dusty Apollo 16 LM footpad. NASA photo AS16-107-17442 (cropped).

Once again, a conspiracy theory is based on the assumption of bungling perpetrators: for some bizarre reason, the most important fakery of the century was assigned to a bunch of sloppy amateurs who made all sorts of mistakes and left evidence in the photographs, and somehow their bosses didn't notice the mistakes before releasing the pictures to the public.

The difference in dust can be explained quite simply without resorting to farfetched tales of colossal incompetence. First of all, the Apollo missions landed in geologically very different sites in order to acquire the broadest possible variety of samples: Apollo 11 and 12 landed on very flat terrain; Apollo 14 touched down in a broad, shallow valley; and Apollo 15, 16 and 17 landed in the highlands of the Moon. Compare, for example, the Apollo 11 site (Figure 8-16) with the Apollo 17 site (Figure 8-17).

It seems reasonable to assume that vastly different locations might have different dust coverings. Indeed, Pete Conrad (Apollo 12) and Dave Scott (Apollo 15) reported that they had to fly on instruments for the final 30 meters (100 feet) of their landing because the dust kicked up by their engine's exhaust obscured their view of the surface, while other LM pilots didn't have the same problem.

Figure 8-16. Composite panorama of the Apollo 11 landing site (photos AS11-40-5930/31/32/33/34/39/40). Credit: NASA/Moonpans.com.

Figure 8-17. Composite panoramas of the Apollo 17 landing site. Credit: NASA/Moonpans.com.

Moreover, some landings were quite rough. Apollo 11 landed very smoothly, but Apollo 14, for example, dragged its landing gear sideways after touchdown. This caused the footpads to scoop up moondust, as shown for example in NASA photo AS14-66-9234. Apollo 15 landed with one footpad in a 1.5-meter (5-ft) deep crater, damaged its engine exhaust bell and came to rest at a steep angle. Its footpads dug quite deeply into the ground and got very dusty.

Finally, dust could also accumulate on the footpads after landing, for example if the astronauts worked close to the LM's landing gear (as in Figure 8-15). As they walked around, they kicked up dust which, in a vacuum and in low gravity, could travel quite far and end up on the footpads.

8.13 The astronauts' footprints are too sharp

IN A NUTSHELL: *No, they're as sharp as they should be in dry, jagged moondust in a vacuum, which behaves quite differently than weathered sand in Earth's atmosphere.*

THE DETAILS: In *NASA Mooned America!*, Ralph Rene claims that *"clear tracks in deep dust require moisture; otherwise they form only indistinct* *depressions* [...] *There can be no moisture on the Moon* [...] *And yet, every picture allegedly taken on the Moon shows clear footprints"* (page 7). In other words, sharply outlined bootprints such as the famous one shown in Figure 8-18 are said to be impossible on the Moon.

Proponents of this claim, however, fail to consider that sand on Earth is exposed to very different conditions than dust on the Moon. First of all, on Earth, the wind, the flow of water and other natural phenomena move and churn the grains of sand against each other constantly, smoothing their surfaces and reducing their friction.

On the Moon this smoothing doesn't occur, and therefore the grains of lunar "sand" (termed *regolith* in geological jargon) are sharp-edged and uneven. Accordingly, they tend to lock together and stick to

Figure 8-18. A footprint left on the Moon by Buzz Aldrin (Apollo 11). Detail of photo AS11-40-5877.

each other far more than Earth sand, much like a stack of smooth river stones will collapse easily while a similar pile of jagged rocks will keep its shape. This leads to higher cohesion and sharper footprints.

Then there's gravity, which is one sixth of the Earth's. Stacked moon-dust particles are pulled down by weaker forces than on our planet and therefore the edges of footprints, for example, hold their shape more easily.

Finally, there's electrostatic attraction. Lunar regolith has a considerable electrostatic charge and therefore its grains tend to cling to each other more than ordinary Earth sand, in the same way that dust clings to an electrostatically charged glass surface, such as an old-style (CRT) television screen.[67]

The sharpness of prints in moondust is confirmed by the Russian unmanned rovers of the Lunokhod series, which landed on the Moon and sent back pictures of their finely detailed wheel tracks (Figure 8-19).

---

67 *Effects of gravity on cohesive behavior of fine powders: implications for processing Lunar regolith*, Otis R. Walton, C. Pamela De Moor and Karam S. Gill, in *Granular Matter*, vol. 9 no. 6 (2007).

In 2008, the *Mythbusters* TV show placed a sample of powdery material, geologically equivalent to lunar regolith, in a vacuum chamber and then pressed a footprint into it, using a replica of an Apollo Moon boot. The result closely resembled the sharp-edged footprints seen in Apollo photographs, despite the higher gravity and the lack of any significant electrostatic charge.

Figure 8-19. Sharp-edged wheel tracks left on the Moon by Soviet Lunokhod 1 in 1970.

8.14 The lunar module hatch was too narrow

IN A NUTSHELL: *No, it wasn't. People who claim that the spacesuit was too wide to pass through the hatch are referring to the width of the suit when spread flat and with the arms at its sides, but the suit is much narrower when worn and moonwalkers crawled through the hatch on all fours and therefore with the arms tucked under their bodies, not at their sides. All this reduced the actual suit width dramatically, allowing it to pass easily through the hatch. Besides, if the whole thing had been faked, it would have been trivial to fake a comfortably bigger LM hatch.*

THE DETAILS: Mary Bennett and David Percy, in their book *Dark Moon*, argue that *"the aperture of the LM is only 32 1/4 inches wide [...]. Surely, it would be very difficult for a pressurised, spacesuited astronaut, fully loaded with his PLSS and measuring over 31 inches in width to exit through such a small and awkward aperture"* (pages 340-341).

The width of the LM hatch quoted by Bennett and Percy is essentially correct, as confirmed by NASA's *Apollo 11 Press Kit* and *Lunar Module Operations Handbook*. However, their measurement of the width of a suited astronaut is definitely wrong, because it refers to the spacesuit laid flat and with the arms at the sides of the flattened torso of the suit (as shown in the photograph on page 341 of *Dark Moon*). Any garment measured in this way will appear to be much wider than when it is being worn, because it's not wrapped around the wearer's body. Try this for yourself: your sweater, when spread flat, is much wider than your body. Basically, Bennett and Percy are confusing girth and width.

This mistake is compounded by the fact that the Apollo astronauts crawled out through the hatch on their hands and knees and therefore held their arms tucked in under their bodies, not at their sides as shown in *Dark Moon*. This reduces further the actual width of the spacesuited astronaut.

There's a very simple way to check all this. The hatch width reported by Bennett and Percy, 32 1/4 inches (82 centimeters), is the width of an average interior house door. The widest part of a suited astronaut's body is at the shoulders, so try standing in a doorway and notice how much clearance you have on either side. Even if you take into account a bulky Apollo spacesuit, there's still room enough to walk through easily. The backpack (PLSS) wasn't a problem, because it was about 51 centimeters (20 inches) wide. If you really want to be thorough, buy or rent a replica Apollo spacesuit (avail-

Figure 8-20. Buzz Aldrin exits from the Lunar Module to walk on the Moon. NASA photo AS11-40-5862 (cropped).

able from specialist dealers), put it on and compare its actual width with the hatch of an original LM, such as the one on display at the National Air and Space Museum in Washington, DC.

Besides, Apollo photographs such as AS11-40-5862 (Figure 8-20), which shows Buzz Aldrin as he exits the lunar module through the hatch, clearly demonstrate that the hatch was wide enough. Exit certainly wasn't easy, but it was feasible.

8.15 The pressurized spacesuits should have ballooned

IN A NUTSHELL: *No, because they had a containment layer, just like present-day spacesuits, and the outer layer wasn't pressurized.*

THE DETAILS: Some Moon hoax proponents wonder how astronauts could flex their fingers inside the bulky gloves of their spacesuits and more generally how they could move at all, since the suits, if pressurized as NASA claims, would have inflated like balloons in the vacuum of space and would have become impossibly rigid. Yet Apollo photographs show astronauts on the Moon moving around quite comfortably, with suits that show no sign of ballooning and are actually flexible and surprisingly creased and saggy.

This objection can be dismissed simply by considering that the American, Russian and Chinese spacesuits currently worn by astronauts during spacewalks on the International Space Station and in Chinese spaceflights are quite obviously flexible and don't balloon, so there must be a way to solve these allegedly unsurmountable problems. That way is essentially the same one introduced by Russian and American spacesuits of the 1960s.

The Apollo spacesuits were pressurized to approximately one third of sea-level pressure; this helped to reduce the suit's tendency to balloon. This lower pressure was countered by a non-elastic containment layer of mesh, integrated in the neoprene layer that formed the so-called *Pressure Garment*, i.e., the airtight part of the suit that enclosed the astronaut's body.

In other words, the suit could only expand until this mesh was taut. If you can imagine a balloon placed inside a bag of netting, or if you look at a garden hose, you have a good example of a pressure containment layer.

Figure 8-21. Gene Cernan checks the fit of the airtight inner layer of the Apollo spacesuit, known as Pressure Garment. *Note the accordion-like joints at the elbows and fingers. NASA photo AP17-72-H-253.*

The fingers, shoulders, knees and elbows of the suit had accordion-like joints that allowed flexing without ballooning. Moreover, the spacesuit was actually *two* suits worn one over the other: the inner Pressure Garment (Figure 8-21) and the white outer unpressurized protective suit (Figure 8-22), designed to withstand fire, abrasion and micrometeoroids and provide thermal insulation.

In summary, the Apollo spacesuits don't look like they're pressurized simply because what we normally see is their outer layer, which indeed wasn't pressurized.

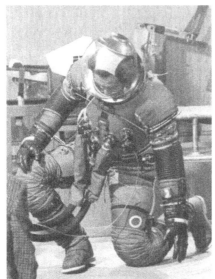 

Figure 8-22. Left: Charlie Duke (Apollo 16) tests the flexing of his Pressure Garment. Right: Ron Evans (Apollo 17) checks the upward reach of his arm while wearing both the inner Pressure Garment and the white outer protective suit.

9. Other alleged anomalies

9.1 The astronauts had guilty looks on their faces

IN A NUTSHELL: *Not guilty, but serious. Hoax theorists cherry-pick the photos in which the Apollo astronauts are serious and solemn and claim that they always had that expression because they felt guilty of their deception. Actually, there are plenty of photographs and film clips in which they smile, joke and laugh.*

THE DETAILS: It is often argued that Armstrong, Collins and Aldrin had suspiciously gloomy, guilty, sad and reluctant expressions as they were held in quarantine after their Moon trip and during their first post-flight press conference (Figure 9-1).

Figure 9-1. Gloomy expressions of Armstrong, Collins and Aldrin (Apollo 11) during their post-flight quarantine and press conference.

There's a good reason why they're serious in that quarantine photo: they're listening to President Nixon's formal speech, so it would have been rather inappropriate for them to be laughing their heads off. Once Nixon changes to a less formal tone, the astronauts smile and laugh with him (Figures 9-2 and 9-3).

Figure 9-2. The Apollo 11 astronauts laughing with Nixon. Detail of NASA photo S69-21365.

The apparently gloomy post-flight press conference image is just a carefully selected frame from the film record of the event, which actually includes many moments of laughter, smiles and outright jokes despite the pressure of it being their first press conference after their historic trip.

Figure 9-3. Another moment of shared laughter of the Apollo 11 crew with Nixon.

Contrary to the claims made by some conspiracy theorists, the other lunar astronauts also were anything but sad and guilty-looking after their flights. In the course of four decades they have been (and still are) part of countless public talks and television events in which they unhesitatingly report their experiences and promote space exploration in many ways, including some unorthodox ones.

Buzz Aldrin, for example, appeared very light-heartedly on *Da Ali G Show* (2003), recorded a rap song with Snoop Dogg (*Rocket Experience*, 2009), was a contestant in the 2010 edition of the US show *Dancing with the Stars* and has guest-starred in TV shows like *30 Rock* (2010), *Numb3rs* (2006) and *The Big Bang Theory* (2012), as well as in the movie *Transformers - Dark of the Moon* (2011). In his autobiography, *Magnificent Desolation*, he has also acknowledged candidly his successful fight against alcohol and depression.

A special mention goes to Alan Bean, Pete Conrad and Richard Gordon, whose video *Apollo 12 Uncensored* is a hilarious collection of anecdotes and jokes about their lunar landing that certainly doesn't appear to suggest guilt or unease.

This Moon hoax claim is probably one of the most significant: it shows very clearly the symptoms of a world vision in which everything, even an ordinary, occasional serious expression, is interpreted as evidence of a colossal conspiracy and the facts are cherry-picked to bend them to that distorted vision.

9.2 Neil Armstrong hid from the media out of guilt

IN A NUTSHELL: *No, he simply picked his media appearances very carefully after the overwhelming barrage of public events that followed the Moon landing. He preferred technical conferences, in which he was anything but shy and indeed proved to have a wry sense of humor.*

THE DETAILS: According to some hoax theorists, Neil Armstrong, first man on the Moon, became a recluse and never appeared on TV, refusing all interviews, after the initial celebrations for the Apollo 11 trip. This absence from the media was allegedly due to his guilt for lying to the entire world.

Figure 9-4. Neil Armstrong in an advert for Chrysler (1979).

The truth is quite different. For example, in the 1970s Armstrong even did TV advertising campaigns for Chrysler (Figure 9-4).

However, it is true that Armstrong chose his media appearances very carefully and protected his own image against anyone who tried to profit from his lunar endeavor. For example, in 1984 he sued Hallmark

Cards for using his name and voice without permission for a Christmas decoration. Proceeds from the settlement, less legal feeds and costs, were donated to Purdue University, Armstrong's alma mater.

In 2005 Armstrong's barber auctioned off the astronaut's hair clippings, which were bought by a collector for 3,000 dollars. Armstrong threatened legal action and the barber donated the proceeds of the auction to a charity.

One of Armstrong's few personal interviews was granted in 2005 to CBS's *60 Minutes* (Figure 9-5) when his biography, curated by historian James Hansen and entitled *First Man: The Life of Neil A. Armstrong*, was published.

Figure 9-5. Neil Armstrong interviewed for 60 Minutes.

Armstrong was an extremely modest and reserved man who preferred to talk about technical matters rather than his personal feelings. He was part of the public inquiry boards for the Apollo 13 accident in 1970 and for the *Challenger* disaster in 1986. These roles placed him once again in the public spotlight at two dramatic times of the United States' space program. He also hosted the documentary *First Flights with Neil Armstrong* in 1991. More recently, he granted extensive technical interviews to the curators of the *Apollo Lunar Surface Journal* and appeared in the documentary *When We Left Earth* (2008).

On a lighter note, in 2009 he celebrated the fortieth anniversary of the first Moon landing by joining Aldrin and Collins at the *John H. Glenn Lecture*, an annual conference held at the National Air and Space Museum in Washington, D.C., and attended the gala for the fortieth anniversary of Apollo 12 at the Kennedy Space Center, where he demonstrated a talent for self-effacing humor.

In 2010 he also spoke publicly quite vehemently against the plans of the Obama administration to restructure NASA.[68] These don't seem to be the choices of someone who is shunning publicity out of guilt.

Moreover, Armstrong wasn't at all impossible to reach: for example, in April 2011 some news reports claimed that he had been a follower of Indian guru Sai Baba, who had just died. So I contacted James Hansen,

---

68 *Neil Armstrong blasts Obama's 'devastating' Nasa cuts*, by Jacqui Goddard, *Times Online*, April 14, 2010.

Armstrong's biographer, to clarify the matter. Within a day, I received a personal e-mail from Neil Armstrong himself, in which he stated that he didn't even know who Sai Baba was and had not communicated in any way with any of his associates or followers. He added that he was not surprised, as many religious organizations had claimed him as a member.

9.3 NASA refuses to deal with the hoax allegations

IN A NUTSHELL: *Actually, NASA has published various rebuttals to the allegations. But the agency has stated that it has no plans to produce any more because it doesn't want to dignify a set of claims that the science community has long dismissed as ridiculous. NASA prefers to work on more positive enterprises and leave to others the task of answering the individual allegations of fakery.*

THE DETAILS: Some doubters find it suspicious that NASA won't simply answer the hoax theorists' questions once and for all and debate them. It's as if it had something to hide, they argue.

In actual fact, NASA has already published quite detailed rebuttals. After the Fox TV program *Did We Land on the Moon?* was broadcast in 2001, the space agency added several pages of debunking material, based on what it had already released in 1977.[69]

However, there's a limit to how much efforts NASA intends to spend in responding to conspiracy theorists. In 2002, in response to the Fox TV program, NASA allocated 15,000 dollars and asked aerospace engineer and spaceflight historian James Oberg to write a book specifically on the matter, aimed mainly at teachers and students. The project was canceled shortly after, following media criticism that it was a waste of taxpayers' money. NASA Administrator Sean O'Keefe stated in November 2002 that *"The issue of trying to do a targeted response to this is just lending credibility to something that is, on its face, asinine."*

Since then, the widespread availability of the Internet has allowed many enthusiasts and experts to reply to the hoax theories directly on their own websites, and NASA has redirected doubters to these debunkers. The *References* section of this book lists some of the most popular debunking sites in various languages.

---

69 *Did U.S. Astronauts Really Land on the Moon?*, in *NASA Facts,* 1977, republished on April 14, 2001; *The Great Moon Hoax,* February 23, 2001; *The Moon Landing Hoax,* March 30, 2001; *Did We Really Land on the Moon? Suggestions for Science Teachers*, March 4, 2001.

Accordingly, any further direct response by NASA has become essentially unnecessary. The ultimate rebuttal is NASA's overwhelmingly vast library of publicly available documents that provide all the details of the reality of the Moon landings.

9.4 The lunar astronauts won't face the doubters

IN A NUTSHELL: *On the contrary, many astronauts have answered the doubters directly, have taken part in TV debates and have granted interviews to hoax believers, even swearing on the Bible in front of the conspiracy theorists' cameras.*

THE DETAILS: A recurring complaint among Moon hoax proponents is that the moonwalkers refuse to debate them and don't answer their questions. This, they say, suggests guilt.

Actually, the astronauts who walked on the Moon have engaged the hoax theorists on several occasions. For example, in 2001 John Young (who flew around the Moon with Apollo 10 and landed on it with Apollo 16) went on NBC's *Today Show* to respond to the conspiracy allegations made by Bill Kaysing. He also asked one very pointed question: *"If it was a hoax, why did we do it more than once?"*

Some moonwalkers have actually accepted to be interviewed at length by hoax proponents. Gene Cernan (Apollo 10, Apollo 17), Alan Bean (Apollo 12) and Edgar Mitchell (Apollo 14) even swore on the Bible, on video, to comply with Bart Sibrel's insistent demands (Figure 9-6).

Figure 9-6. Edgar Mitchell, Gene Cernan and Alan Bean swear on the Bible as requested by hoax theorist Bart Sibrel. Stills from Sibrel's Astronauts Gone Wild *(2004).*

Others have preferred to reply to these demands with a punch, as in the case of Buzz Aldrin after Sibrel accused him of being *"a coward and a liar"*, or with a knee to the butt, as delivered by Edgar Mitchell again to Sibrel at the end of the interview in which he had sworn on the Bible. Both episodes are documented in Sibrel's video *Astronauts Gone Wild* (2004).

Usually, however, lunar astronauts dismiss the hoax allegations with a few poignant words, such as those chosen by Gene Cernan for the David Sington documentary *In the Shadow of the Moon* (2007):

> *I was there, I made the footprints on the moon, and no one can take that away from me.*

9.5 NASA documents aren't available

IN A NUTSHELL: *Not true. NASA has always provided access to copies of its technical documents, photographs and film footage for anyone willing to file a formal request and pay for duplication and postage. Now that documents can be distributed at no cost via the Internet, an immense amount of NASA data is available with just a few mouse clicks.*

THE DETAILS: Bill Kaysing, on page 7 of his book *We Never Went to the Moon*, asks this question: *"Why is it that NASA's Apollo records are not classified, but are also not available to the general public?"*

This criticism was perhaps excusable when Kaysing wrote the first edition of his book, in 1974, but today NASA's Apollo documents are easily available on the Internet: tens of thousands of pages of manuals, technical diagrams, reports, and all the photographs of all the Apollo flights. A partial list of these archives is in the *References* section at the end of this book.

Kaysing's claim, however, was factually incorrect even when it was first made: even then, NASA already provided all public records to anyone who requested them and paid the duplication and postage fees. Such requests, however, were rather

Figure 9-7. The cover of the design report on the Apollo navigation computer. The stamps indicate release to the public in 1973.

rare, since just one of the manuals of the Lunar Module, the *Apollo Operations Handbook – Lunar Module, LM 10 and Subsequent*, has over 1700 pages, so duplication costs were high.

Some documents were kept confidential for a few years because they discussed military technologies (such as used in the Apollo 11 lunar camera) or technologies that could be used for military purposes by potential enemies, but even these were soon declassified.

For example, even the documentation related to a truly state-of-the-art item like the Apollo guidance and navigation computer was declassified and made available to the public already in 1973, just four years after the first Moon landing and less than one year after the end of the lunar missions (Figure 9-7).

9.6 The Saturn V blueprints have been "lost"

IN A NUTSHELL: *No, they're preserved on microfilm at the Marshall Space Flight Center and on paper at Rocketdyne and in US federal archives. The F-1 engines of the giant rocket are being studied in detail and used as engineering templates for the next generation of spacecraft. Three whole Saturn V rockets are on public display, available to anyone who cares to examine them.*

THE DETAILS: John Lewis, in his 1996 book *Mining the Sky*, reported that he had tried in vain to obtain the blueprints of the Saturn V rocket: *"My attempts to find them several years ago met with no success: the plans have evidently been 'lost'. The fleet has been destroyed. The plans are gone".* Some hoax theorists have built on this report to claim that the blueprints were destroyed to hide the fact that the Saturn V actually didn't work and couldn't reach the Moon as NASA instead claimed.

However, in 2000 NASA clarified that the blueprints still exist as microfilm at the Marshall Space Flight Center in Huntsville, Alabama,[70] and the Federal Archives in East Point, Georgia, store approximately 82 cubic meters (2,900 cubic feet) of Saturn documents and Rocketdyne (the manufacturer of the main engines of all three Saturn V stages) has preserved dozens of volumes of Saturn-related information as part of its knowledge retention program.

Moreover, the fleet has not been *"destroyed".* There are three full, original Saturn V rockets on display and freely accessible to the public: one at the Kennedy Space Center in Florida, one at the Johnson Space Center in Houston, Texas, and one at the U.S. Space & Rocket Center in Huntsville, Alabama (Figure 9-9).

---

70 *Saturn 5 Blueprints Safely in Storage,* Space.com, March 13, 2000.

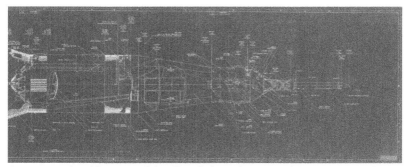

Figure 9-8. A detail from one of the allegedly lost schematics of the Saturn V. Credit: Up-ship.com.

Figure 9-9. An original Saturn V on display at the U.S. Space & Rocket Center in Huntsville, Alabama. Credit: Spacecamp.com.

9.7 NASA tampers with the recordings, there's no delay

IN A NUTSHELL: *NASA doesn't do any tampering, but documentary makers do. To keep the narrative flowing, they often summarize or edit footage. That's why, for example, sometimes in documentaries there's no speed-of-light delay in Apollo's Earth-Moon communications. But the unabridged reference recordings and transcripts published by NASA have the delay.*

THE DETAILS: In some footage of the Moon landings, the astronauts appear to answer the radio messages from Earth too quickly. Radio waves, traveling at the speed of light, take about a second and a quarter to cross the gap between the Earth and the Moon, so there should be at least an equivalent pause between the words uttered in Mission Control in Houston and the replies from the astronauts on the Moon. If there's no delay, the radio transmissions must have been fake, argue some conspiracy theorists.

A less conspiratorial explanation is that the footage has been edited for conciseness or pacing with respect to the original recordings. Indeed, the lack of delay occurs in documentaries, but not in NASA's source material. With very few exceptions, documentaries tend to omit unnecessary dialogue and use mismatched images to achieve a more dramatic and interesting narration by focusing on key moments. There's no real intent to deceive, but the end result is that many documentaries are not as faithful as one might expect.

For example, the Apollo 11 lunar landing is often portrayed so that it seems that the very first words spoken on the Moon were *"Tranquility Base here, the Eagle has landed".* Actually, if you go to the original recordings and transcripts (available at the *Apollo Lunar Surface Journal* website), it turns out that those famous words were preceded by a substantial chunk of technical reporting.

Here's the unabridged transcript, starting from the very first contact with the lunar surface:

> *102:45:40 Aldrin: Contact Light.*

Aldrin is telling Mission Control that the Lunar Contact warning light has turned on: this means that at least one of the 173-centimeter (68-inch) probes under the footpads of the Lunar Module has touched the ground. Technically, these are the first words spoken on the Moon.

Once the LM has settled on the surface, the series of technical status reports continues, as the spacecraft is prepared for its stay on the Moon:

> *102:45:43 Armstrong: Shutdown.*

> *102:45:44 Aldrin: Okay. Engine Stop.*

> *102:45:45 Aldrin: ACA out of Detent.*

> *102:45:46 Armstrong: Out of Detent. Auto.*

> *102:45:47 Aldrin: Mode Control, both Auto. Descent Engine Command Override, Off. Engine Arm, Off. 413 is in.*

Only at this point does Mission Control speak out: Charlie Duke, future Apollo 16 astronaut, is working as Capcom for Apollo 11. He is one of the few people who talk directly to the crew in space:

102:45:57 Duke: We copy you down, Eagle.

102:45:58 Armstrong: Engine arm is off. [pause] *Houston, Tranquility Base here. The Eagle has landed.*

It's quite obvious that these status reports are of no interest to the average viewer: that's why they often get cut in documentaries.

Another frequent example of a cut for narrative purposes occurs seconds later: Charlie Duke, momentarily tongue-tied by the excitement of the event, mispronounces the new name of the Lunar Module, i.e., *Tranquility Base*. He starts to say *"Roger, Twan...",* then pauses and corrects himself: *"...Tranquility. We copy you on the ground. You got a bunch of guys about to turn blue. We're breathing again. Thanks a lot."* In most documentaries this flub is edited out.

Even the famous phrase *"One small step..."* is often presented in the wrong context: it's usually heard as we see Neil Armstrong jump down the ladder of the LM. But actually, in the original video recording Armstrong jumps down and lands on the LM footpad, without touching the ground, describes his surroundings, hops up the ladder again (to test that he will be able to get back up at the end of the moonwalk), jumps down again, and only then does he cautiously place his left foot on the surface of the Moon and utter the historic words (Figure 9-10).

Figure 9-10. Armstrong is about to set foot on the Moon. Frame from the partially restored edition of the live TV broadcast.

Conspiracy theorists persistently make the mistake of considering documentaries to be equivalent to official records. They are not; the only true reference material is constituted by the original raw data and footage.

The extent to which even prize-winning films, such as *For All Mankind*, present inaccurately and misleadingly images and sounds of the Apollo missions is detailed by spaceflight historian James Oberg's article *Apollo 11 TV Documentary Misrepresentations* (*Wall Street Journal*, 1994).

9.8 The Moon rock donated to Holland is fake

IN A NUTSHELL: *Of course it is: it's not a NASA Moon rock. NASA has never authenticated it (there are no documents tracing its origins), it's far too big to be a donated lunar sample, and its background story is nonsensical. It was reportedly donated privately in 1969 to a retired prime minister instead of being given, as was customary, to a representative of the then-current Dutch government; it wasn't put on public display as a Moon rock would have deserved; and real donated Moon rocks were encapsulated in transparent plastic, while this one is not. Everything points to a mistake or to a hoax orchestrated by two Dutch artists in 2006.*[71]

THE DETAILS: In August 2009, several media outlets began reporting that the curators of the Dutch national museum in Amsterdam, the Rijksmuseum, had discovered that an exhibit that had been presented for years as an Apollo 11 Moon rock was actually a chunk of petrified wood (Figure 9-11).

The reports stated that the alleged Moon rock had been donated on October 9, 1969 by J. W. Middendorf II, who was the US ambassador to the Netherlands at the time, to former Dutch prime minister, Willem

Figure 9-11. The fake "Moon rock" and its descriptive plaque.

Drees, during the world tour of the Apollo 11 astronauts following their historic mission. When Drees died, in 1988, the item was reportedly put on display in the museum.

However, in 2006 Arno Wielders, a physicist and aerospace entrepreneur, saw it and warned the museum that it was highly unlikely that NASA had donated such a large, priceless Moon rock just three months after returning from the Moon and before any further samples were brought back by later Apollo flights.

The investigation conducted in 2009 by Xandra Van Gelder, chief editor of the museum's *Oog* magazine, confirmed that the exhibit was a fake. Van Gelder reported that NASA hadn't authenticated the specific item but had merely stated that it was likely that the Netherlands had received a Moon rock, since the US had donated small samples to over

---

71   I am indebted to Diego Cuoghi for sharing his research into many of the details of this story.

100 countries in the early 1970s. In actual fact, the real Dutch Moon rock was at the Boerhaave museum.

The fakery, if intended, wasn't particularly subtle. The alleged Moon rock was huge, about 55 by 20 millimeters (2.2 by 0.8 inches), compared to the tiny samples usually donated to foreign countries by the United States. The reddish color of the item was completely different from the usual color of lunar samples. Petrologist Wim van Westrenen, of the Amsterdam Free University, reported that he was immediately aware that something was wrong. Spectroscopic and microscopic inspection of a fragment found quartz and cell-like structures typical of petrified wood. Also, real samples were encapsulated in plastic and accompanied by a flag and an inscription that clearly identified them as Moon rocks (Figure 9-12), whereas the descriptive plaque of the fake doesn't even say it's a lunar sample and spells *center* with an incongruous British spelling (*centre*).

Van Gelder also noted that the history of the item was suspicious. Real samples would be donated to the people of a country through a representative of the then-current government, not to a former prime minister who in 1969 had been out of office for eleven years. The US ambassador explained that he had received the exhibit from the US State Department, but he could not recall the details of the matter.

Another questionable issue is the fact that such a rare and important item surfaced only during an *"art exhibition"* organized in 2006 by Rotterdam artists Liesbeth Bik and Jos van

Figure 9-12. At the top, encapsulated in clear plastic, a genuine sample of Moon rock donated to the Netherlands by the US. Credit: Museumboerhaave.nl.

der Pol and not during a science-oriented event. The exhibition was rather tongue-in-cheek, since it asked visitors what they thought of the museum's plans to open an exhibition center on the Moon. However, it is true that on October 9, 1969 the Apollo 11 astronauts were in Amsterdam on an official visit.

All this leads to two likely scenarios. Perhaps the item was indeed donated by the US ambassador to the former prime minister during the visit of the Apollo 11 astronauts and was misidentified by him or his family as a Moon rock instead of a sample from a petrified forest of the United States. That would explain the ambassador's donation to a politician no longer in office: J. W. Middendorf II would have been at liberty to procure and donate a piece of petrified wood from his home state, for example. If so, when Drees died, his family bequeathed the item to the Rijksmuseum in good faith.

Another possibility is that the two Dutch artists knowingly or unwittingly used a piece of petrified wood as a stand-in for a Moon rock for their exhibition and the item was later mislabeled as a genuine Moon rock. An intentional hoax might explain the fact that they reported in 2007 that *"in a drawer they saw a very small rock with a note with it. On that note it said that this stone came from the moon."* Yet the photographs of the note show that it doesn't say that the stone is a lunar specimen.

Figure 9-13. The "Moon rock" as shown in the Rijksmuseum catalog (where it was classified as fake).

Either way, it is unquestionable that the item was not formally authenticated by NASA and that anyone arguing that this is evidence of faking the trips to the Moon would have to explain why the perpetrators of a conspiracy on which the worldwide standing of the US depended would be so dumb as to manufacture such a crude and easily detectable fake.

9.9 Astronaut Grissom was killed to keep him quiet

IN A NUTSHELL: *Unproven and unlikely. The accident in which Grissom was allegedly killed to stop him from revealing the problems of the Apollo spacecraft actually revealed those problems in a tragic way that nobody could ignore. Killing him in a cabin fire that would expose the very troubles that had to be kept hidden doesn't sound like a particularly bright problem-solving approach.*

THE DETAILS: In the Fox TV program *Did We Land on the Moon?*, Scott Grissom, son of astronaut Gus Grissom, who died with Ed White and Roger Chaffee in the fire of their Apollo 1 capsule during a ground test on January 27, 1967, stated that the spacecraft *"was intentionally sabotaged"*.

Figure 9-14. Scott Grissom in the documentary Did We Land on the Moon? *(2001).*

Some Moon hoax proponents claim that Grissom was killed because he was an outspoken critic of the Apollo program and was about to announce that the spacecraft would never be able to get to the Moon.

In other words, allegedly Gus Grissom was going to disclose that the Apollo spacecraft was dangerously unsafe and unreliable and so someone decided to shut him up by making him die in an onboard fire that disclosed to everyone that the Apollo spacecraft was dangerously unsafe and unreliable. A flawless plan.

Scott Grissom's accusations are not backed by any hard evidence. The Fox TV program says that *"the cause of the fire is still a mystery and the capsule remains locked away at a military base"*, but this statement is twice incorrect and misleading.

First of all, the primary cause of the fire is known quite precisely: seconds before the first report of fire by the crew, telemetry tapes recorded a short-circuit in the spacecraft cabin, which was built with materials that became highly flammable in a high-pressure (1.13 atm, 16.7 psi), pure-oxygen environment such as the one used for the specific test that was being run on that fatal day. In such conditions, the slightest spark, for example due to static electricity or faulty wiring, could trigger a raging blaze, and it did.

The crew was trapped in the spacecraft by the complicated double hatch, which opened inward and therefore was pressed shut by the sudden internal pressure build-up caused by the heat. Grissom, White and Chaffee died within seconds due to inhalation of toxic gases from the fire.

The tragedy forced NASA and its contractors to review all their procedures and rethink the redesign of the spacecraft that was already in progress, focusing on the need to minimize the risk of fire. In the course of twenty-one frantic months, all flammable materials were replaced by self-extinguishing ones, the nylon spacesuits were replaced with fire- and heat-resistant models, a hatch that could open outward in less than ten seconds was introduced and the onboard atmosphere was changed to 60% oxygen and 40% nitrogen at sea level pressure during liftoff and 0.3 atm (5 psi) of pure oxygen for the remainder of the flight. Apollo 7 was the first flight to introduce these fixes.

Secondly, the Apollo 1 capsule is not *"locked away at a military base"*, as if to suggest some secret that has to be kept under wraps: records show that at the end of the inquiry into the accident the capsule was taken to NASA's Langley Research Center in Hampton, Virginia, where it remained until 2007. After that date it was placed in an environmentally controlled warehouse at the same center, which is not a military base (NASA is a civilian agency), although there is a military facility nearby.

Figure 9-15. The remains of the Apollo 1 spacecraft. Source: Chariots for Apollo.

The mystery, in other words, is entirely fabricated by Fox TV's sensationalist scriptwriters.

The alleged motive makes no sense also because Grissom was far from being a lonely voice in the desert as regards the flaws of the Apollo spacecraft. Indeed, a major redesign of the spacecraft was already in progress and NASA's post-accident report stated openly that *"deficiencies in design, manufacture, installation, rework and quality control existed in the electrical wiring... No design features for fire protection were incorporated... Non-certified equipment items were installed in the Command Module at time of test."*[72]

9.10 NASA whistleblower Thomas Baron was murdered

IN A NUTSHELL: *Safety inspector Thomas Baron died in a car accident after testifying in writing before Congress and after publishing his criticism of the safety of the Apollo spacecraft. Getting rid of an embarrassing witness after he has testified seems to be a rather ineffective scheme.*

---

72 *Report of Apollo 204 Review Board – Findings, Determinations and Recommendations* (1967).

THE DETAILS: Thomas Ronald Baron e was a safety and quality inspector who worked at the Kennedy Space Center from September 1965 to November 1966. He reported to his superiors many acts of worker negligence, poor workmanship and disregard for safety rules.

His reports, however, were not based on direct observation, but on second-hand notes from other people, and this caused them to be taken lightly. He submitted some of his remarks to NASA at the end of 1966 in a 55-page report; some of his warnings were heeded, while

Figure 9-16. Thomas Baron.

others were considered groundless. Baron felt disregarded and sidelined and so leaked his criticism directly to the press. This decision led North American Aviation (the manufacturer of the Apollo command modules) to fire him in January 1967.

Baron began to draft on his own a more detailed 500-page report. After the Apollo 1 fire, which took the lives of Grissom, White and Chaffee on January 27, 1967, Baron delivered this report to the committees of the US Congress that were investigating the disaster and on April 21, 1967 testified before a subcommittee governed by Congressman Olin Teague. One week after testifying, Baron and his family were killed when their car was struck by a train at a level crossing. His full-length report was never made public and has since vanished.

If the facts are told in this way, they certainly lend themselves to a conspiracy theory: Baron was killed to silence him and make sure that nobody found out that the Apollo project was in deep trouble or was a sham.

However, the theory clashes with a basic logic flaw: Baron died *after* he had talked to the press, *after* delivering his extended report to Congress, *after* testifying before the commission subcommittee, and *after* the very serious problems in the design of the Apollo command module had become public in the most tragic and inescapable way: with the death of three astronauts. Silencing Baron at this point would have been absolutely useless.

Moreover, while the nature of the accident that killed Baron and his family might seem freakish and suspicious at first glance, if you consider the logistics of coordinating a train to pass at the exact time when Baron's car is passing and making sure Baron can't see it and avoid being struck, it seems an absurdly complicated way to go about eliminating an embarrassing witness.

What happened to the 500-page report is unclear. The transcripts of Baron's testimony indicate that the report was discussed and that the Congress committee was reluctant to include it as an official record because its size made it awkward and costly to duplicate and print it, especially if the report included hearsay, which would have been legally inadmissible anyway.

NASA and North American Aviation, the organizations that had most to lose from its publication, never had the opportunity to destroy it, since Baron gave it directly to the Congressmen. It is unknown whether the report was returned to Baron or simply discarded.

Figure 9-17. Gus Grissom's coffin at the Arlington cemetery, escorted by Alan Shepard, John Glenn, Gordon Cooper and John Young. Photo 67-H-141. Scan by Ed Hengeveld.

Either way, it mattered little whether the report was saved or not: NASA and especially North American Aviation were already in the spotlight for the Apollo 1 disaster and their omissions had already been made public. Baron's report would have made no difference before the coffins of Grissom, Chaffee and White (Figure 9-17).

9.11 Ten mysterious deaths among the astronauts

IN A NUTSHELL: *No, they weren't mysterious. Being a test pilot of experimental, high-performance aircraft and spacecraft has always been dangerous and deadly. Test pilots died often, in the Fifties and Sixties, outside of the American space program as well, as witnessed by any aviation history book. Moreover, two of these ten astronauts had nothing to do with the Apollo project: the compilers of this death list are cooking the books.*

THE DETAILS: The Fox TV program *Did We Land on the Moon?* states that *"Between 1964 and 1967, a total of ten astronauts lost their lives in freak accidents. These deaths accounted for an astonishing 15% of NASA's astronaut corps."*

Bill Kaysing then adds that *"to keep something that's a lie wrapped up and covered over, you've got to eliminate all the people that can talk about it".* The implication is that these *"freak accidents"* were staged to keep under wraps the secret that the Apollo missions would be faked. Conspiracy theorists, here, are no longer talking about doctored photographs: they're openly making accusations of murder.

But let's fact-check this claim of ten mysterious deaths. The program shows photographs of pilots without identifying them, so it takes some patient historical research to find their names and check whether they did die in freak accidents and were part of the Apollo program. Further details on these men are in the chapter *Remembering the fallen*, but here are the key facts.

Figure 9-18. Theodore C. Freeman.

Theodore Cordy Freeman. USAF captain, aeronautical engineer and experimental aircraft test pilot. He died in 1964, two years before the first test flight of the Apollo spacecraft and three years before the first flight of a Saturn V, in a plane crash caused by a bird strike. He had been selected as an astronaut for the Gemini and Apollo projects but was never assigned to a specific mission.

Figure 9-19. Edward G. Givens, Jr.

Edward Galen Givens, Jr. USAF major and test pilot, selected and trained by NASA in 1966 as an astronaut for the *Apollo Applications Program*, a planned series of flights that were intended to follow the first lunar landing. He was on the backup crew of Apollo 7. He died in a car accident in 1967.

Figure 9-20. Robert H. Lawrence, Jr.

Robert Henry Lawrence, Jr. USAF major and test pilot, selected in June 1967 for the *Manned Orbiting Laboratory* project, which intended to place military space stations in Earth orbit to perform reconnaissance of enemy territories. He died on December 8, 1967 in the crash of his F-104 trainer, flown by his student. He was not involved in the Apollo program.

Figure 9-21. Clifton C. Williams, Jr.

Figure 9-22. Elliot M. See, Jr.

Figure 9-23. Michael J. Adams.

Figure 9-24. Charles A. Bassett II.

Figure 9-25. Virgil I. Grissom, Ed H. White and Roger B. Chaffee.

Clifton Curtis Williams, Jr. Major of the Marines and test pilot, chosen for NASA's third group of astronauts in 1963. He was part of the backup crew of Gemini 10 and Apollo 9. He died in 1967 when the T-38 supersonic trainer that he was flying developed a malfunction and crashed.

Elliot McKay See, Jr. US Navy engineer and test pilot, selected as an astronaut by NASA in 1962. He also supervised the design and development of spacecraft guidance and navigation systems. He had been chosen to command Gemini 9, but died on February 28, 1966 together with astronaut candidate Charles Bassett when their T-38 jet crashed during a low-visibility instrument-only landing.

Michael James Adams. USAF major and test pilot, selected as astronaut for the *Manned Orbiting Laboratory* military project. He died on November 15, 1967, when his X-15 experimental hypersonic rocket plane broke up as it was flying at five times the speed of sound. He was not involved in any way with the Apollo project.

Charles Arthur "Art" Bassett II. USAF captain and test pilot. Member of NASA's third group of astronauts, selected in October 1963. He was assigned to Gemini 9 together with Elliot McKay See, but died with See on February 28, 1966, in the crash of their T-38 trainer.

Virgil "Gus" Grissom, Ed H. White, Roger B. Chaffee. As already described in the previous chapters of this book, these three astronauts died together in a fire on the launch pad, during a spacecraft systems test, on January 27, 1967.

To sum up, two of the allegedly suspicious deaths involved military astronauts (Michael James Adams and Robert Henry Lawrence) who had nothing to do with the Apollo project; four (Charles Bassett, Elliott See, Theodore Freeman and Clifton Williams) died in three accidents with T-38 supersonic training jets (they were test pilots); Ed Givens died in a car crash; and Gus Grissom, Ed White and Roger Chaffee died in the Apollo 1 fire.

Ten deaths over three years was sadly par for the course in the high-risk world of test pilots in those days, as Tom Wolfe's *The Right Stuff* mercilessly recounts, so statistically there's nothing particularly suspicious about these events. What *is* suspicious, instead, is that the Fox TV list includes two people who were not part of the Apollo project. It's easy to create an atmosphere of mystery if you inflate the number of deaths by 20%.

10. Alternative realities

Sometimes Moon hoax proponents realize that their alleged evidence entails absurdities or contradictions and try to justify them with other allegations. This generates a vast web of accusations that go beyond the details of the Apollo missions and enter the realm of politics and history. If you need to discuss Moon hoax theories, it is advisable to be familiar with these alternative interpretations of reality in order to avoid their pitfalls and spot their fallacies.

10.1 The Soviets were bribed to keep quiet

When a Moon hoax believer is asked to explain why the Soviets didn't denounce the alleged US fakery, one frequent reply is that the Soviet government was silenced by a bribe it couldn't refuse. Ralph Rene, in *Nasa Mooned America!*, claims that this bribe was a huge amount of grain sold below cost by the United States to Russia in 1972.

However, a little fact-checking of history files shows that there was no secret deal between the two rival countries: on the contrary, the Soviet Union contrived a clever plan to covertly purchase on the free market, through shell companies, 30% of the US grain crop and even managed to take advantage of the US government's farming export incentives. The press aptly called this scam *The Great Russian Grain Robbery*, as a reference to the famous British great train robbery of 1963.

Contrary to Rene's claims, the grain wasn't sold below cost, but the huge purchase triggered a market rush which tripled the price within a year. The Russians even managed to pull a similar trick again in 1975.[73]

It should be noted that US grain sales to Russia were not unusual: smaller negotiated deals had been made even during President Kennedy's term and West European countries had also been involved.

In other words, Rene is reversing cause and effect in order to make the events fit his preconceptions: the US didn't sell the grain below cost, but rather the Russian purchase made grain prices rise later on.

---

73 *What Land Crash?* by Marcia Zarley Taylor, AgWeb.com (2007); *Another Soviet Grain Sting*, in *Time*, Nov. 28, 1977.

There's also a bigger picture to be considered: if a discounted sale of grain was really all it took to keep the Russians quiet and convince them to lose face in the space race, then why wasn't this leverage used to obtain other, perhaps more useful results, such as keeping the Russians out of the Vietnam War or ending the nuclear arms race? Instead of solving a contradiction, this justification merely leads to an even bigger absurdity.

This bribery scenario also entails a further increase in the number of participants to the conspiracy and in the consequent risk of someone, sooner or later, spilling the beans: the Russians, too, would have to be in on the fakery and would have to keep the secret flawlessly for over forty years.

Moreover, if the Russians were paid off to let the US win the race to the Moon, why did they bother to design and build a rival Moon rocket, the giant N1, that they would never use (Figure 10-1)?

Figure 10-1. A Soviet N1 rocket under construction.

10.2 The Moon rocks were faked

Some conspiracy theorists argue that the rock samples allegedly returned from the Moon were actually created in a laboratory so that they would fool even the experts: an easy task, they say, since there were no other Moon rock samples to which they could be compared. As an alternative, meteors of lunar origin found on Earth were used. It is alleged that only trusted geologists were allowed to examine the samples, which were tightly controlled with the excuse that they were rare and valuable.

The facts, however, don't support these claims: every year, approximately 400 samples from the Apollo Moon rocks are given out to the public for scientific and educational purposes. Requesting a sample is a fairly simple procedure.[74]

---

74 www-curator.jsc.nasa.gov/lunar/sampreq/index.cfm.

For example, the *Lunar Sample Disk Kit,* containing Apollo Moon rocks encapsulated in transparent material, is available to any teacher that follows a three-hour certification course.[75]

Many samples of these Moon rocks have been donated to museums in over 100 countries of the world and are on public display (Figure 10-3).

Moreover, it is incorrect to claim that no comparisons were possible, because the Soviet probes Luna 16, 20 and 24 returned lunar soil samples to Earth between 1970 and 1976.

Figure 10-2. A cross-section from the Lunar Petrographic Educational Thin Section Set, *which can be requested by any geology faculty.*

Figure 10-3. A Moon rock sample returned to Earth by Apollo 17 and on public display at the Museum of Transportation in Luzern, Switzerland. Credit: PA.

The idea to use lunar meteorites found on Earth and pass them off as samples brought back by the Apollo astronauts is shot down by the fact that the Apollo samples have many features that lunar meteorites can't have. One of the most conspicuous is that the surface of the Apollo Moon rocks is pockmarked with minute craters produced by the high-speed impact of micrometeoroids (Figure 10-4).

---

75 *www.nasa.gov/centers/goddard/visitor/loan/.*

This feature could not be replicated in a laboratory in the 1960s and is not observed in lunar meteors found on Earth because the heat and friction of their fiery dive through the atmosphere erodes their surface.

The characteristics of the Apollo rocks also confirm their nonterrestrial origin: they lack water-bearing minerals and show none of the geologic changes that characterize Earth's rocks. For example, here's the opinion of Steven Dutch, professor of geology at the University of Wisconsin, who examined the Apollo samples personally and replied to the allegations of fakery:

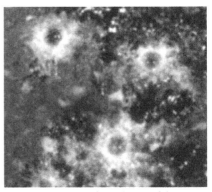

Figure 10-4. An enlarged view of the tiny craters produced by micrometeoroids on Moon rocks.

Water is ubiquitous on earth - it's present in magma, rocks deep in the crust are changed by hot fluids, and rocks near the surface are altered by surface water. Olivine in particular is easily altered. In the second picture [Figure 10-5], *the olivine is fractured but the fractures are absolutely clean. You simply do not see unaltered olivine on earth.*

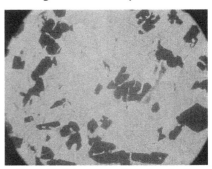

Figure 10-5. A cross-section of an Apollo Moon rock photographed by Steven Dutch, University of Wisconsin.

This could not have been faked. These rocks have grains easily visible to the unaided eye, which means they cooled slowly. To have made these materials synthetically would have required keeping the rocks at 1100 C for years, cooling them slowly at thousands of pounds per square inch pressure. It would have taken years to create the apparatus, years more to get the hang of making the materials, and then years more to create the final result. Starting from Sputnik I in 1957, there would not have been enough time to do it. And, you'd have to synthesize several different types of rock in hundred-pound lots.

...Why create absolutely water-free rocks? Nobody was expecting that - it would have been much easier to fake rocks with water in them (for one thing, you could use terrestrial rocks) and nobody would have been suspicious. And you'd have to put in exactly the right amounts of radioactive elements and daughter products to get the rocks to date radiometrically at 4 billion years old - older than any terrestrial rocks. And you'd have to anticipate the development of new dating methods not in use in 1969 and make sure those elements are present in the correct abundance. And it's not like adding carrots to a stew, either. To mimic the results of potassium-argon dating, you'd have to add inert argon gas and trap it just in the potassium-bearing minerals, and in exact proportion to the amount of potassium.

– from a review of *Conspiracy Theory: Did We Go to the Moon?*

10.3 Stanley Kubrick shot the fake footage

The name of movie director Stanley Kubrick, author of *2001: A Space Odyssey*, is mentioned often as the creator of the faked Apollo footage. However, his biography clearly shows that his whereabouts at the time when he was supposed to be shooting the Apollo fakery were well-known. He was busy shooting *2001* from 1964 to 1968 and then focused on the preproduction of *Napoleon*, which was never completed because United Artists went broke, and on directing *A Clockwork Orange* (1971). Famous for his obsessive attention to image composition and cinematography and for his glacially slow production pace, Kubrick simply wouldn't have had the time to direct the dozens of hours of moonwalk footage needed to cover six Moon landings (leaving aside the problem of how to fake them with 1960s visual effects technology).

Moreover, since the early Sixties, Kubrick no longer lived in the United States. He lived in the United Kingdom, where he shot all of his movies (including *2001*) and had a well-known fear of travel, especially in aircraft. This would have made any participation to the fakery even more complicated.

Kubrick was probably aware of the allegations of his involvement in a movie simulating the Moon trips (Arthur C. Clarke, co-writer of the *2001* screenplay with Kubrick, certainly was: he even wrote a facetious letter to NASA's chief administrator, demanding prompt payment for the job). It is probably not coincidental that Danny, one of the key characters in Kubrick's 1980 movie *The Shining*, wears a sweater that depicts a rocket and the words *"Apollo 11 USA"* (Figure 10-6).

Some Moon hoax theorists, such as Jay Weidner,[76] instead argue that this choice of sweater isn't an in-joke but is actually a silent act of confession by Kubrick, therefore bizarrely justifying one conspiracy claim by means of another one.

One astute objection to the claim that Kubrick shot the fake visual record of the Apollo mis-

Figure 10-6. Danny wears an Apollo-themed sweater in The Shining (1980).

sions has been suggested by Christian Blauvelt of Hollywood.com: *"the moon footage would have looked a hell of a lot better if Kubrick really had directed it."[77]*

10.4 The Apollo astronauts never left Earth orbit

Another popular twist on the Apollo fakery claims is the idea, championed for example by Bart Sibrel, that the Apollo astronauts did indeed go to space on their Saturn V rockets and returned with the splashdowns that the world watched on TV, but didn't go all the way to the Moon: they hid in Earth orbit.

In this way, it is argued, they didn't have to cope with the allegedly lethal radiation of the Van Allen belts and they were able to shoot the TV and film footage in which they are seen to be weightless inside the spacecraft. This solved the problem of simulating weightlessness, and only the footage on the Moon would have to be faked, greatly reducing the workload and the number of participants involved in the hoax. The spacecraft would actually be fully functional and would actually fly, and only a small group of people would need to know the actual flight plan.

The liftoff would be real, and so would the reentry, and the astronauts would actually be in space, where nobody could bump into them by mistake and where they would be subjected to the physiological effects of weightlessness.

---

76 *Secrets of The Shining: Or How Faking the Moon Landings Nearly Cost Stanley Kubrick his Marriage and his Life*, by Jay Weidner (2009), Archive.org.

77 *Get Thee to the Geek: 20 Things You Didn't Know About 2001: A Space Odyssey*, by: Christian Blauvelt, April 9, 2013, Hollywood.com.

Conspiracy theorists make it sound easy, but this scenario clashes with the basic fact that the lunar TV and film footage of the Apollo missions was nevertheless impossible to fake with 1960s-era movie effects.

There's also the problem that the astronauts' radio and TV transmissions would arrive from Earth orbit instead of from deep space, and this would entail a very conspicuous difference in the aiming of any radio antenna that received these signals. An orbit around the Earth below the Van Allen belts last no more than a couple of hours and therefore the antennas would have to swing rapidly to chase the spacecraft as it moved across the sky, whereas real lunar transmissions would instead require them to stay

Figure 10-7. What's a Lunar Module doing in Earth Orbit? Nothing mysterious: it's the Apollo 9 test flight. Photo AS09-21-3183.

trained on the Moon. The wrong aiming would be obvious not only to local technicians but also to anyone nearby, who would wonder why the giant dish-like antennas were not pointed at the Moon.

Moreover, the Soviets, who were competing with the United States for the prestige of the first Moon landing, would have been able to detect the fakery by using their own radio telescopes.

Ham radio operators such as Sven Grahn,[78] who listened in on the radio transmissions from the Apollo spacecraft, also would have noticed that the signals were not coming from the Moon or its vicinity: they would have found that the signal vanished periodically when the spacecraft, as it orbited around the Earth, went beyond the local horizon.

There's another objection that renders the Earth-parking scenario visibly absurd: the Apollo spacecraft would have been observable from the ground by any amateur astronomer. Even small satellites can be spotted because they reflect sunlight and therefore stand out as bright moving specks against the dark sky after sunset or before dawn. A vehicle of the size of Apollo (with or without the S-IVB stage) would

---

78 *Tracking Apollo-17 from Florida,* by Sven Grahn, *www.svengrahn.pp.se.*

have been very easy to spot, giving away the secret.

For example, the International Space Station, the Chinese Tiangong-1 space station or the Russian Soyuz spacecraft, which orbit the Earth at much higher altitudes than those alleged for the Apollo spacecraft, are visible to the naked eye and can be photographed in detail with a good telescope (as demonstrated magnificently by Thierry Legault's images at Astrophoto.fr) and their transit times and paths are easily available. Indeed, the Apollo flights were spotted in this way not only during their brief period in Earth orbit but also during their journeys to the Moon and back by professional and amateur astronomers all over the world.

The photographs shown in Figure 10-8, for example, were taken by the Smithsonian observatory in Maui on December 21, 1968 and show Apollo 8, the first manned mission to leave low Earth orbit and fly around the Moon, as it fires its engine to accelerate toward the Moon. The subsequent dumping of the residual fuel from the S-IVB stage was even visible to the naked eye and was documented by many amateur astronomers in the United Kingdom.

Figure 10-8. Ignition of the S-IVB stage of Apollo 8. Credit: Smithsonian observatory, Maui.

During the Apollo 13 crisis, the initial explosion released a cloud of oxygen that was documented visually from Earth. NASA, moreover, resorted to help from the professional astronomers of the Chabot observatory in Oakland to determine the exact position of the crippled spacecraft so as to calculate the last firing of the lunar module engine, used as an emergency retrorocket, and bring back safely the three astronauts. Details of these and other Apollo sightings are in Bill Keel's *Telescopic Tracking of the Apollo Lunar Missions.*[79]

---

79 *www.astr.ua.edu/keel/space/apollo.html.*

Figure 10-9 shows, at the center, the command module, the service module and the lunar module of Apollo 13, over 23,000 kilometers (14,300 miles) from Earth, en route to the Moon, before the accident. The other four dots are the fairing panels that enclosed the lunar module and had been jettisoned.

The picture was taken through the 60-centimeter (24-inch)

Figure 10-9. The Apollo 13 spacecraft en route to the Moon. Credit: James W. Young.

telescope of Table Mountain, in California. The diagonal streaks are stars, distorted by the motion of the telescope to chase the spacecraft during the five minutes of the exposure of the film. The same observatory saw the Apollo 8 S-IVB stage and command and service module when it was nearly 320,000 kilometers (200,000 miles) from Earth.[80]

It should be noted that the locations and events reported and recorded by amateur and professional astronomers correspond perfectly to the ones described in NASA's technical documents for the individual missions.

10.5 The radio and TV signals came from an orbiting satellite

Another frequent conjecture among Moon hoax theorists is that the live TV broadcasts and the radio communications were prerecorded and then sent from an unmanned satellite that orbited the Earth or the Moon.

An Earth-orbiting satellite would have been out of the question, however, for the same reasons mentioned earlier: the Soviet space surveillance system and ham radio users worldwide would have been capable of intercepting the direct feed from the satellite and would have realized that its signal wasn't coming from the Moon because its source changed position constantly. Even a geostationary orbit would have revealed the trick, because it wouldn't have followed the orbital motion of the Moon.

---

80   *The Apollo 13 CSLM*, W7ftt.net.

Placing the transmitter in orbit around the Moon or on the lunar surface would have solved these problems, but it would have left another very conspicuous clue to the fakery: the frequency of the radio transmissions from a moving spacecraft varies depending on the speed with which it moves toward or away from the receiving station, just like the sound of an ambulance siren changes pitch as it approaches or moves away. This variation, known as *Doppler effect*, would have been detectable by any well-equipped radio enthusiast.

The transmitter would have to travel through space (or vary its transmission frequency artificially) by following exactly the mission profile stated by NASA, simulating not only the trip but also every lunar orbit, which entailed an increase and a decrease in the distance to Earth, with a consequent continuous frequency variation. A second transmitter, simulating exactly the movements of the lunar module when it detached from the command and service modules, would also have been necessary.

To add to the complexity of this concept, it would have been necessary to transmit not only the radio and TV communications but also fake telemetry data that reported the state of the spacecraft to Mission Control. All these data would have to be created from scratch with perfect authenticity and would have to match exactly the speed and direction of the spacecraft, which would have been detectable by means of the Doppler effect.

Worse still, any mistake in the characteristics of the transmissions from the fake spacecraft would have exposed the conspiracy.

Moreover, the deep space monitoring and transmission network wasn't entirely controlled by NASA or the US government. For example, most of the radio communications of the various missions and in particular the live TV broadcast of the first landing on the Moon went through the Australian radio telescopes of Parkes and Honeysuckle Creek, which were operated by local engineers.

These weren't nameless minions; they were (and many still are) very real people, who don't mince words about their role in the Apollo project and about the conspiracy theorists who accuse them of collusion. Here's what Mike Dinn, deputy manager of the radio monitoring station of the Manned Spaceflight Network in Honeysuckle Creek, Australia, during Apollos 7 to 13, has to say:

...as I was the Australian citizen employed by the Australian government responsible for running the operations at the prime Australian tracking site here near Canberra I can vouch for the scientific/engineering fact that we pointed our antenna at the trajectory to, at and

*from the moon and transmitted and received radio signals contain-
ing commands, telemetry, television together with navigation info
from antenna angles, Doppler frequencies and two way range delays.
Impossible to fake.*

*I actually talked with Apollo 8 on the way out (see ALSJ for details)
and my assistant ops man John Saxon spoke to Young and Duke on
the lunar surface during Apollo 16.*[81]

10.6 The mistakes were left in on purpose by whistleblowers

One of the most interesting and creative justifications in the alternative
vision of reality proposed by conspiracy theorists, both regarding the
Moon landings and other historical events, is the so-called *whis-
tleblower theory.*

Sooner or later the conspiracy theorist has to deal with the fact that
there are, paradoxically, just *too many* apparently revealing mistakes in
his reconstruction of the events. If this was supposed to be a colossal
deception, organized by the highest levels of government, with access
to vast funding and resources and top experts in fakery, and if the nation's reputation was at stake, why is the resulting conspiracy riddled
with blatant blunders and amateurish mistakes?

A typical answer to this conundrum is to explain away the missing
stars and fluttering flags by arguing that these flubs were left in *intentionally* by the perpetrators of the conspiracy. They were ashamed of
the deception into which they had been forced and so they tried to
warn people through these mistakes. Astute observers and true free
thinkers would detect these coded messages and reveal the truth to
the world.

The logical flaw of this explanation is that it uses a totally unproven
conspiracy theory to prop up another conspiracy theory and it implies
that the organizers of the fakery were so dumb that they didn't notice
the telltale mistakes that had been left in by the whistleblowers. It is
rather difficult to believe that nobody along the chain of command of
the conspiracy would notice, for example, a letter "C" left conspicuously
on a rock or the crosshairs drawn behind objects.

This conspiracy-within-a-conspiracy theory also entails assuming that
all the experts in the science fields touched by the Apollo missions are

---

81   Interview with Mike Dinn by Steven Dutch (*www.honeysucklecreek.net/people/dinn.html*);
     my personal communication with Dinn, 2010.

blind and incompetent: today's astronauts, aerospace engineers, astronomers, including those of countries that don't exactly hold the United States in high regard, would all have to be so dumb that they fail systematically to notice the alleged intentional errors that conspiracy enthusiasts, despite knowing little or nothing about spaceflight or astronomy, claim to find so easily.

Unfortunately, the kind of person who is convinced that he or she is the only one who has the insight and the intelligence to grasp the truth that is hidden to others usually is unable to abandon this pathological world view and will resort often to an ever-expanding web of conspiracies to hold on to that view. In such cases, arguing over details is pointless: the problem is not in the Moon landings, but in the denialist's overall mindset.

11. UFOs and Moon landings

One of the many contradictions of Moon hoax theories is that some claim that the Apollo landings never happened, while others argue that the Apollo flights not only did happen but even encountered extraterrestrial spacecraft and there were even secret missions to the Moon.

It's important to be acquainted with these theories of secret flights and alien encounters, because they are part of the classic repertoire of hardcore conspiracy theorists and reveal clearly the typical errors of the conspiracist mindset. Most importantly, however, they're very amusing to bring up in a Moon hoax discussion and then watch the ensuing colorful argument among the various factions of conspiracy theorists.

11.1 UFOs in Apollo photographs

Some UFO enthusiasts claim that the photographs taken on the Moon by the astronauts are authentic and show the presence of alien vehicles. For example, Ufocasebook.com includes, in the section entitled *The Best UFO Pictures Ever Taken*, three photographs of the Apollo 16 mission (Figure 11-1).[82]

It's worth noting that these enthusiasts claim that these photographs were *really* taken on the Moon, in contrast with "classic" conspiracy theorists, who deny the Moon landings. Putting the two groups of believers in the same room might turn out to be entertaining.

The "UFOs" that can be seen in these photographs and in many other images from the Apollo missions are not flying saucers that NASA nonchalantly left in the pictures, hoping that nobody would notice them: they're simply reflections of the Sun inside the camera lens. These reflections are known as *lens flares* and occur on Earth, too, although usually they are less noticeable because on Earth the sky is very bright when the Sun is up. On the Moon, the sky is black even when the Sun is above the horizon, so any lens flare stands out starkly against the blackness.

---

82 ufocasebook.com/bestufopictures3.html.

The photos shown in Figure 11-1 are, top to bottom, AS16-114-18423, AS16-114-18422 and AS16-109-17804, all from the Apollo 16 flight. They're incomplete versions of those images, cropped so as to not show an important detail.

It turns out that in the uncropped high-resolution original scans of these photographs, the "UFOs" are actually two in each image and are always aligned in the direction of the Sun, the position of which can be determined by tracing the directions in which the shadows converge. These are typical indications of a lens flare.

In the third photo, in particular, the lens flare would stand out unmistakably if someone hadn't removed the upper part of the picture, because the second "UFO" is actually *in front* of the sunshade on the astronaut's helmet (Figure 11-2).

It's rather hard to believe that the pictures were cropped so conveniently just by chance or that the vehicles used by aliens for their Moon trips are the size of horseflies.

The visual records of the Apollo flights include dozens of photographs affected by lens flares. In the color photos, the rainbow

Figure 11-1. Alleged UFOs in Moon photographs according to Ufocasebook.com.

effect produced by the different refraction of the various colors inside the lens is an obvious giveaway that the alleged alien spacecraft is merely a byproduct of the camera lens and is not a real object.

However, not all the "UFOs" that can be spotted in the Apollo photographs are camera-generated. Some are real objects that are difficult to interpret correctly without knowing the technical context: for example, they are often parts of the spacecraft that were jettisoned after use or flakes of the vehicle's covering that peeled off and traveled alongside it by inertia.

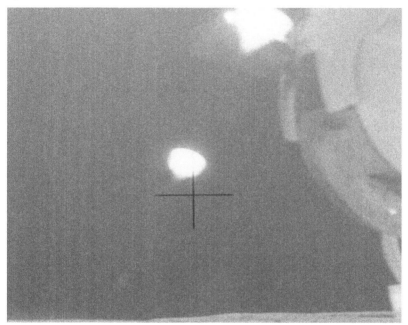

Figure 11-2. Detail of photo AS16-109-17804, including the part that is cropped in the version shown by Ufocasebook.com. Note the raised sunshade on the helmet and another "UFO" on the sunshade.

Fragment break-off was quite frequent. Figure 11-3 shows the S-IVB stage of Apollo 8 after its separation from the command and service module: note the swarm of bright debris that surrounds the jettisoned stage.

Figure 11-4 instead shows a piece of Mylar covering that detached from the Apollo 10 command module and floated outside the spacecraft. Astronaut John Young estimated it to be about 50 centimeters (a foot and half) long.

Figure 11-3. The third stage of Apollo 8. NASA photo AS08-16-2583.

Without knowledge of this context and with no distance references to estimate the size of the object, it's easy to imagine the flake to be a mysterious alien vehicle. It is not surprising that this is one of the most frequently mentioned Apollo images among UFO enthusiasts. However, a more thorough perusal of the Apollo archives reveals at least two more photographs (AS10-28-3989 and 3900) of the same fragment as it slowly turns. If these photos are combined to create a stereo pair, they clearly show that the object is small and close to the viewer.

Figure 11-4. NASA photo AS10-28-3988 (Apollo 10).

11.2 Buzz Aldrin saw a UFO

This remarkable claim stems from a statement made by Buzz Aldrin (Apollo 11) in the documentary *First on the Moon: The Untold Story* (2005). Here's what he says verbatim:

> There was something out there that was close enough to be observed... and what could it be?... Mike [Collins] decided he thought he could see it in the telescope, and he was able to do that, and when it was in one position it had a series of ellipses. But when you made it real sharp it was sort of L-shaped. That didn't tell us very much... Obviously the three of us were not gonna blurt out "Hey, Houston, we've got something moving alongside of us, we don't know what it is, you know, can you tell us what it is?" We weren't about to do that! 'Cause we know that those transmissions would be heard by all sorts of people, and who knows what somebody would have demanded that we turn back because of aliens or whatever the reason is. So we didn't do that, but we did decide we'd just cautiously ask Houston where... how far away was the S-IVB... And a few moments later, they came back and said something like it was six thousand miles away because of the maneuver, so we really didn't think we were looking at something that far away, so we decided that after a while watching it, it was time to go to sleep, and not to talk about it anymore until we came back, in debriefing.

Aldrin's expression clearly reveals his amusement (Figure 11-5) as he tells this anecdote; he doesn't speak in the solemn tone that one might expect for such a world-shaking revelation as an alien encounter. Nevertheless, the documentary dwells on his words and also shows a blurry image of an object (not the one seen by Apollo 11, but another one observed during

Figure 11-5. Buzz Aldrin recounts his "UFO" encounter in First on the Moon: The Untold Story *(2005).*

another Moon trip) while the narrator states that the object seen by Aldrin was never identified certainly.

At first sight, it would seem that an Apollo astronaut is claiming that he saw an extraterrestrial spacecraft and decided, together with his crewmates, to keep quiet about it. That's the way many UFO sites present this story. But a little fact-checking reveals that the conspiracy of silence was perpetrated not by the astronauts, but by the authors of the documentary, perhaps seeking a dramatic scoop.

The most likely and thoroughly non-extraterrestrial explanation of the sighting had in fact been given directly by Aldrin during the interview he recorded for the documentary, but it was cut, as Aldrin told David Morrison of the NASA Astrobiology Institute.[83] The astronaut explained to the documentary makers that the object that was chasing them was quite likely to be one of the four fairing panels that enclosed the Lunar Module, as shown in Figure 11-6.

During liftoff from Earth and for the initial part of the trip to the Moon, the Lunar Module sat on top of the S-IVB stage (the cylinder at the bottom left in Figure 11-6) and below the command and service module, protected by these four panels. As the spacecraft continued its voyage toward the Moon, the command and service module separated from the S-IVB stage and turned

DOCKING AND SEPARATION OF SPACECRAFT FROM S IVB

Figure 11-6. Extraction of the Lunar Module. Detail of NASA drawing S-66-5107.

around to face the stage. The fairing panels opened out and detached from the S-IVB and then the command and service module docked with the lunar module and pulled it away from the stage.

---

83 *Ask an Astrobiologist, July 26, 2006, Astrobiology.nasa.gov.*

The docked command and service module and the lunar module (the actual Apollo spacecraft) then moved away from the S-IVB, which was commanded from Earth to fire its engines to set it on a trajectory that avoided any risk of collision with the spacecraft.

The fairing panels, however, were already uncoupled from the S-IVB stage and therefore were not affected by the trajectory change and diligently obeyed Newton's laws of motion, continuing by inertia along the same path as the Apollo spacecraft, like seagulls trailing a ship, until the spacecraft fired its main engine to change course, as shown also in Figure 10-9.

Aldrin subsequently confirmed the true nature of the sighting on several occasions, for example on the *Howard Stern Show* of August 15, 2007. In a TV interview for the Science Channel he asked for the opportunity to explain to the viewers that he had not seen an alien spacecraft, but the TV channel refused his request. The tale of the astronaut who says he saw a UFO is too good to be put down and so it continues to circulate unchecked, despite the fact that the matter had already been clarified and discussed thirty-five years earlier during the debriefing mentioned by Aldrin, as recorded on pages 6-33 to 6-36 of the *Apollo 11 Technical Crew Debriefing* of July 31, 1969.

It's quite ironic that the astronauts, during their flight, chose not to discuss the issue over the radio because they were concerned that their remarks might be misinterpreted but this choice was then construed as evidence that they were hiding something. Just as they expected, their words were grossly misunderstood.

11.3 A secret Moon mission recovered an alien spaceship

Another popular UFO-related claim is that there was a secret military mission to the Moon, named Apollo 20, that was performed by a joint Russian-American crew to recover an alien spacecraft found on the Moon.

A man named William Rutledge claims that he was one of the members of this crew together with US astronaut Leona Snyder and Russian cosmonaut Alexei Leonov. According to his tale, a Saturn V rocket departed in secret in 1976 from the Vandenberg military base in California and reached the far side of the Moon, where the photographic reconnaissance performed by Apollo 15 had discovered a giant extraterrestrial spaceship.

Evidence of this alien vehicle was said to be visible even in public photo atlases of the Moon, for example in the detail of NASA photo AS15-P-9625 shown in Figure 11-7. The alleged spaceship is the elongated sunlit shape at the center of the picture, surrounded by deep shadow.

This claim is highly suspicious: if the presence of an extraterrestrial vehicle on the Moon was so top secret that it prompted a covert joint Russian-American mission, then why was its picture released (for example in the LPI photo atlas)?[84] Since images of the far side of the Moon were available at the time only if NASA or the Soviet Union chose to publish them, it would have been trivially easy to censor them and keep the secret.

Figure 11-7. The alleged alien spaceship.

Rutledge's tale, however, continues with many technical details that appear quite plausible to the layperson and includes rather shocking videos, which even show a humanoid alien corpse (Figure 11-8) and close-ups of the extraterrestrial vehicle.

Many UFO researchers, however, have investigated Rutledge's story and shown that it is just a well-orchestrated hoax

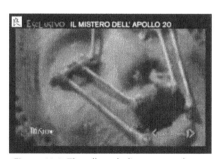

Figure 11-8. The alleged alien corpse shown by Italian TV program Mistero.

created by French artist Thierry Speth, as detailed for example in the report published by the Italian UFO investigators of the *Centro Ufologico Nazionale* (National UFO Center).[85]

For example, the alleged video footage of the alien spaceship includes a very terrestrial-looking spring, and in one of the videos of the interior of the lunar module the background can be seen through an astronaut, revealing the fact that the astronaut was superimposed using visual effects. The alleged alien corpse turns out to be one of Speth's sculptures.

84 *www.lpi.usra.edu/resources/apollo/frame/?AS15-P-9625.*
85 *www.cun-veneto.it/apollo20.htm.*

In addition to these clear indications of fakery, it is technically absurd to think that a giant Saturn V rocket could depart from California without anyone noticing its thunderous liftoff and bright climb through the sky and without being spotted by the world's professional and amateur astronomers as it flew to the Moon, as occurred for the other Apollo missions.

A launch from Vandenberg, on the west coast of the United States, would have entailed another problem: Moon rockets usually lift off along a west-to-east trajectory, in order to take advantage of the substantial speed boost provided by the Earth's rotation (1470 kilometers per hour, or about 910 miles per hour at the latitude of the Kennedy Space Center). But a west-to-east Vandenberg launch would mean that the climb to space would be visible from the entire US and, most importantly, that the massive S-IC first stage, once spent, would fall somewhere in the continental United States, and any malfunction of the rocket would cause it to fall onto populated areas. That's the reason why Florida was chosen as a launch site: any spent or malfunctioning boosters fall safely into the Atlantic Ocean.

An east-to-west trajectory, climbing over the Pacific, would not only entail the loss of the natural boost of the Earth's rotation, but would cause an equivalent speed penalty, as the rocket would have to accelerate against the Earth's motion. A polar orbit (to the north or to the south) would still have to do without the rotational boost and this would reduce considerably the Saturn V's payload capacity.

As regards the alleged alien spaceship, the high-resolution original photographs (Figure 11-9) show that it's just an elongated depression of the lunar surface. The appearance of a smooth, artificial-looking shape is an artifact of the low-quality copies often used by UFO enthusiasts and hoax perpetrators.

Figure 11-9. Detail of NASA photo AS15-P-9625. Scan from the Arizona State University archive.

11.4 The astronauts found alien structures on the Moon

One of the many UFO-centered tales regarding the Apollo missions alleges that Neil Armstrong and Buzz Aldrin, the two moonwalkers of Apollo 11, found alien artifacts on the Moon. Overwhelmed by their discovery, they started reporting it excitedly to Mission Control over the public radio link, while Mission Control tried to shut them up and told them to switch to a secure channel.

According to the proponents of this story, the radio transmissions from the Moon had a built-in delay designed to allow censorship and so the discovery was never made public. Some radio enthusiasts, however, allegedly managed to intercept the direct radio signal from the astronauts and recorded it, and so the amazing extraterrestrial discovery was leaked. Here's the transcript of the astronauts' excited exchange, which is also available as an audio file:

Astronaut 1: Ha! What is it?

Astronaut 2: We have some explanation for that?

Houston: We have none, don't worry, continue your program!

Astronaut 1: Oh boy it's a, it's, it, it is really something [garbled] fantastic here, you, you could never imagine this!

Houston: Roger, we know about that, could you go the other way, go back the other way!

Astronaut 1: Well it's kind of [garbled] ha, pretty spectacular... God... what is that there?

Astronaut 1: It's [garbled], what the hell is that?

Houston: Go Tango, Tango!

Astronaut 1: Ha! There's kind of light there now!

Houston: Roger, we got it, we (watched it), lose communication, Bravo Tango, Bravo Tango, select Jezebel, Jezebel!

Astronaut 1: ...ya, ha! ... but this is unbelievable!

The claim is actually very easy to debunk. First of all, the voices in the recording are completely different from Armstrong and Aldrin's. The beeps (formally known as *Quindar tones*) that separate the astronauts' voices from the orders from Mission Control are different from the real ones, and so are the background noise and the type of distortion. Also, there's no sign of the 2.6-second delay between the voice from Mission Control and the replies of the astronauts that inevitably occurs due to the round trip to Earth-Moon distance, covered by the radio signal at the speed of light.

Most importantly, it turns out that the original source of the alleged recording is actually a 1977 British parody documentary, *Alternative 3*.

Another version of this exchange was published by an American-Canadian tabloid, the *National Bulletin*, on September 29, 1969, under the title *Phony Transmission Failure Hides Apollo 11 Discovery... MOON IS A UFO BASE!* It's not clear whether this was an attempt at parody like *Alternative 3*, but it certainly has the same implausible setting and is replete with meaningless technobabble such as *"orbit scanned"* or *"In 625 to the fifth, auto-relays set"*, which might be impressive to the layperson but are dead giveaways for experts in the field.

The issue of the badly faked beeps is a good opportunity to dispel some frequently repeated myths about them. First of all, the beeps could not be heard by the astronauts and were not used to indicate that it was the other party's turn to talk. Instead they controlled the transmission of the radio signals from Earth via transmitters located in various countries, which were used as the Earth's rotation brought them within line-of-sight reach of the spacecraft. They were linked to Mission Control in Houston, Texas, via analog telephone lines, which were affected by interference and noise, so it was necessary to mute the transmitter locally, at the transmission station, instead of closing the microphone in Houston. Essentially, the Quindar tones were remote control signals sent over the telephone lines.

These signals are still used for some space communications. They take their name from Quindar Electronics, Inc.,which provided the equipment that generated these tones and responded to their commands. The tones are 250 milliseconds long at 2,525 Hz for the activation tone (transmission start) and 2,475 Hz for the deactivation tone (transmission stop). A filter eliminated the tones from the signal sent to the Apollo spacecraft and therefore the astronauts usually didn't hear them. However, during some flights, such as Apollo 8, the filtering didn't always work fully and the piercing beeps reached the astronaut's ears.

11.5 Astronaut Ed Mitchell's UFO claims

Apollo 14 Lunar Module pilot and moonwalker Edgar Mitchell is often presented as an authoritative UFO witness, but he has made it very clear that he does not support the claims that he saw direct evidence of extraterrestrial presence while he was in space or on the Moon or that NASA was involved in some kind of coverup:

The notion that there are structures on Mars or the Moon is bonkers. I can attest to the latter -- I've been there. We saw no structures at the landing site and none was reflected in my helmet, as has been alleged.[86]

I, nor any crew I was on (I was on three Apollo crews), received any briefing before or after flights on UFO events, saw anything in space suggesting UFOs or structures on the moon, etc. We did it just like we said in official reports. My only claim to knowledge of these events is from the individuals, mostly of yesteryear, who were in government, intelligence, or military; were there, saw what they saw, and now believe it should be made public. But I claim no first hand knowledge, nor have any.[87]

On the other hand, he has gone on record saying that he believes that extraterrestrial spacefarers have visited Earth and that there is a government coverup on the UFO phenomenon:

I happen to be privileged to [...] be in on the fact that we have been visited on this planet and the UFO phenomenon is real, although it's been covered up by our governments for quite a long time [...] I have been deeply involved in certain committees and certain research programs with very credible scientists and intelligence people that do know the real inside story [...] The Roswell crash was real and a number of other contacts have been real and ongoing.[88]

The evidence to back up these claims is, as Mitchell himself readily acknowledges, not first-hand and is based on statements by other people that Mitchell believes to be reliable but cannot corroborate. Currently there is no publicly available hard evidence and therefore this fascinating issue remains a matter of opinion.

---

86 *UFOs: It's a coverup*, by Tom Rhodes, *Ottawa Citizen*, October 11, 1998.

87 *Ed Mitchell Most Unhappy With Greer Using His Name As Disclosure Witness*, Rense.com, 2001.

88 *Astronaut Says Aliens Are Real*, Kerrang Radio (2008).

12. How to debate a Moon hoax believer

12.1 One word of advice

Don't. Never, ever try to change the mind of a Moon hoax *believer*, i.e., someone who claims to be absolutely, instinctively sure that the Moon landings were faked in one way or another. It would be a waste of time: you can't use rationality to dispel an irrational belief.

Debating a *doubter* instead can be very constructive. A doubter is still open to reasoned argument and to clearly presented evidence. Many people have doubts about the Moon landings simply because they're not familiar with the subject and have heard the hoax theories. Since they lack the tools to determine who's right and who's wrong, they take the only sensible course: they remain doubtful.

There's only one situation in which it's worth debating a Moon hoax believer: in front of a doubter. A calm, well-documented discussion will often allow the doubter to realize that the hoax believer's arguments are seductive but ultimately inconsistent and irrational.

However, some Moon hoax theories may seem quite plausible and convincing at first, and it's easy to get lost in the technical details. What you need is something that clearly reveals the absurdities of these theories.

Here is a series of questions that in my experience are effective in rapidly exposing the untenability of Moon hoax beliefs. These question force believers to justify their ideas with explanations that they cannot give without contradicting themselves. Moreover, they often produce a very intense and sometimes aggressive emotional reaction, which is worth a thousand pages of technical exposition in making it clear, to the doubter who observes the debate, who is rationally, serenely right and who is hopelessly, aggressively wrong.

These same questions, especially the first one, are also useful as a starting point for a debate with doubters. They force them to question the consistency and plausibility of their doubts, at least enough to want to know more about the subject, for example from the book you're reading.

To avoid writing *"he or she"* repeatedly, I'll assume that the hoax believer/doubter is male, which in any case is true most of the time. No sexism is implied; that's just the way it is.

12.2 If you've only got time for one question

Moon hoax claims often surface in situations where there's no time to have an extensive debate. If all you have time for is one question, try this one.

> **There isn't a single astronaut, from any country, who agrees with Moon hoax theories. Many are personal friends of the moonwalkers or trained with them. Are you saying that these highly skilled space professionals, who have actually been in space, are too dumb to realize that they were being hoaxed by a bunch of liars riding a fake rocket? And are you implying that you're smarter than an astronaut? Seriously?**

If you know the name of an astronaut from your country, mention it; e.g., *"Are you implying that you're smarter than Canadian astronaut Chris Hadfield, who spent six months in space working on the International Space Station?"* Make it personal.

Then walk away or change the subject.

12.3 Questions for hoax believers

One of the most effective ways to flummox a Moon hoax theorist is to ask him to provide technically documented answers (i.e., provide specific, authoritative technical sources) for the following questions – and do so without being self-contradictory. You should never accept arguments that begin with *"We all know that…"*: always ask for sources and documents to back up every claim. Without them, the theorist's claims are nothing more than hot air. Remember to always ask *"Do you have an authoritative source for that?"*

Some hoax theorists try personal attacks by asking you if *you're* qualified to talk about the Moon landings. They might ask you if you're an aerospace engineer or have a science degree or other qualifications that entitle you to speak authoritatively. If you do, say so, of course; but in any case, make it very clear that your personal qualifications aren't really relevant, since the authenticity of the Moon landings is supported overwhelmingly by the international technical and scientific community. Then ask the conspiracists what qualifications they have or what authoritative backing *they* can provide. They won't have any.

Never allow a hoax theorist to control the discussion by changing the subject and moving on to another claim when he is stumped: this is a typical trick. Be calm but firm: you've asked a specific question, you have the right to an answer. If the hoax supporter dodges the question, ask it again, and point out his attempt to elude it. If he then caves in and starts to submit another objection by saying *"Yes, but..."*, remember to make it very clear that his *"Yes"* means that he's conceded the point and admitted that he was wrong. If he's wrong on that point, maybe he's wrong on the others.

Don't get bogged down in arguments over the technical minutiae of the missions: they don't provide any insight to anyone who is not well acquainted with spaceflight. Conspiracy theorists love to split hairs on insignificant details. Don't reply by offering further technical details, but ask them to get to the point. Just say *"And so?"*: the hoax proponent will have to explain why the technical detail on which he is dwelling is so important. Usually he will fail, and this will show how inconsistent his vision actually is and will bring the debate back to more general and less arcane issues.

Remember that the best way to show how ridiculous these theories are is to let a Moon hoax theorist babble on and then calmly ask a few pointed questions. Most of all, be serene. Let your tone of voice make it clear to everyone who is being sensible and logical and who is being hysterical and obsessive, and show that you don't really care whether you change his mind or not. Conspiracy theorists want you to argue and get mad: don't rise to the bait. Have fun and consider the debate an opportunity to talk about the greatness and wonder of spaceflight.

Now let's move on to the questions.

How many missions were faked?

Was it just the first Moon landing, or all of them, or all the flights that went to the Moon, or maybe all manned flights in space? What about the Soviet ones? The Chinese ones? Whatever he says, the Moon hoax theorist is going to paint himself in a corner.

If he claims that *all* the lunar flights were faked, including the ones that didn't land, then he's saying that *nine* missions to the Moon were hoaxes – not just the six lunar landings, but also Apollo 8, 10 and 13, which went all the way to the Moon and flew around it.

The complexity of faking perfectly not one, not six, but *nine* entire flights is overwhelming: the amount of photographs, movie and TV footage, radio transmissions and scientific data that would have to be simulated flawlessly increases to the point of absurdity. Likewise, the number of people that would have to be in the know and kept gagged for over four decades, with nobody ever blabbing, becomes ludicrously large. Especially if you consider that all this incredibly complicated, top-secret trickery would have to be achieved by the US government – which, let's face it, has a less than stellar record at keeping secrets and accomplishing complex tasks.

If the conspiracy theorist claims that only the Moon landings (i.e., the Apollo flights from 11 onward) were faked, then this implies that he believes that the previous missions were real and therefore that the photographs taken during those missions are authentic. These photos quash many of the objections based on photographs, such as the allegedly suspicious lack of stars, the fogging or melting of the film due to radiation or heat, and many of the technical objections: for example, deep space radiation and the Van Allen belts can't have been unsurmountable obstacles if Apollo 8 went safely through both on its way to the Moon. If he says that Apollo 8 wasn't faked, then the whole argument that 1960s space technology wasn't up to the task of going to the Moon gets thrown out.

If instead the claim is that only the first Moon landing (Apollo 11) was faked to save face and meet Kennedy's end-of-the-decade deadline, but the subsequent ones were real, then the hoax theorist has to explain why the first landing had to be faked at great risk when the second one (Apollo 12, which, he argues, was real) took place *just four months later*, in November of 1969, still within the deadline.

And if he claims that the subsequent lunar missions were real, then the photographs, TV and movie footage shot during those later missions can be used as reference to disprove the allegations of anomalies in the Apollo visual record.

Can you explain in detail what you think really happened without contradicting yourself?

In over forty years, no conspiracy theorist has been able to provide a detailed and consistent alternative version of the events. Sooner or later, his description contradicts itself or requires entirely groundless, unproven assumptions. The only consistent, documented version of the events surrounding the Moon landings is the one presented by the overwhelming majority of historians and backed up by tons of technical evidence: we went to the Moon nine times and landed on it with manned spacecraft six times.

A Moon hoax believer might argue that he doesn't have to provide a complete alternative version and that all he has to do is prove that the "official" version is false. Fine: but in over four decades, conspiracy theorists have failed even to accomplish this simpler task and provide at least one item of irrefutable evidence of the alleged fakery.

Moreover, it's not true that hoax theorists don't offer alternative versions of the events: the claim that the "official" version is false *is* an alternative version. As such, it must not be self-contradicting, so ask the theorist for a detailed explanation of how he thinks things really happened and then wait for the contradictions to appear. Ask him to paint the full picture: it's the best way to find whether it makes any sense.

Were the Moon photographs faked or not?

For example, ask the hoax believer or doubter to consider the famous picture of Buzz Aldrin saluting the American flag on the Moon (Figure 12-1): was the flag added by photo editing or was it really there?

Figure 12-1. Aldrin salutes the US flag. Photo AS11-40-5874 (cropped).

No matter how the conspiracy theorist replies, he's going to end up contradicting himself. If he answers that the photograph was faked by adding the flag, then this implies that it was actually taken on the Moon, otherwise it would have been easier to just put the flag on the movie set in the first place or, if the flag photo op had been somehow inexplicably forgotten, just go back to the movie set and take more pictures.

If he claims that the flag was really there but the picture was shot in a studio, then ask why didn't they also fake a nice photograph of Neil Armstrong saluting the flag, while they were at it. After all, Armstrong was the commander of the mission and the first man to set foot on the Moon, yet there isn't a single decent picture of him on the lunar surface, and virtually all the Apollo 11 photos show Aldrin. How come?

How come not one of the 400,000 people who worked on the Apollo project has ever confessed to the hoax, not even on his or her deathbed?

The Saturn V rocket and the Apollo spacecraft were designed and built by private contractors like Boeing and Grumman, not by some secretive NASA skunk works. If the claim is that the technology of the 1960s was not up to the job, then the conspiracy theorist has to explain why not one of the thousands of highly skilled workers and engineers who were part of the Apollo project has ever spilled the beans and why not one of the equally skilled testing crews ever noticed that the spacecraft was an unworkable dummy.

If the argument is that they realized what was going on but kept quiet to avoid repercussions, then the theorist must explain why there haven't been any deathbed confessions, anonymous leaks or at least some inadvertent disclosure by a blundering, disgruntled or drunken employee. Even the CIA, the NSA or the most ruthless organized crime syndicates can't achieve this level of absolute compliance. All it would take is one person like Chelsea Manning (formerly Bradley Manning) or Edward Snowden and the whole plot would be exposed.

If instead the hoax theorist claims that fully functional vehicles were built to fool the engineers and were launched to fool the public but weren't actually used to go to the Moon, that still leaves the problem of the other engineers who had to alter these vehicles to fake the flights: if there was no crew on board, for example, then someone had to design, test and install the extra hardware needed to pilot the spacecraft from Earth, land it on the Moon, send fake radio transmissions and data from the Moon to fool the radio astronomers on Earth (especially the Soviet ones), pick up Moon rocks, and so forth, and then keep perfectly quiet forever.

The fake rocket theory also contradicts the claim that the Apollo project was created and faked to divert its billions of dollars to covert government operations. Fake or not, lots of giant Saturn rockets still had to be seen lifting off from the pads in Florida, and giant rockets, plus all their supporting hardware and ground crews, don't come cheap, especially if they actually have to get to space. Then there would be the expense of faking the radio signals, shooting the fake Moon footage, manufacturing the Moon rocks, counterfeiting millions of pages of technical documents, paying everybody to keep quiet, and so on. Faking the Moon landings probably would have been just as expensive as actually going to the Moon.

If human flight to the Moon is physically impossible, why did the Russians try so hard to do it?

Any Moon hoax theorist has to contend with the fact that the Soviet Union worked hard and secretly spent billions trying to put a cosmonaut on the Moon before the United States. This covert attempt, known as N1-L3, ran late due to technical glitches and political squabbling and was abandoned when Neil Armstrong and Buzz Aldrin set foot on the Moon. The Russians also had a separate, simpler lunar fly-around project, named L1, which was almost ready but was canceled when Americans became the first to orbit around the Moon with Apollo 8.

True, the N1 rockets exploded four times out of four. But the fact remains that the Soviets believed that it was technically possible to take human beings to the Moon and that all the natural obstacles, such as the Van Allen belts, deep space radiation or temperature extremes on the Moon, could be overcome.

How come the Soviets didn't realize the hoax and didn't expose it to the world?

The spies and the electronic eavesdropping outposts of the Soviet Union would have been quite capable of detecting any attempt at faking the flight trajectories and the radio and TV transmissions from the Moon by broadcasting them from somewhere else. The Soviets had every reason to want to expose any fraud perpetrated by their enemy and humiliate the United States before the world. Yet they kept quiet and even congratulated America for the Moon landings. How come?

Some hoax theorists argue that the silence of the Soviets was bought by the United States by giving them massive amounts of desperately needed grain, as mentioned in Chapter 10, or by threatening to reveal Russia's hidden space failures, such as the alleged deaths of the cosmonauts that preceded Yuri Gagarin, who according to this theory wasn't the first human being to fly in space but merely the first one to come back alive.

Of course, using one unproven conspiracy theory to justify another one isn't a very sound approach to finding out the truth. Moreover, history shows that during the Cold War the United States and Russia seldom had any qualms about exposing each other's atrocities and deceptions, so it seems rather unlikely that they somehow reached a gentleman's agreement about human spaceflight, which in the 1960s was a crucial aspect of political propaganda and prestige.

How many photographs and how many hours of live TV and movie footage would have had to be faked?

Ask the conspiracy theorist to give an estimate of the numbers involved in faking the photos and the footage of the Apollo missions. He probably will be quite far from the actual figures. You should point out that the photographs that were taken on the Moon and therefore allegedly would have to be faked are *over 6,500*. Just the TV and film footage shot on the lunar surface by the Apollo 16 mission amounts to *over fourteen hours*, and there were six Moon landings.

You should also point out that all this visual record would have to be faked without any of the errors in continuity or inconsistencies that occur regularly in movies and TV shows.

Using 1960s special effects, how did they prevent the film crew and equipment from being reflected in the astronauts' mirror-like visors?

Ask the Moon hoax proponent to explain in detail how this remarkable result could be achieved using only the non-digital visual effects available at the time of the Moon landings. Point out that the astronauts' visors often reflect quite clearly the details of the ground and of the nearby equipment and vehicles and therefore would have revealed any film crew and their bulky 1960s-era television and film cameras, especially in close-ups.

The only plausible way to conceal the crew and their equipment would have been not to use them at all: in other words, use only the still, TV or movie camera shown in the visor's reflection and have another astronaut-actor hold it, or mount it on a tripod or a replica of the Rover. But this would have entailed renouncing any extra equipment needed to create the special effects. These constraints would therefore make it even harder to achieve a credible level of fakery.

For example, the "cameraman" would have had to wear a spacesuit and the movie set would have had to include the so-called "fourth wall", the one behind the camera, and simulate the lunar sky and terrain through a full circle. All this would have to be achieved in a vacuum, with all the safety risks that this entailed, to obtain the correct swinging of the flag and the parabolic motion of the dust kicked up by the astronauts. All this leads to the next question.

Using 1960s special effects, how did they obtain the parabolic, swirl-free motion of the dust kicked up by the astronauts or by the Moon buggy?

This effect can only be obtained in a vacuum, so ask the conspiracy theorist for a technical description of how it would have been possible to achieve it without actually taking people and a buggy to the Moon and filming them there. Of course, no digital tricks would be allowed, because there was no broadcast-quality computer graphics in the 1960s.

How big was the set?

The Apollo TV footage includes long, unbroken sequences such as the one summarized in Figure 12-2 and taken from the Apollo 16 moonwalks. Note how the astronauts walk a great distance away from the camera without reaching the end of the alleged movie set. The boulder in the background turns out to be actually as big as a house. Ask the conspiracy theorist how this effect could be obtained on Earth.

Figure 12-2. Apollo 16: Young and Duke visit House Rock, which is 220 meters (720 feet) away from the camera and is behind the astronaut on the right in the first image. In the last image, the arrow indicates one of the helmets of the astronauts.

You see revealing mistakes everywhere: why would the fakery be so amateurish?

Ask the hoax theorist to explain why a conspiracy on which no less that the world reputation of the entire United States depended would have been entrusted to a bunch of bungling amateurs who made such egregious (alleged) mistakes as forgetting to add the stars or letting the flag flutter in the nonexistent lunar wind. Then ask to explain how come not one of their supervisors and project managers noticed their blunders.

How come not one professional spaceflight expert agrees with you?

Are they all bribed or threatened into silence? How does this world-wide cover-up work, exactly? Does everyone who earns a degree in aerospace engineering or becomes an astronaut get a visit from the Men in Black, warning him or her not to talk about the Apollo fakery? And what happens to those who refuse to cooperate? Are they murdered? Are their brains zapped and stealthily reprogrammed?

Ask the conspiracy theorist how come all the alleged anomalies in the photographs, in the film and video recordings and in the technology of the Apollo project are seen as evidence of fakery only by people with no significant aerospace qualifications, while those who actually work in the field have no doubt whatsoever about the reality of the Moon landings. Is it really believable that unskilled amateurs can find real anomalies that these experts have failed to notice and admit? And isn't it rather arrogant for a Moon hoax theorist to imply that by watching a few Youtube videos and looking at a few low-quality photos he or she can outsmart an astronaut or an aerospace engineer with years of practical experience?

13. Real secrets
of the Moon landings

Moon hoax theories have a huge advantage over dry technical reports: they're great stories to tell. However, there's no need to make up absurd tales of conspiracy to bring out the excitement and wonder of an actual trip to the Moon.

Many details of the Apollo missions were not revealed or discussed publicly at the time of the flights because they were private, embarrassing or politically inappropriate. NASA was keen to project a squeaky-clean, flawlessly heroic image of its astronauts, and the press was somewhat complicit in this patriotic intent, so the unsavory or less uplifting aspects of Moon missions were left untold. This chapter is just a teaser of the some of these rarely shared stories.

13.1 Aldrin's pause on the LM ladder

For decades, people who studied the recordings of the live TV broadcast of the first moonwalk were puzzled by Buzz Aldrin's long pause halfway down the ladder (Figure 13-1) before he joined Neil Armstrong on the surface of the Moon.

Was it dictated by fear? Was it a moment of disorientation caused by motion in an unconfined environment with unfamiliar one-sixth gravity? Was it an instant of spiritual contemplation

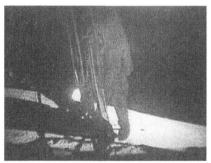

Figure 13-1. Aldrin pauses on the ladder.

of the amazing site? No such thing. Aldrin explained the true nature of this mysterious pause in the 2007 documentary *In the Shadow of the Moon*.

> *We had it in our flight plan that we'd take the first 10-15 seconds down at the bottom of the ladder, sort of hold on to the edge of the landing gear and just sort of check our stability and so forth... So*

that's when I decided to take that period of time to, uh, to take care of a bodily function of slightly filling up the urine bag... so that I wouldn't be troubled with having to do that later on... Everybody has their firsts on the Moon, and that one hasn't been disputed by anybody.

13.2 Suspicious corrosion

In a complex endeavor such as space launch, countless things can go wrong. Usually it's the unexpected problems that cause the greatest trouble.

For example, the *Reliability Bulletin* of March 8, 1968 (Figure 13-2) reported serious corrosion problems in the stainless steel pipes of pads 34 and 37 at the Kennedy Space Center.

The report revealed the cause of the corrosion: the combined effects of uric acid and chloride. While the chloride came from the launch site environment, the uric acid did not:

Figure 13-2. The pipe corrosion report reveals an unexpected source of acid.

The occasional practice of personnel relieving themselves from the umbilical tower has been suspected for some time... Personal interviews at the launch site confirmed the likely human source based on observed practices.

In another somewhat similar case, reported in *Memorable Moments - My Years with the Apollo Program* by John T. Everett, the hydrogen leak detector of the launch tower was triggered, causing the activation of the water sprinkler safety system, which led to several million dollars' worth of damage. It later emerged that the highly sensitive detector had reacted to the *"gaseous emissions of* [a] *robust engineer"* from Chrysler who was changing a component in the vicinity..[89]

---

89 http://www.technologysite.org/HomePageFiles/MemorableMomentsApollo4Small.pdf.

13.3 Smuggling on the Moon: the Sieger covers

Scott, Worden and Irwin, the astronauts of the Apollo 15 flight (Figure 13-3), took to the Moon 398 stamped letters in addition to the 243 authorized by NASA for commemorative philatelical purposes.

They did this on behalf of H. Walter Eiermann, who in turn was working for a German stamp collector, Hermann Sieger. The agreement was that one hundred of these covers would be sold by the astronauts to Eiermann for 7,000 dollars, deposited on a foreign account for each astronaut, while the other 298 would be kept by the crew as souvenirs.

Figure 13-3. David Scott, Alfred Worden and James Irwin. NASA photo AP15-S71-22401 (cropped).

Eiermann, however, sold his covers to Sieger, who put them on sale shortly after the Apollo 15 flight. Financial gain from the flights by the Apollo crews was no longer permitted (contrary to what had happened with the Mercury astronauts), and the event led to a public scandal that also involved Jack Swigert (Apollo 13). Swigert, Scott and Worden were removed from service as astronauts and Irwin left NASA to start religious preaching.

13.4 Secretive commemoration

Near the end of their historical moonwalk, while Neil Armstrong was still on the surface and Buzz Aldrin had already reentered the LM, the two astronauts had a rather cryptic exchange of words over the open radio channel. Armstrong asked Aldrin, *"How about that package out of your sleeve? Get that?"*

"No," answered Aldrin tersely. *"OK, I'll get it when I get up there,"* Armstrong replied. After a brief pause, Aldrin asked *"Want it now?"* and Armstrong answered *"Guess so".* Another pause and then Armstrong asked *"OK?"* and Aldrin answered *"OK".* Nothing more was said about the *"package".*

They were referring guardedly to a set of commemorative items to be left on the Moon: an Apollo 1 patch, in honor of Gus Grissom, Ed White and Roger Chaffee, who had died in a fire in their spacecraft during a preflight test; an olive branch sculpted in gold, identical to those that the two Apollo 11 moonwalkers had taken to the Moon for their wives and for Michael Collins' wife (Figure 13-4); and a small silicon disk that contained written messages from several heads of state from all over the world and other data.

This was the official content list of the package, as reported in NASA press release 69-83F on July 13, 1969. But according to Aldrin's book *Men from Earth*, published twenty years later, there were also other politically very sensitive items: two Soviet medals, one in honor of cosmonaut Vladimir Komarov, who had died at the end of his Soyuz 1 flight due to parachute failure, and one for Yuri Gagarin, the first man to orbit the Earth, who had perished in a plane crash in 1968.

Figure 13-4. A gold olive branch similar to the one left on the Moon by the Apollo 11 crew. Detail of NASA photo S69-40941.

This was a gesture of chivalry among spacefarers that at the time of the Cold War, when the Soviet Union was seen as a deadly enemy, might not be appreciated by many and therefore was kept confidential.

13.5 Naked women on the Moon

In November 1969, Apollo 12's Alan Bean and Charles "Pete" Conrad landed on the Moon while Richard Gordon remained in lunar orbit. It became clear immediately that this was not going to be a solemn expedition. Conrad's first remark as he stepped off the ladder of the LM set the tone by referencing humorously Neil Armstrong's timeless words: *"Man, that may have been a small one for Neil, but that's a long one for me!"* Conrad was referring both to his own short stature and to a bet made with Italian journalist Oriana Fallaci to prove to her that the astronauts' words were not scripted by NASA.

But roughly two and a half hours into their moonwalk, things took a strange turn: the two astronauts began giggling so much that there was some concern that their oxygen supply might be malfunctioning or that they had been affected by some mysterious space sickness.

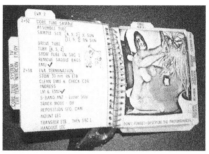

Figure 13-5. Alan Bean's cuff checklist, with Playmate Cynthia Myers, Miss December 1968.

Conrad explained the somewhat alarming laughter in the December 1994 issue of *Playboy*. The two lunar astronauts had a so-called *cuff checklist* (basically a small ring binder with laminated fireproof sheets, strapped to their left sleeve) as a reminder of the procedures to be performed. It was a simple and effective solution.

However, Dave Scott and Jim Irwin, members of the mission's backup crew, had arranged a prank: they had inserted Playmate photographs, photocopied onto fireproof paper, among the pages of the cuff checklists, adding captions full of *double entendres*.

Conrad found Miss September 1967, Angela Dorian, with the caption *"Seen any interesting hills & valleys?"*, and Miss October 1967, Reagan Wilson (*"Preferred tether partner"*); Bean found Miss December 1968, Cynthia Myers (*"Don't forget – describe the protuberances"*, Figure 13-5), and Miss January 1969, Leslie Bianchini (*"Survey - Her activity"*).

Richard Gordon, in the Command Module orbiting the Moon, also found a Playmate hidden on board, in the form of the current month's *Playboy* calendar page, featuring DeDe Lind (formerly Miss August 1967), which had been fixed with Velcro inside one of the Command Module's cabinet doors.

This is not a legend or a colorful anecdote: the Playmate pictures from the cuff checklist are on NASA's website and the calendar page provided to Gordon was auctioned among the Apollo 12 memorabilia in January 2011..[90]

While this might be seen as just a curious case of nudity on NASA's usually very prudish website and as the first instance of erotica taken to another world, it also shows that despite the hype and heroic rhetoric that often surrounds them, astronauts are, after all, very human beings, with the same urges and weaknesses as the rest of us.

And this is what makes their accomplishments so great.

Figure 13-6. Pete Conrad. His cuff checklist is open on the page with Reagan Wilson, Miss October 1967. Detail from NASA photo AS12-48-7071.

---

90 *Apollo 12 Playboy Stowaway to be Auctioned*, by Ian O'Neill, *Discovery News*, January 11, 2011.

13.6 The President's speech in case of Moon disaster

In 1999 it was disclosed that famed journalist and presidential speech-writer William Safire had drafted a message that then President Nixon would have read to the nation if Armstrong and Aldrin had been stranded on the Moon with no way to get home. H. R. Haldeman was the Chief of Staff of the White House at the time.

Ao: H.R. Haldeman

from: Bill Safire

July 18, 1969

IN EVENT OF MOON DISASTER:

Fate has ordained that the men who went to the moon to explore in peace will stay on the moon to rest in peace.

These brave men, Neil Armstrong and Edwin Aldrin, know that there is no hope for their recovery. But they also know that there is hope for mankind in their sacrifice.

These two men are laying down their lives in mankind's most noble goal: the search for truth and understanding.

They will be mourned by their families and friends; they will be mourned by the nation; they will be mourned by the people of the world; they will be mourned by a Mother Earth that dared send two of her sons into the unknown.

In their exploration, they stirred the people of the world to feel as one; in their sacrifice, they bind more tightly the brotherhood of man.

In ancient days, men looked at the stars and saw their heroes in the constellations. In modern times, we do much the same, but our heroes are epic men of flesh and blood.

Others will follow, and surely find their way home. Man's search will not be denied. But these men were the first, and they will remain the foremost in our hearts.

For every human being who looks up at the moon in the nights to come will know that there is some corner of another world that is forever mankind.

PRIOR TO THE PRESIDENT'S STATEMENT:

The President should telephone each of the widows-to-be.

AFTER THE PRESIDENT'S STATEMENT, AT THE POINT WHEN NASA ENDS COMMUNICATIONS WITH THE MEN:

A clergyman should adopt the same procedure as a burial at sea, commending their souls to "the deepest of the deep," concluding with the Lord's Prayer.

14. Remembering the fallen

Many men and women have lost their lives during spaceflight and for this reason have been commemorated by the media and by the general public. However, there are also many people who were selected as astronauts or cosmonauts and worked on these missions but died before reaching space. Their sacrifice and their contributions are often neglected, and the fate of one of them was made public only several years later, when the secrets of the Soviet space program were exposed.

The *In memoriam* subsection of the introduction to this book listed the names of these forgotten spacefarers; here is some information about them, as a supplement to the details already given in this book for some of these brave men and women.

Michael James Adams

A USAF major and test pilot, Adams was selected as an astronaut for the MOL (*Manned Orbiting Laboratory*) military project, which was intended to provide manned space stations to be used for monitoring and reconnaissance of the territory of potential enemies.

The MOL project was canceled before any actual launches were made, but Adams still flew into space when he piloted the X-15 experimental hypersonic rocket plane and reached an altitude of 81 kilometers (266,000 feet) on November 15, 1967. This qualified him as an astronaut even according to USAF criteria, which were stricter than NASA's.

This flight, however, was fatal: a malfunction of the electrical systems of the X-15 and an initial disorientation caused the spacecraft to assume an incorrect attitude, which induced a spin at Mach 5 (five times the speed of sound). The stresses overwhelmed the airframe, which broke up, killing Adams. He was the only fatality of the highly experimental X-15 program, which included Neil Armstrong among its pilots. Many of the records set with the X-15 are still unbeaten.

Michael P. Anderson, David M. Brown, Kalpana Chawla, Laurel B. Clark, Rick D. Husband, William C. McCool, Ilan Ramon

The seven members of the crew of Space Shuttle *Columbia* died on February 1, 2003 during reentry. At liftoff, a fragment of the thermal insulation of the Shuttle's external tank had struck and damaged the thermal protection of the leading edge of the spacecraft's wing. The red-hot air that formed around the spacecraft during reentry penetrated the wing and partially melted its internal structure, which broke up catastrophically as *Columbia* was flying at 15 times the speed of sound at an altitude of approximately 55 kilometers (181,000 feet), killing the entire crew instantly.

Charles Arthur Bassett II and Elliot McKay See, Jr.

Charles Bassett II was a USAF captain, test pilot and member of the third group of astronauts chosen by NASA in October 1963; Elliot See was a US Navy engineer and test pilot and member of the second group of astronauts, selected in September 1962, in addition to being in charge of supervising the design and development of guidance and navigation systems for US spacecraft.

Bassett and See were assigned to the Gemini 8 mission, but on February 28, 1966 they died in the crash of their T-38 training jet as they attempted an instrument landing in low visibility conditions. Bassett was 34 years old; See was 38.

Valentin Bondarenko

Lieutenant Valentin Bondarenko was a fighter pilot in the Soviet air force. On April 28, 1960 he was selected for the first group of 29 cosmonauts and on May 31st of the same year he began training to fly the Vostok 1, the same spacecraft on which Yuri Gagarin would perform the first manned orbital flight in the history of mankind.

On March 23, 1961, at the end of the third day of a two-week experiment in a pressure chamber at the Institute for Biomedical Studies in Moscow, Bondarenko removed from his body the sensors that monitored his vital functions and cleaned himself with a wad of cotton impregnated with alcohol. He tossed the cotton, which fell onto an electric heater and caught fire, igniting the cosmonaut's woolen clothing. In the pure oxygen environment of the chamber, the flames raged uncontrollably, with devastating results.

It took half an hour to open the door of the chamber. By then, Bondar-enko had suffered third-degree burns on all of his body except for his feet, partly protected by his flight boots. He died in hospital after 16 hours of agony at the age of 24. According to some historical sources, the man assigned to stand by him and report his condition was Yuri Gagarin. Three weeks later, Gagarin flew in space and into the history books, presumably as a replacement for Valentin Bondarenko.

The Praesidium of the Supreme Soviet awarded Bondarenko the Order of the Red Star on June 17, 1961 and the Soviet defense minister issued secret orders that his family be *"given all that is necessary, as befits the family of a cosmonaut".*

The horrible death of the young pilot was kept secret until 1980. His face was deleted from the official Soviet photographs of the first six cosmonauts. Cosmonaut Alexei Leonov, questioned about the censor-ship of these photos and the rumors of cosmonauts who had died in secret, lied repeatedly to Western journalists. Bondarenko's death was revealed in Russia only in 1986, twenty-seven years later, by an article penned by Yaroslav Golovanov on *Izvestia*. No Soviet vehicle ever used a pure-oxygen atmosphere. A crater on the far side of the Moon bears his name.

Roger B. Chaffee, Virgil I. "Gus" Grissom, Ed H. White

On January 27, 1967, Grissom, White and Chaffee, astronauts of the Apollo space program, were on the launch pad, inside their Apollo 1 spacecraft, for a routine static systems test to prepare for their space-flight when fire broke out in the cabin. The pure-oxygen environment at atmospheric pressure turned the fire instantaneously into an inferno, which killed the three astronauts in less than thirty seconds. The sud-den cabin pressure increase jammed the hatch, which opened inward, blocking any attempt at escape and rescue.

The tragedy had an enormous impact on public opinion in the United States and forced NASA to rethink drastically its procedures and im-prove the redesign of the Apollo spacecraft that was already in pro-gress, introducing for example a hatch that could be opened easily and outward, removing most of the flammable components and using a mixed nitrogen and oxygen atmosphere for the launch phase. These modifications made the Apollo spacecraft much safer and more reli-able than they were initially. In a way, the success of the lunar missions is a direct consequence of the sacrifice of Grissom, White and Chaffee.

Georgi Dobrovolski, Viktor Patsayev, Vladislav Volkov

These three Soviet cosmonauts had completed successfully the first visit to Salyut 1, the first space station in the history of spaceflight, and were beginning their maneuvers for reentry on June 30, 1971, when the cabin of their Soyuz 11 spacecraft depressurized in a few seconds due to a damaged valve at an altitude of 168 kilometers (551,000 feet).

The valve was out of reach and the cosmonauts were not wearing pressure suits due to the tightness of the cabin and therefore died by suffocation. Dobrovolski was 43; Patsayev was 38; Volkov was 35. Their ashes are in the Kremlin, in Moscow.

Theodore Cordy Freeman

A USAF captain, aeronautical engineer and test pilot of experimental aircraft, Freeman was a member of the third group of astronauts selected by NASA in October 1963. He died on October 31, 1964, when the windshield of the T-38 aircraft he was piloting was struck by a goose and windshield fragments were ingested by the engines; Freeman ejected, but his altitude was insufficient and his parachute didn't have time to open. He was 34 years old. Freeman was the first designated US astronaut to die during the space program.

Edward Galen Givens, Jr.

A USAF major and test pilot, Givens was selected in April 1966 for the fifth group of astronauts, composed of 19 men. He completed his astronaut training and was assigned to the backup crew of Apollo 7.

His group was intended to provide the astronaut pilots for the Apollo Applications Program, which at the time was intended as a series of ten Moon landings and thirty flights to space stations in Earth orbit. Almost all the other members of this group went to space on Apollo, Skylab or Shuttle flights, but Ed Givens died in a car accident on June 6, 1967. He was 37 years old.

Gregory Jarvis, Christa McAuliffe, Ronald McNair, Ellison Onizuka, Judith Resnick, Francis "Dick" Scobee, Michael J. Smith

The entire crew of Space Shuttle *Challenger* died during liftoff on January 28, 1986.

One minute and thirteen seconds after their spacecraft had left the launch pad, one of the gaskets of the lateral solid-propellant boosters broke due to the intense cold that it had experienced overnight on the pad, allowing a tongue of flame to strike the external tank, full of liquid oxygen and hydrogen. The tank ruptured and its fuel ignited catastrophically while the Shuttle was at an altitude of approximately 15 kilometers (48,000 feet) and America was watching helplessly as the tragedy was broadcast live on national television.

The aerodynamic stresses broke up the Shuttle, but the cabin remained almost intact, protecting the astronauts (who had no usable means of escape) until impact occurred in the ocean at over 330 kilometers per hour (200 mph).

The *Challenger* disaster was the first loss of a US crew during spaceflight.

Vladimir Komarov

Komarov's Soyuz 1 spacecraft departed from the Baikonur cosmodrome on April 23, 1967, and showed problems right after the climb to space. One of its solar panels failed to open, leading to a shortage of onboard power and making attitude corrections difficult. After thirteen orbits, the automatic stabilization system had failed completely and the manual one was only partially functional.

The decision was taken to abort the mission, and five orbits later the spacecraft began reentry. The drogue parachute open properly, but the main chute did not, due to a faulty pressure sensor. Komarov opened the spare parachute, which caught in the drogue chute that had not been jettisoned. The spacecraft was slowed only partially and struck the ground at approximately 140 kilometers per hour (90 mph), killing Komarov instantly.

Robert H. Lawrence, Jr.

A USAF major and test pilot, Robert Lawrence was chosen in June 1967 for the third group of US Air Force astronauts that were intended to fly in space as part of the MOL military space station project. He thus became the first African-American designated astronaut.

He provided important contributions to the space program, as his test flights with modified aircraft were fundamental in developing the steep, unpowered glide paths that would be used by the Space Shuttle.

Lawrence, however, never flew in space. He died on December 8, 1967, in the crash of the F-104 supersonic trainer piloted by his trainee pilot as he was teaching him to perform a so-called "flare", one of the experimental landing maneuvers used by the spaceplanes of the period, such as the X-15, and developed and mastered by Lawrence. He was 31.

His name is on the Space Mirror Memorial at the Kennedy Space Center but is not among those left on the Moon on a commemorative plaque placed by the Apollo 15 astronauts in 1971. One of the reasons is that the Pentagon uses the "astronaut" designation only for those who have flown to an altitude of 80 kilometers (50 miles) or more; being merely selected does not qualify. His mission patch was taken to space by the Shuttle *Atlantis* during the STS-86 flight.

Clifton Curtis Williams, Jr.

A major of the US Marines and a test pilot, Williams was selected for NASA's third astronaut group in October 1963 and was assigned to the backup crews of Gemini 10 and Apollo 9.

He died on October 5, 1967, at the age of 35, when a mechanical failure of his T-38 supersonic trainer rendered the controls unusable and the plane entered an uncontrolled roll. Williams ejected, but he was flying too low and too fast for the ejector seat to work.

The Apollo 12 mission commemorated his loss with a patch bearing four stars (one for each of the astronauts who flew, plus one for Williams). Alan Bean, who had been his commander in the backup crew of Gemini 10, placed Williams' astronaut wings pin on the Moon.

15. References

Due to space and legibility constraints, it has not been possible to indicate explicitly the technical source of each fact reported in the preceding chapters. However, I have carefully kept track of all the sources in my notes, so if you need to know where I found a specific item of information, just e-mail me at *paolo.attivissimo@gmail.com*.

The main reference sources are listed in the following pages and are also useful as further reading on the subject. Many are available directly on the Internet: for the sake of brevity, I have not included links to all of them.

15.1 NASA reports, footage and photos on digital media

A full collection of the Apollo 11 photographs, digitized at the highest publicly available resolutions, and of the original uncropped color versions of the images used in this book is freely downloadable from MoonHoaxDebunked.com.

15.2 Public photo archives

Apollo Archive
  apolloarchive.com
  Photographs, timelines, schematics, simulators and many other documents.

Apollo Image Atlas (70mm)
  www.lpi.usra.edu/resources/apollo/catalog/70mm/
  Archive of the Apollo photographs taken on 70 mm film.

Apollo Image Atlas (35 mm Nikon)
  www.lpi.usra.edu/resources/apollo/catalog/35mm/
  Photographs taken on 35 mm film during the Apollo 17 flight.

Apollo Image Atlas (Metric Camera)
  www.lpi.usra.edu/resources/apollo/catalog/metric/

Photos from the automatic lunar surface mapping camera installed in the service module of Apollo 15, 16 and 17.

Apollo Image Atlas (Panoramic Camera)
www.lpi.usra.edu/resources/apollo/catalog/pan/
Photographs from the automatic panoramic lunar surface mapping camera installed in the service module of Apollo 15, 16 and 17.

Apollo Lunar Surface Closeup Camera (ALSCC)
www.lpi.usra.edu/resources/apollo/catalog/alscc/
Catalog of the stereo images of lunar soil taken by the closeup camera during the Apollo missions.

Gateway to Astronaut Photography of Earth
eol.jsc.nasa.gov
Despite the name, this site includes very high-resolution scans of the Apollo mission photographs, including the photos taken on the Moon.

LIFE Magazine
images.google.com/images?q=Apollo+source%3Alife
Pictures of the Apollo program taken from the well-known US magazine.

Lunar Orbiter Photo Gallery
www.lpi.usra.edu/resources/lunarorbiter
Collection of the lunar mapping images taken by the Lunar Orbiter automatic probes launched by the United States (1966-67).

Lunar Orbiter Photographic Atlas of the Moon
www.lpi.usra.edu/resources/lunar_orbiter
Lunar atlas based on the photographs taken by the Lunar Orbiter probes.

Lunar Panoramas
spacemodels.nuxit.net/Panoramas/index.htm
Panoramas created by merging digitally the original Apollo photographs taken on the Moon.

NASA Images
www.nasaimages.org
An immense catalog of photographs from all aspects of the US space program.

NIX - NASA Image Exchange
nix.nasa.gov
One of NASA's primary audio, photo and video archives.

Ranger Photographs of the Moon
www.lpi.usra.edu/resources/ranger
Lunar photographs taken by the United States' Ranger probes
(1961-65).

Science Photo
www.sciencephoto.com
Commercial catalog of science photographs, including images from
the space programs of several countries.

15.3 Technical reference sites

Apollo 11 Onboard Audio
www.nasa.gov/mission_pages/apollo/40th/apollo11_audio.html
Recordings and transcripts of the onboard conversations during the
Apollo 11 flight.

Apollo Artifacts
www.apolloartifacts.com
Vast private collection of Apollo spaceflight-related items.

Apollo Bibliography
history.nasa.gov/alsj/apollo.biblio.html
Photographs, documents, software, models, reference books and
sites.

Apollo Flight Journal
history.nasa.gov/afj/
Highly detailed and richly commented timeline of the Apollo flights,
including transcripts of all the radio communications and onboard
conversations.

Apollo Lunar Surface Journal
www.hq.nasa.gov/alsj
A full timeline of the lunar excursions, with commented transcripts
of every word, photograph and action of the moonwalkers.

Apollo Saturn Reference Page
www.apollosaturn.com
Technical documents related to the Saturn V booster.

Apollo Technical Data Library
www.cs.indiana.edu/sudoc/image_30000061709352/30000061709352/pdf/techdata.htm
Specific documents and manuals of the command module, of the

lunar module and of the Saturn V launcher; preliminary and final reports and press kits for each mission.

Apollo TV
www.apollotv.net
Information on the television coverage of the Apollo missions.

Chariots for Apollo: A History of Manned Lunar Spacecraft
http://www.hq.nasa.gov/office/pao/History/SP-4205/contents.html
A meticulously detailed history of the Apollo spacecraft.

Clementine Color Images of the Moon / Clementine Lunar Map
ser.sese.asu.edu/MOON/clem_color.html
www.nrl.navy.mil/clm
Collections of the images acquired by the United States' Clementine lunar probe (1994).

Consolidated Lunar Atlas
www.lpi.usra.edu/resources/cla
Photographic atlas of the Moon.

Deepcold
www.deepcold.com
Military space projects of the United States and the Soviet Union.

Encyclopedia Astronautica
Astronautix.com
Vast collection of technical and historical information on Russian and American manned spaceflights.

HORIZONS
ssd.jpl.nasa.gov/horizons.cgi
A NASA site that allows to calculate the apparent size, phase and position of any celestial body of our solar system as seen from any other body on any date (e.g., the appearance of the Earth as seen from the Moon).

Kàguya/Selene
wms.selene.jaxa.jp
www.jaxa.jp/projects/sat/selene/index_e.html
Technical data, photographs and videos from the Japanese Kaguya/Selene lunar probe (2007-2009).

Lunar Reconnaissance Orbiter
lunar.gsfc.nasa.gov
centauri.larc.nasa.gov/lro
Sites of the probe that obtained the first images of the Apollo spacecraft on the Moon in 2009.

Moonport
www.hq.nasa.gov/office/pao/History/SP-4204/cover.html
History of the lunar launch facilities of the United States.

NASA JSC Transcript Collection (Mercury to Apollo)
www.jsc.nasa.gov/history/mission_trans/mission_transcripts.htm
Collected transcripts of the radio communications of US manned spaceflights.

NASA Office of Logic Design
klabs.org/history/history_docs/mit_docs/index.htm
Archive of documents related to the navigation and control computers of the Apollo spacecraft.

NASA Technical Reports Server
ntrs.nasa.gov
Huge collection of technical reports covering the entire US space program and the scientific knowledge gained from spaceflight.

PBS Race to the Moon
www.pbs.org/wgbh/amex/moon/index.html
Extensive site providing additional information in support of the PBS documentary *Race to the Moon.*

Radiation Effects and Analysis
radhome.gsfc.nasa.gov/top.htm
One of the main archives for documents regarding the effects of radiation in relation to spaceflight, managed by the Goddard Spaceflight Center.

Russian Space Web
www.russianspaceweb.com
News and history of the Russian space program.

The Apollo Program (1963-1972)
nssdc.gsfc.nasa.gov/planetary/lunar/apollo.html
Archive of the National Space Science Data Center, containing documents on all the Apollo missions, including the unmanned test flights.

The Space Race
www.thespacerace.com
Site dedicated to the Mercury, Gemini and Apollo projects; not affiliated with NASA.

Unmanned Spaceflight
www.unmannedspaceflight.com
Site focusing on news regarding space missions by unmanned vehicles.

We Choose the Moon
www.wechoosethemoon.org
Interactive site celebrating the fortieth anniversary of the first
manned Moon landing, with detailed animations, sounds and
videos of all the key phases of the Apollo 11 mission.

Working on the Moon: Lessons from Apollo
workingonthemoon.com/index.html
Documents and experiences of the Apollo lunar excursions, reex-
amined for their usefulness for future manned missions to the
Moon.

15.4 Technical books and documents

35 Years Ago, "One Small Step...". Jack Yanosov. In QST, February 2005.

Adventures in Celestial Mechanics: A First Course in the Theory of Orbits.
Victor G. Szebehely, University of Texas Press, Austin (1989).

*ALSEP Data Handling Estimates. BellComm Memorandum for File B69
05062.* R.J. Pauly (1969).

An Annotated Bibliography of the Apollo Program. Edited by Roger D.
Launius and J.D. Hunley and published as *Monographs in Aerospace History*, n.o 2 (1994).

An Introduction to Celestial Mechanics. Moulton, Forest R.. Dover Publications, New York (1970).

An overview of medical-biological radiation hazards in earth orbits.
Stauber, M. C.; Rossi, M. L.; Stassinopoulos, E. G., Goddard Space Flight
Center (1984).

Apollo 7 – The NASA Mission Reports, Robert Godwin, Apogee Books;
ISBN 1896522645.

Apollo 8 – The NASA Mission Reports, Robert Godwin, Apogee Books;
ISBN 1896522661.

Apollo 9 – The NASA Mission Reports, Robert Godwin, Apogee Books;
ISBN 1896522513.

Apollo 10 – The NASA Mission Reports, Robert Godwin, Apogee Books;
ISBN 1896522688.

*Apollo 10 Color Television, Westinghouse Defense and Space Center News
Release* (1969).

Apollo 10 Optical Tracking, in *Sky and Telescope*, July 1969, pages 62-63.

Apollo 11 – The NASA Mission Reports, Volume 1, Robert Godwin, Apogee Books; ISBN 189652253X.

Apollo 11 – The NASA Mission Reports, Volume 2, Robert Godwin, Apogee Books; ISBN 1896522491.

Apollo 11 – The NASA Mission Reports, Volume 3, Robert Godwin, Apogee Books; ISBN 1896522858.

Apollo 11 Photography, 70-mm, 16-mm and 35-mm Frame Index, National Space Science Data Center (1970).

Apollo 11 Technical Air-to-Ground Voice Transcription. Manned Spacecraft Center (1969).

Apollo 12 – The NASA Mission Reports, Volume 1, Robert Godwin, Apogee Books; ISBN 1896522548.

Apollo 12 – The NASA Mission Reports, Volume 2, Robert Godwin, Apogee Books; ISBN 1894959167.

Apollo 13 – The NASA Mission Reports, Robert Godwin, Apogee Books; ISBN 1896522556.

Apollo 13 Television. Westinghouse press release, 1970.

Apollo 14 – The NASA Mission Reports, Robert Godwin, Apogee Books; ISBN 1896522564.

Apollo 15 – The NASA Mission Reports, Robert Godwin, Apogee Books; ISBN 1896522572.

Apollo 15 Final Lunar Surface Television Operations Plan. NASA Manned Spacecraft Center (1971).

Apollo 16 – The NASA Mission Reports, Robert Godwin, Apogee Books; ISBN 1896522580.

Apollo 17 – The NASA Mission Reports, Robert Godwin, Apogee Books; ISBN 1896522599.

Apollo Black-and-White Television Scan Converter. M.V. Sullivan, *SMPTE Journal*, vol. 79, pages 621-625 (1970).

Apollo Color Television Camera. L.L. Niemyer, Jr., Westinghouse Defense and Space Center (1969).

Apollo Color Television Subsystem: Operation and Training Manual. Westinghouse (1971).

Apollo Experience Report – TV Systems. Paul P. Coan, Manned Spaceflight Center Television Subsystem Manager, *NASA Technical Note TN D-7476* (1973).

Apollo Lunar Landing Launch Window: the Controlling Factors and Constraints. Robin Wheeler, *Apollo Flight Journal.*

Apollo Lunar Television Camera: Operations Manual. Stan Lebar, Westing house Defense and Space Center (1968).

Apollo Unified S-Band System. K.E. Peltzer, Goddard Space Flight Center (1966).

Apollo: Race to the Moon. Charles Murray and Catherine Bly Cox. Touchstone Books (1990); ISBN 9780671706258.

Apollo: The Definitive Sourcebook. Richard W. Orloff, David M. Harland. Springer (2006); ISBN 0387300430.

Apollo - The Lost and Unflown Missions. David Shayler. Springer (2002); ISBN 9781852335755.

Communications on the Moon. In *Electronics World* (August 1969).

Comparison of Measured LM/EVA Link Transmission Losses on Apollo 15 with Predicted Values. BellComm Memorandum for File B71 12012. I.I. Rosenblum (1971).

EVA Communications from Surveyor III Site on Apollo 12. BellComm Memorandum for File B69 10020. I.I. Rosenblum (1969).

EVA VHF Communications with LM on Apollo 15 Traverses. BellComm Technical Memorandum TM-71-2034-2. I.I. Rosenblum (1971).

First Color TV from Space. Warren C. Wetmore, in *Aviation Week and Space Technology,* pages 18-20 (May 26, 1969).

Full Moon. Michael Light, Alfred A. Kropf (1999); ISBN 0375414940.

Fundamentals of Astrodynamics. Roger R. Bate, Donald D. Mueller, and Jerry E. White. Dover Publications, New York (1971).

Genesis: The Story of Apollo 8. Robert Zimmerman. Random House, New York (1998).

Ground Control Television Television Engineering Notebook. Richard Bohlmann et al., Manned Spacecraft Center (4/1971 - 4/1972).

Ground-Controlled Television Assembly: Final Report. RCA R-3901-F (1972).

Ground-Controlled Television Assembly: Interim Final Report. RCA R-3838F (1972).

Ground-Controlled Television Assembly: Operation and Checkout Manual. RCA (1971).

How Apollo Flew to the Moon, David Woods, Praxis Publishing (2008); ISBN 9780387716756.

Journey to the Moon: The History of the Apollo Guidance Computer. Hall, Eldon C. American Institute of Aeronautics and Astronautics, Reston, Va. (1996).

Liftoff: The Story of America's Adventure in Space. Michael Collins, Grove Press, New York (1988).

Live TV from the Moon, Dwight Steven-Boniecki (2010). Apogee Books; ISBN 9781926592169.

Lunar Module Reference. World Spaceflight News, Progressive Management (2000).

Lunar Television Camera: Pre-Installation Acceptance Test Plan. NASA/MSC-SESD-28-105 (1968).

Lunar TV Camera: Statement of Work (Final Draft). NASA/MSC (1966).

Mankind's Giant Leap. Robert Hotz, in *Aviation Week and Space Technology*, page 17 (July 28, 1969).

Manned Space Flight Network (MSFN) Postmission Report on the AS-506 (Apollo 11) Mission. Goddard Spaceflight Center (1970).

Moon Lander: How We Developed the Lunar Module. Thomas J. Kelly. Smithsonian History of Aviation and Spaceflight Series, Dominick Pisano et al., eds. Smithsonian Institution Press, Washington, D.C. (2001).

Moon Missions: Mankind's First Voyages to Another World. William F. Mellberg, Plymouth Press, Michigan (1997).

Moonfire: The Epic Journey of Apollo 11. Norman Mailer and Colum McCann, Taschen GmbH (2010); ISBN 978-38-3652-077-5.

Network Controller's Mission Report Apollo 11 (1969).

On the Radiation Hazards of Space Flight. James A. Van Allen, University of Iowa, in *Physics and Medicine of the Atmospheres and Space*, O. O. Benson Jr and Hubertus Strughold, John Wiley & Sons (1960).

Optical Observations of Apollo 12, in *Sky and Telescope*, February 1970, pages 127-130.

Optical Observations of Apollo 8, Harold B. Liemon, in *Sky and Telescope*, March 1969, pages 156-160.

Photography Equipment and Techniques - A Survey of NASA Developments. Albert J. Derr, Technology Utilization Office, NASA (1972).

Proceedings of the Apollo Unified S-Band Technical Conference, Goddard Space Flight Center, July 14-15, 1965. K.E. Peltzer, Goddard Spaceflight Center (1965).

Radiation Hazards to Crews of Interplanetary Missions: Biological Issues and Research Strategies. Task Group on the Biological Effects of Space Radiation, Space Studies Board, Commission on Physical Sciences, Mathematics, and Applications of the National Research Council. National Academy Press (1997).

Radiation Plan for the Apollo Lunar Mission (1969).

Red Star in Orbit, James E. Oberg. Random House (1981); ISBN 0394514297.

Remembering the Space Age, Steven J. Dick (ed.) (2008); ISBN 9780160817236.

Report of Apollo 204 Review Board (1967).

Review of Particle Properties, Particle Data Group, Lawrence Berkeley Laboratory (1999).

Shooting the Apollo Moonwalks, Sam Russell, in *Apollo Lunar Surface Journal.*

Star-Crossed Orbits, James E. Oberg (2002). McGraw Hill; ISBN 0071374256.

Summary of Medical Experience in the Apollo 7 Through 11 Manned Spaceflights. C.A. Berry, in *Aerospace Medicine* 41 (May 1970): 500-19.

The Apollo 13 Accident, in *Sky and Telescope,* July 1970, page 14.

The Apollo Guidance Computer - Architecture and Operation, Frank O'Brien (2010). Praxis Publishing Ltd; ISBN 9781441908766.

The Color War Goes to the Moon. Stan Lebar, in *Invention & Technology,* Summer 1997.

The Lunar Television Camera. E.L. Svensson, in *Westinghouse Engineer* no. 3, pages 46-51 (March 1968).

The Probability of an ALSEP Accepting an Erroneous Command – BellComm Memorandum for File B69 12007. J.E. Johnson (1969).

The Radiation Environment. J. Barth, Goddard Spaceflight Center.

Theory of Orbits. Victor G. Szebehely, Academic Press, New York (1967).

Tracking Apollo to the Moon. Lindsay Hamish, Springer-Verlag London (2001).

Trajectories in the Earth-Moon Space with Symmetrical Free Return Properties. Arthur J. Schwaninger, *NASA Technical Note D-1833* (1963).

TV Show of the Century: A Travelogue with No Atmosphere. Stanley Lebar and Charles P. Hoffman, in *Electronics* (1967).

Where No Flag Has Gone Before: Political and Technical Aspects of Placing a Flag on the Moon. Anne Platoff, *NASA Contractor Report 188251* (1993).

Where No Man Has Gone Before: A History of NASA's Apollo Lunar Expeditions. William David Compton. Dover Publications (2010); ISBN 9780486478883.

15.5 Biographies

A Man on the Moon: The Voyages of the Apollo Astronauts. Andrew Chaikin. Penguin Books, New York (1994). Republished by Penguin (2007); ISBN 014311235X.

All-American Boys: An Insider's Look at the U.S. Space Program. Walter Cunningham. First edition: MacMillan (1977); ISBN 0025292404. Reissue: Ipicturebooks (2010); ISBN 1876963247.

Apollo EECOM - Journey of a Lifetime. Sy Liebergot and David Harland. Apogee Books (2006); ISBN 9781894959889.

Carrying the Fire: An Astronaut's Journeys. Michael Collins. Farrar, Strauss, and Giroux (1974). Republished by Cooper Square Press (2001); ISBN 081541028X.

Countdown: An Autobiography. Frank Borman and Robert J. Serling. Silver Arrow Books (1988); ISBN 0688079296.

Failure Is Not an Option. Gene Kranz. Berkeley Publishing Group, New York (2000). Republished by Simon & Schuster (2009); ISBN 1439148813.

Falling to Earth – An Apollo Astronaut's Journey to the Moon. Al Worden and Francis French. Smithsonian Books (2011); ISBN 9781588343093.

First Man: The Life of Neil A. Armstrong. James R. Hansen. Simon & Schuster (2006); ISBN 074325631-X.

Flight: My Life in Mission Control. Chris Kraft. Plume (2002); ISBN 0452283043.

From the Trench of Mission Control to the Craters of the Moon. Glynn Lunney, Jerry Bostick, David Reed, Charles Deiterich, Maurice Kennedy, William Boone, William Stoval. Blurb.com (2011).

Magnificent Desolation. Buzz Aldrin and Ken Abraham. Harmony Books (2009); ISBN 9780307463456.

Moon Shot: The Inside Story of America's Race to the Moon. Alan Shepard and Deke Slayton. Turner Publishing (1994); ISBN 1570361673.

Moondust: In Search of the Men Who Fell to Earth. Andrew Smith. Bloomsbury (2005); ISBN 0747563691.

Moonwalker. Charlie and Dotty Duke. Oliver-Nelson Books (1990); ISBN 0840791062.

The Last Man on the Moon. Eugene Cernan and Don Davis. St. Martin's Press, New York (1999); ISBN-10: 0312263511.

Two Sides of the Moon: Our Story of the Cold War Space Race. David Scott and Alexei Leonov. Pocket Books (2004); ISBN 0743450671.

15.6 Moon-related items, documents and memorabilia for purchase

Astronaut Store
www.astronautstore.org
Models, flight items and autographs. Site managed by the Mercury astronauts.

Collectionspace
www.collectionspace.it
Rare books, meteorite samples, autographs, flight items and models (in Italian).

Collectspace
www.collectspace.com
Autographs, items from space missions and models.

Footagevault
www.footagevault.com
High-definition digital transfers of spaceflight film and TV footage.

Kennedy Space Center
www.thespaceshop.com
Space-themed models, clothes, pins and other collectibles.

Moonpans.com
www.moonpans.com
Panoramic posters created by stitching together digitally the original photographs shot on the Moon.

Orbitec
www.orbitec.com
Regolith simulant (technical replica of moondust, used for testing lunar vehicles and instruments).

Spacecraft Films
www.spacecraftfilms.com
DVDs and Blu-rays containing the unabridged original footage of the flights; documentaries on the American space program.

Up-Ship.com
www.up-ship.com/drawndoc/drawndocspacesaturn.htm
Prints and technical blueprints of the Apollo spacecraft, of the Saturn rockets and of many other built or designed space vehicles.

15.7 Books by Moon hoax proponents

Dark Mission: The Secret History of NASA. Richard Hoagland and Mike Bara (2007). Feral House; ISBN 1-9325-9526-0.

Dark Moon: Apollo and the Whistle-Blowers. Mary Bennett and David S. Percy (2001). Adventures Unlimited Press; ISBN 0-9328-1390-9.

Der Mond ist ganz anders! Widersprüche und Falschaussagen. Gernot L. Geise (1985, 2003). EFODON e.V., Hohenpeißenberg; ISBN 3-9804300-6-5.

Die dunkle Seite von Apollo. Wer flog wirklich zum Mond? Gernot L. Geise (2002, 2006). Michaels-Verlag; ISBN 3-89539-607-9.

Die Schatten von Apollo. Hintergründe der gefälschten Mondflüge. Gernot L. Geise (2003). Michaels-Verlag, Edition EFODON; ISBN 3-89539-612-2.

Lumières sur la Lune – La NASA a t-elle menti! Philippe Lheureux (2002). Editions Carnot; ISBN-10 2912362490. Published in English as *Moon Landings: Did NASA lie?* Philippe Lheureux (2003). Carnot USA Books; ISBN-10 1592090419.

NASA Mooned America! Ralph Rene, self-published (1994).

One Small Step? The Great Moon Hoax and the Race to Dominate Earth from Space. Gerhard Wisnewski (author) and Johanna Collis (translator) (2008). Clairview Books; ISBN 1905570120.

We Never Went to the Moon. Bill Kaysing, self-published (1974).

We Never Went to the Moon: America's Thirty Billion Dollar Swindle. Bill Kaysing and Randy Reid (1976). Health Research Books; ISBN 0-7873-0487-5.

15.8 Websites supporting the Moon hoax theories

Atmosphärenfahrt-Index – die Beweise für die Mondlüge
www.geschichteinchronologie.ch/atmosphaerenfahrt-index.html
(in German)

Aulis Online
www.aulis.com

Moonmovie
www.moonmovie.com

Wagging the Moondoggie
davesweb.cnchost.com

15.9 DVDs, videos and TV shows supporting hoax claims

A Funny Thing Happened on the Way to the Moon. Bart Sibrel (2001).

Apollo 11 Press Conference. Bart Sibrel (2004).

Apollo 11: Monkey Business. Bart Sibrel (2004).

Apollo One Accident Report. Bart Sibrel (2007).

Astronauts Gone Wild. Bart Sibrel (2004).

Conspiracy Theory: Did We Land on the Moon? Fox TV (2001).

Was it Only a Paper Moon? James M. Collier (1997).

What Happened on the Moon - An Investigation Into Apollo. David Groves and David Percy (2000).

15.10 Parodies that hoax proponents believe are true

Alternative 3 by Christopher Miles (Anglia Television, 1977).

Capricorn One by Peter Hyams (Associated General Films, 1978).

Dark Side of the Moon (Opération Lune) by William Karel (Arte France/Point du Jour, 2002).

Moontruth (The Viral Factory, 2002).

15.11 Books with rebuttals to Moon hoax claims

Bad Astronomy: Misconceptions and Misuses Revealed, from Astrology to the Moon Landing "Hoax". Phil Plait (2002). J. Wiley & Sons, ISBN 0471409766.

15.12 Neutral or debunking DVDs, videos and TV shows

For All Mankind (Apollo Associates/FAM Productions, 1989).

In the Shadow of the Moon (Discovery Films/FilmFour, 2007).

Moonwalk One (NASA/The Attic Room Ltd, 1970/2009).

Mythbusters – NASA Moon Landing (no. 104, August 27, 2008).

Penn & Teller: Bullshit! – Conspiracy Theories (no. 3-03, May 9, 2005).

The Truth Behind the Moon Landings (Discovery Science, 2003).

When We Left Earth: The NASA Missions (Dangerous Films, 2008).

Live from the Moon (Spacecraft Films, 2010).

15.13 Moon hoax debunking sites

AboveTopSecret
   www.abovetopsecret.com

ApolloHoax
   www.apollohoax.net

Bad Astronomy
   www.badastronomy.com/index.html

Clavius
   www.clavius.org (also available in German at *www.clavius.info*)

Rocket and Space Technology
   www.braeunig.us/space/

16. Apollo by the numbers

16.1 Apollo landing sites

Figure 16-1. The Apollo landing sites. A11 - Mare Tranquillitatis (Sea of Tranquility), July 1969; A12 - Oceanus Procellarum (Ocean of Storms), November 1969; A14 - Fra Mauro, February 1971; A15 - Mare Imbrium (Sea of Rains), July 1971; A16 - Descartes Highlands, April 1972; A17 - Taurus-Littrow Valley, December 1972. Photo credit: PA.

16.2 The Apollo missions

Missions are listed chronologically. CM = Command Module; LM = Lunar Module; CDR = Commander; LMP = Lunar Module Pilot; CMP = Command Module Pilot.

AS-201 ("Apollo 201")

Crew: none.

Launcher: Saturn IB.

LM: none.

Lunar orbit: none.

CM and LM call signs: not assigned (CM was present; LM was not).

Launch and return dates: February 26, 1966.

Lunar landing date and time: none.

Lunar landing site: none.

Number of moonwalks: none planned.

Mission duration: 37 minutes.

Time spent on the Moon: none planned.

Number of photographs taken: none. Automatic onboard movie cameras shot footage to acquire technical data.

Quantity of Moon rocks: none planned.

Rover: none.

Notes: This was the first flight of a Saturn IB launcher, which consisted of an uprated version of the first stage of the Saturn I (launched successfully 10 times between October 1961 and July 1965) and a new second stage, the S-IVB, which would later become the third stage of the Saturn V. The flight was suborbital, reaching a maximum altitude of 488 kilometers (303 miles), and carried into space a Block I Apollo command and service module that had been modified specifically for this launch.

This mission tested the ignition and restarting of the service module engine and tested the structure and heat shield of the command module with a reentry that was slower (29,000 km/h, 18,000 mph) but steeper than those planned for manned lunar missions.

AS-203

Crew: none.

Launch vehicle: Saturn IB.

LM: none.

Lunar orbit: none planned.

CM and LM call signs: none (no CM or LM present).

Launch and return dates: July 5, 1966.

Lunar landing date and time: none.

Lunar landing site: none.

Number of moonwalks: none planned.

Mission duration: 6 hours and 20 minutes.

Time spent on the Moon: none planned.

Number of photographs taken: none. Automatic onboard TV and movie cameras recorded the behavior of the hydrogen in the fuel tanks.

Quantity of Moon rocks: none planned.

Rover: none.

Notes: This flight was numerically out of sequence because it was scheduled initially as the third launch of the Saturn IB booster but was moved up due to delays in preparing the second scheduled flight.

AS-203 tested the behavior of the Instrument Unit and of the S-IVB stage, particularly of its fuel settling systems, in weightless conditions. It was also the first orbital flight of an S-IVB. The Apollo spacecraft was replaced with an aerodynamic fairing.

The system that provided continuous venting of the liquid hydrogen of the S-IVB was found to generate a modest but constant thrust that was sufficient, as expected, to settle the hydrogen in the tanks, preventing any weightless sloshing of the fuel, which would have prevented the stable supply of fuel to the engine. This was a key requirement in order to allow restarting of the J-2 engine of the S-IVB stage during a trip to the Moon.

AS-202

Crew: none.

Launch vehicle: Saturn IB.

LM: none.

Lunar orbit: none planned.

CM and LM call signs: not assigned (CM present, LM not present).

Launch and return dates: August 25, 1966.

Lunar landing date and time: none.

Lunar landing site: none.

Number of moonwalks: none planned.

Mission duration: 1 hour 33 minutes.

Time spent on the Moon: none planned.

Number of photographs taken: none. Automatic onboard movie and TV cameras shot footage to acquire technical data.

Quantity of Moon rocks: none planned.

Rover: none.

Notes: The main goals of this mission were testing the heat shield of the command module and performing structural qualification of the Saturn IB for carrying astronauts. Fuel cells were used for the first time as onboard power supply.

The command and service modules reached a maximum altitude of 1,144 kilometers (711 miles) along its suborbital path. The engine of the service module was started several times to demonstrate its restarting capability, which was essential for the maneuvers planned for flights to the Moon.

Reentry followed the intended trajectory, which made the Apollo command module "bounce" off the atmosphere, gaining altitude before final descent. This maneuver produced a double impact with the atmosphere and therefore generated a double peak in the heating of the heat shield which was very similar to the peak that would occur during crew return from the Moon. External temperature was estimated at 1,482 °C (2,700 °F); cabin temperature was 21 °C (70 °F).

Apollo 1 (AS-204)

Crew: Virgil Grissom (CDR), Edward White (Senior Pilot), Roger Chaffee (Pilot).

Launch vehicle: Saturn IB.

LM: none.

Lunar orbit: none planned.

CM and LM call signs: not assigned (CM present, LM not present).

Launch and return dates: January 27, 1967.

Lunar landing date and time: none.

Lunar landing site: none.

Number of moonwalks: none planned.

Mission duration: not applicable.

Time spent on the Moon: none planned.

Number of photographs taken: none.

Quantity of Moon rocks: none planned.

Rover: none.

Notes: The Apollo 1 flight, the first crewed mission of the Apollo program, was scheduled for liftoff on February 21, 1967, but the prime crew, consisting of Grissom, White and Chaffee, died in a fire inside the command module during a rehearsal of the countdown procedures on January 27, 1967.

The specific source of the fire was never pinpointed, but many materials used on board were flammable in the pure oxygen atmosphere at high pressure (1.13 atm, 16 psi) used for the test and combustion was initiated by an electrical short-circuit. Just seventeen seconds elapsed between the crew's first report of flames and the final radio transmission from the spacecraft. The internal overpressure made it impossible to open the hatch and attempt any rescue until the pressure buildup ruptured the vehicle, far too late to save the crew.

This disaster delayed the manned part of the Apollo project by 20 months. The Saturn IB launcher assigned to the Apollo 1 mission was later used for the first test flight of the lunar module (Apollo 5). The name Apollo 1 was reserved by NASA and removed from the progressive numbering of the missions in honor of the three dead astronauts.

Apollo 4 (AS-501)

Crew: none.

Launch vehicle: Saturn V.

LM: present, but only as an engineering mockup.

Lunar orbit: none planned.

CM and LM call signs: not assigned (CM and LM both present).

Launch and return dates: November 9, 1967.

Lunar landing date and time: none.

Lunar landing site: none.

Number of moonwalks: none planned.

Mission duration: 8 hours 37 minutes.

Time spent on the Moon: none planned.

Number of photographs taken: 715 (with 70 mm automatic still camera). Automatic onboard movie cameras shot footage to acquire technical data.

Quantity of Moon rocks: none planned.

Rover: none.

Notes: This was the first flight of the Saturn V and qualified it for carrying astronauts. The noise generated at liftoff was so powerful that the launch tower was damaged severely and the buildings of the control center and the press room shook so much that ceiling panels fell around CBS reporter Walter Cronkite.

The Apollo capsule reached a maximum distance from Earth of 18,092 kilometers (11,240 miles) and was turned so as to expose one half to the Sun and keep the other half in shadow, creating the maximum temperature differential and assessing the ability of the spacecraft to withstand these extremes. Radiation shielding was also tested. The Service Module engine was restarted to accelerate the vehicle and create the worst possible reentry conditions that might occur during a return from the Moon. A Lunar Module engineering mockup was carried on board.

The spectacular movie footage of the separation of the interstage ring of this flight is often used in documentaries and movies but attributed to other missions.

Apollo 5 (AS-204R)

Crew: none.

Launch vehicle: Saturn IB.

LM: present, but legs were not installed.

Lunar orbit: none planned.

CM and LM call signs: not assigned (CM absent, LM present).

Launch and return dates: January 22-23, 1968.

Lunar landing date and time: none.

Lunar landing site: none.

Number of moonwalks: none planned.

Mission duration: 11 hours 10 minutes.

Time spent on the Moon: none planned.

Number of photographs taken: none.

Quantity of Moon rocks: none planned.

Rover: none.

Notes: The primary goal of this mission was to test in Earth orbit the Lunar Module and the Instrument Unit in the configuration that would be used for the Saturn V. The LM was legless because the legs weren't ready. The Saturn IB launcher from the Apollo 1 mission was reused.

This flight verified that the LM was able to adjust the thrust and orientation of the descent engine and to separate the descent stage from the ascent stage even in the extreme case of an abort during descent to the Moon.

The LM used for this flight suffered from many problems and delays. During a test on another LM being built, the windows had exploded due to the internal pressure, so this mission flew with aluminum panels to close the window openings.

The LM control software shut down the engine earlier than required and ground control had to intervene manually, but the flight was nonetheless considered a success.

Apollo 6 (AS-502)

Crew: none.

Launch vehicle: Saturn V.

LM: present, but only as an engineering mockup.

Lunar orbit: none planned.

CM and LM call signs: not assigned (CM and LM present).

Launch and return dates: April 4, 1968.

Lunar landing date and time: none.

Lunar landing site: none.

Number of moonwalks: none planned.

Mission duration: 9 hours 57 minutes.

Time spent on the Moon: none planned.

Number of photographs taken: 370 (with 70 mm automatic still camera). Automatic onboard movie cameras shot footage to acquire technical data.

Quantity of Moon rocks: none planned.

Rover: none.

Notes: This second test flight of the Saturn V aided in human-rating the giant launcher and testing the new Command Module hatch.

Violent longitudinal oscillations ("pogo"), intolerable for a crew, occurred during liftoff. One of the fairing panels of the Lunar Module suffered a structural failure and pieces of its covering came off. In the second stage, one engine shut down prematurely due to excessive vibrations and another one was shut down due to incorrect wiring; the onboard systems were forced to compensate for the error, leading to an orbit that was significantly different from the planned one.

These and other malfunctions and errors prevented completion of the original flight plan, which would have taken the spacecraft to a distance equal to the Moon's. The flight also used dedicated instruments to test radiation exposure inside the cabin. The often-used footage of the inter-stage ring separation is taken from this flight and from Apollo 4.

Apollo 7 (AS-205)

Crew: Wally Schirra (CDR), Walter Cunningham (LMP), Donn Eisele (CMP).

Launch vehicle: Saturn IB.

LM: not present.

Lunar orbit: none planned.

CM and LM call signs: not assigned (CM present, LM absent).

Launch and return dates: October 11-22, 1968.

Lunar landing date and time: none.

Lunar landing site: none.

Number of moonwalks: none planned.

Mission duration: 10 days 20 hours 9 minutes.

Time spent on the Moon: none planned.

Number of photographs taken: 532. Live TV broadcasts were also made.

Quantity of Moon rocks: none planned.

Rover: none.

Notes: This was the first manned flight of the Apollo spacecraft, 21 months after the Apollo 1 disaster, and tested all of its systems in Earth orbit. An orbital rendezvous was performed by using the S-IVB stage as a target, but no actual docking was carried out. The crew performed the United States' first live TV broadcast from space.

The astronauts came down with a head cold, which was particularly unpleasant in weightlessness, and this contributed to a sort of rebellion against the orders from Mission Control, especially on the matter of wearing helmets and gloves during reentry, as the crew was concerned that they would be unable to clear their noses and throats from the mucus accumulated in their heads, which would suddenly start flowing due to deceleration. Mission Control was instead concerned that any unexpected depressurization of the cabin would be lethal if the astronauts weren't wearing their full reentry gear. The astronauts made the final decision and went through reentry without helmets and gloves.

Apollo 7 was the first US flight to use a mixed-gas atmosphere (65% oxygen, 35% nitrogen) instead of pure oxygen.

Apollo 8 (AS-503)

Crew: Frank Borman (CDR), William Anders (LMP), James Lovell (CMP).

Launch vehicle: Saturn V.

LM: present as a test article. Weight on Earth: 9,026 kg (19,900 lb).

Lunar orbit: yes (10 orbits).

CM and LM call signs: not assigned (CM and LM present).

Launch and return dates: December 21-27, 1968.

Lunar landing date and time: none.

Lunar landing site: none.

Number of moonwalks: none planned.

Mission duration: 6 days 3 hours 0 minutes.

Time spent on the Moon: none planned.

Number of photographs taken: 1,100. Live TV broadcasts were made and movie footage was shot.

Quantity of Moon rocks: none planned.

Rover: none.

Notes: Apollo 8 was truly groundbreaking: the first manned flight of a Saturn V, the first manned mission to fly significantly far from the Earth and the first manned flight around the Moon. The mission gave mankind the first photographs of the entire Earth taken by astronauts and the first live TV transmission of a crew from lunar orbit. Borman, Lovell and Anders were the first human beings to see the far side of the Moon with their own eyes.

This flight tested successfully the long-range communication and navigation equipment and methods needed for a mission to the Moon. The astronauts, however, were affected by headaches, vomiting and diarrhea in addition to sleeping problems, worsened by staggered sleep shifts and an excessive workload.

As the crew orbited the Moon, they read the first verses of the *Book of Genesis* live on TV, setting the record for the most watched broadcast in history (approximately 1 billion people in 64 countries).

Apollo 9 (AS-504)

Crew: James McDivitt (CDR), Russell Schweickart (LMP), David Scott (CMP).

Launch vehicle: Saturn V.

LM: present (LM-3). Weight on Earth: 14,530 kg (32,034 lb).

Lunar orbit: none (mission in Earth orbit).

CM and LM call signs: *Gumdrop, Spider.*

Launch and return dates: March 3-13, 1969.

Lunar landing date and time: none.

Lunar landing site: none.

Number of moonwalks: none planned.

Mission duration: 10 days 1 hour 0 minutes.

Time spent on the Moon: none planned.

Number of photographs taken: 1,373. TV broadcasts were made and movie footage was shot.

Quantity of Moon rocks: none planned.

Rover: none.

Notes: This was the first flight of the complete Apollo spacecraft, including the Lunar Module, the first internal crew transfer between the two vehicles (from the Command Module to the Lunar Module and back), and the first docking, undocking and re-docking of the CM and LM. Schweickart performed the first spacewalk in a fully autonomous spacesuit (all previous spacewalks had used suits that depended on the spacecraft for cooling and oxygen).

McDivitt and Schweickart performed the first manned flight of a spacecraft that was unable to reenter the atmosphere and used the LM's engines to fly up to 183 kilometers (114 miles) away from the CM and test the separation of the LM's ascent and descent stages.

The mission tested thoroughly and successfully the Apollo spacesuit and the Lunar Module, which were vital components for the Moon landings, as well as the communications, rendezvous, docking and crew transfer procedures. All these goals were achieved despite Schweickart's bouts of nausea and vomiting.

Apollo 10 (AS-505)

Crew: Tom Stafford (CDR), Gene Cernan (LMP), John Young (CMP).

Launch vehicle: Saturn V.

LM: present (LM-4). Weight on Earth: 13,941 kg (30,735 lb).

Lunar orbit: yes (31 orbits).

CM and LM call signs: *Charlie Brown*, *Snoopy*.

Launch and return dates: May 18-26, 1969.

Lunar landing date and time: none.

Lunar landing site: none.

Number of moonwalks: none planned.

Mission duration: 8 days 0 hours 3 minutes.

Time spent on the Moon: none planned.

Number of photographs taken: 1,436. TV transmissions were broadcast and movie footage was shot.

Quantity of Moon rocks: none planned.

Rover: none.

Notes: This flight was a dress rehearsal of the actual Moon landing. It was the first lunar flight of the complete Apollo spacecraft and tested the LM, which undocked from the Command and Service Module for eight hours and descended to 14,450 meters (47,400 feet) from the surface of the Moon, with Stafford and Cernan on board, along a path that simulated the actual landing trajectory. The descent stage was then jettisoned and the astronauts used the ascent stage to climb back to the CM and dock, achieving the first rendezvous in lunar orbit. The first color TV transmissions from space were also broadcast.

Apollo 10 demonstrated Mission Control's ability to handle two spacecraft simultaneously at lunar distances, checked all the lunar descent procedures (except for the actual landing) and tested the LM's landing radar.

This flight holds the record for the highest speed ever attained by a crewed spacecraft: 39,937 km/h (24,815 mph), during the return from the Moon.

Apollo 11 (AS-506)

Crew: Neil Armstrong (CDR), Buzz Aldrin (LMP), Michael Collins (CMP).

Launch vehicle: Saturn V.

LM: present (LM-5). Weight on Earth: 15,095 kg (33,728 lb).

Lunar orbit: yes (30 orbits).

CM and LM call signs: *Columbia*, *Eagle*.

Launch and return dates: July 16-24, 1969.

Lunar landing date and time: July 20, 1969 20:17:39 GMT.

Lunar landing site: *Mare Tranquillitatis* (Sea of Tranquility).

Number of moonwalks: one (2 hours 31 minutes 40 seconds).

Mission duration: 8 days 3 hours 18 minutes.

Time spent on the Moon: 21 hours 36 minutes.

Number of photographs taken: 1,408, of which 339 on the Moon (121 of which were taken during the moonwalk). TV transmissions were broadcast and color movie footage was shot.

Quantity of Moon rocks: 21.55 kg (47.5 lb).

Rover: none.

Notes: This was mankind's first manned landing on the Moon and the first return of samples and of very high resolution photographs from another celestial object, including panoramas, stereo images and extreme close-ups of the ground.

During landing, the onboard computer was overloaded with data and the automatic navigation system attempted to take the LM into an area strewn with boulders. Armstrong took control and steered the vehicle (with computer assistance) to a less dangerous area, but this deviation took so long that the LM landed with less than a minute of fuel left. The mission was a complete success and allowed the United States to keep President Kennedy's promise, made only eight years earlier, to land a man on the Moon and return him safely.

Armstrong and Aldrin's moonwalk began on July 21, 1969 at 2:56:15 GMT (22:56:15 EDT), 6 hours 39 minutes after landing. The maximum distance of the astronauts from the LM was approximately 60 meters (200 feet).

Apollo 12 (AS-507)

Crew: Pete Conrad (CDR), Alan Bean (LMP), Dick Gordon (CMP).

Launch vehicle: Saturn V.

LM: present (LM-6). Weight on Earth: 15,223 kg (33,652 lb).

Lunar orbit: yes (45 orbits).

CM and LM call signs: *Yankee Clipper, Intrepid.*

Launch and return dates: November 14-24, 1969.

Lunar landing date and time: November 19, 1969 6:54:35 UTC.

Lunar landing site: *Oceanus Procellarum* (Ocean of Storms).

Number of moonwalks: 2 (3 hours 56 minutes; 3 hours 49 minutes).

Mission duration: 10 days 4 hours 36 minutes.

Time spent on the Moon: 1 day 7 hours 31 minutes.

Number of photographs taken: 2,119, of which 583 on the Moon. Color TV transmissions were broadcast and color movie footage was taken.

Quantity of Moon rocks: 34.3 kg (75.7 lb).

Rover: none.

Notes: The second manned Moon landing demonstrated that pinpoint touchdown was possible: the LM landed just 185 meters (600 feet) from its target, the Surveyor 3 probe. This was the first (and so far the only) time that a manned mission visited another space vehicle on another celestial body and returned some of its parts.

During liftoff, the Saturn V booster was struck twice by lightning, leading to multiple malfunctions. Only John Aaron's rapid reaction in Mission Control solved a situation that was leading to an extremely dangerous mission abort.

A color TV camera was used for the live broadcast of the moonwalk, but the camera failed because it was pointed briefly at the Sun, damaging its sensor.

This mission placed on the Moon instruments that were powered by a small nuclear generator, which kept them active for years, providing a constant stream of science data, which was later cross-referenced with the data from subsequent Apollo flights. Conrad and Bean walked up to 411 meters (1,350 feet) away from the LM.

Apollo 13 (AS-508)

Crew: James Lovell (CDR), Fred Haise (LMP), John Swigert (CMP).

Launch vehicle: Saturn V.

LM: present (LM-7). Weight on Earth: 15,192 kg (33,493 lb).

Lunar orbit: scheduled but replaced by a fly-around, setting the absolute manned record for distance from Earth at 400,171 km (248,654 miles).

CM and LM call signs: *Odyssey, Aquarius.*

Launch and return dates: April 11-17, 1970.

Lunar landing date and time: scheduled but not performed.

Lunar landing site: Fra Mauro (not reached).

Number of moonwalks: None. EVAs were scheduled but not performed.

Mission duration: 5 days 22 hours 54 minutes.

Time spent on the Moon: None. Scheduled but not performed.

Number of photographs taken: 604 (none on the Moon). Color TV transmissions were broadcast and color movie footage was shot.

Quantity of Moon rocks: None. Collection was scheduled but not performed.

Rover: none.

Notes: A vital oxygen tank in the Service Module burst at 3:07:53 UTC on April 14, 1970, three days after liftoff from Earth on the way to the Moon, 322,000 kilometers (200,000 miles) from Earth. This depleted dramatically the oxygen reserves and the power available, since Apollo's fuel cells depended on the tank's oxygen to generate electricity. The historically famous phrase *"Houston, we have a problem"* was actually uttered by Swigert as *"OK, Houston, we've had a problem"*; Lovell then repeated *"Houston, we've had a problem".* The plight of the Apollo 13 astronauts was followed live on TV all over the world.

To save the astronauts, all the systems of the command module were shut down, producing an intense cold inside the spacecraft, and the Lunar Module's reserves and engine were used. The emergency trajectory forced Lovell, Haise and Swigert to fly all the way to the Moon, swing around it and then finally fly back to Earth, where they landed, in very poor physical shape but still standing, three days and 15 hours after the beginning of their ordeal.

Apollo 14 (AS-509)

Crew: Alan Shepard (CDR), Edgar Mitchell (LMP), Stuart Roosa (CMP).

Launch vehicle: Saturn V.

LM: present (LM-8). Weight on Earth: 15,279 kg (33,685 lb).

Lunar orbit: yes (34 orbits).

CM and LM call signs: *Kitty Hawk, Antares.*

Launch and return dates: January 31-February 9, 1971.

Lunar landing date and time: 12 May, 1971 9:18:11 UTC.

Lunar landing site: Fra Mauro.

Number of moonwalks: 2 (4 hours 47 minutes; 4 hours 34 minutes).

Mission duration: 9 days 0 hours 1 minutes.

Time spent on the Moon: 1 day 9 hours 3 minutes.

Number of photographs taken: 1,338, of which 417 on the Moon. Color TV broadcasts were made and color movie footage was shot.

Quantity of Moon rocks: 42.3 kg (93.2 lb).

Rover: none. However, a manually propelled cart, termed MET (Modular Equipment Transporter), was used.

Notes: During descent to the Moon, a false contact sent an incorrect signal to the LM's computer, bringing the spacecraft close to an automatic abort of the mission. Changes to the onboard software, performed on the fly to avoid this risk, caused a failure of the radar altimeter, which however recovered just in time to achieve landing.

At 47, Shepard set the record for the oldest moonwalker. In addition to their science tasks, Shepard hit some golf balls with a club he assembled by attaching a genuine #6 iron to the handle of the contingency sample tool and Mitchell threw the handle of a tool as if it were a javelin. Roosa carried on board the CM several hundred tree seeds, which were planted after the flight returned to Earth, giving rise to the so-called "Moon trees". This was the first mission to use red stripes on the legs, arms and helmet to identify the commander (Apollo 13's suits already had this feature but were never used). Shepard and Mitchell set the walking distance record from the LM at 1.5 kilometers (about one mile) but were unable to climb to the destination of their second moonwalk, the 300-meter (1,000-ft) wide Cone Crater. Images of the landing site taken in 2009 revealed that after traveling approximately 400,000 kilometers (250,000 miles) the two astronauts missed Cone Crater by just 30 meters (about 90 feet).

Apollo 15 (AS-510)

Crew: David Scott (CDR), James Irwin (LMP), Alfred Worden (CMP).

Launch vehicle: Saturn V.

LM: present (LM-10). Weight on Earth: 16,437 kg (36,238 lb).

Lunar orbit: yes (74 orbits).

CM and LM call signs: *Endeavour, Falcon.*

Launch and return dates: July 26-August 7, 1971.

Lunar landing date and time: July 30, 1971 22:16:29 UTC.

Lunar landing site: near *Mare Imbrium* (Sea of Rains).

Number of moonwalks: 3 (6 h 32 m; 7 h 12 m; 4 h 49 m) plus a stand-up EVA: Scott, wearing his spacesuit, stood up through the LM's top docking hatch and scanned the surrounding area visually and photographically for 33 minutes.

Mission duration: 12 days 7 hours 11 minutes.

Time spent on the Moon: 2 days 18 hours 54 minutes.

Number of photographs taken: 2,640, of which 1,151 on the Moon. Color TV transmissions were made (including the liftoff of the LM from the Moon) and color movie footage was also shot.

Quantity of Moon rocks: 77.3 kg (170.4 lb).

Rover: Yes, driven for a total of 27.9 km (17.3 miles).

Notes: This flight included the first use of the Rover lunar car, which allowed a far greater exploration range of up to 5 kilometers (3.1 miles) and made Scott the first car driver on another celestial object. Scott and Irwin were the first moonwalkers to perform three excursions and sleep on the Moon without wearing their spacesuits, which were improved and less rigid. They collected the *Genesis Rock*, one of the oldest Moon rocks returned to Earth, over 4 billion years old.

Worden launched a science subsatellite from the Service Module in lunar orbit. During the return trip, he performed the first deep-space spacewalk to recover the film canisters of the automatic mapping cameras.

During the third moonwalk, Scott dropped simultaneously a feather and a hammer to confirm Galileo's theory that different bodies fell at the same rate in a vacuum. He also secretly placed on the Moon a small sculpture, the *Fallen Astronaut*, to honor the Russian and American space travelers whose deaths were publicly known at the time.

Apollo 16 (AS-511)

Crew: John Young (CDR), Charles Duke (LMP), Kenneth Mattingly (CMP).

Launch vehicle: Saturn V.

LM: present (LM-11). Weight on Earth: 16,437 kg (36,237 lb).

Lunar orbit: yes (64 orbits).

CM and LM call signs: *Casper, Orion.*

Launch and return dates: April 16-27, 1972.

Lunar landing date and time: April 21, 1972 2:23:35 UTC.

Lunar landing site: Descartes highlands.

Number of moonwalks: 3 (7 h 11 m; 7 h 23 m; 5 h 40 m).

Mission duration: 11 days 1 hour 51 minutes.

Time spent on the Moon: 2 days 23 hours 2 minutes.

Number of photographs taken: 2,801, of which 1,787 on the Moon. Color TV transmissions were made (including the liftoff of the LM from the Moon) and color movie footage was also shot.

Quantity of Moon rocks: 95.7 kg (211 lb).

Rover: yes, for a total of 26.7 km (16.6 miles).

Notes: Young and Duke were the first astronauts to explore the highlands of the Moon. They spent a total of 20 hours on the Moon outside the LM and traveled for 26.7 km (16.6 miles) on the Rover, reaching a maximum distance of 4.6 km (2.8 miles) from their spacecraft. Young set the land speed record with the Rover, at 17.1 km/h (10.6 mph). Duke became the youngest moonwalker (he was 36). Apollo 16 had the highest elevation of the Sun above the horizon (48.7°).

During the first of their three moonwalks, the Apollo 16 astronauts collected the heaviest single sample, which weighed 11 kg (24 lb) and was named i in honor of Bill Muehlberger, director of geology operations for this mission. A photographic spectrograph/telescope, sensitive to far ultraviolet radiation, which on Earth is mostly blocked by the atmosphere, was used for the first time.

Mattingly, during the return trip, performed an hour-long spacewalk approximately 310,000 km (192,000 miles) from Earth while Duke leaned out of the Command Module hatch to help him. Mattingly's wedding ring, lost in the cabin a few day earlier, started to float out of the hatch, but Duke managed to catch it before it became lost in space.

Apollo 17 (AS-512)

Crew: Gene Cernan (CDR), Harrison Schmitt (LMP), Ron Evans (CMP).

Launch vehicle: Saturn V.

LM: present (LM-12). Weight on Earth: 16,448 kg (36,262 lb).

Lunar orbit: yes (75 orbits).

CM and LM call signs: *America, Challenger.*

Launch and return dates: December 7-19, 1972.

Lunar landing date and time: December 11, 1972 19:54:57 UTC.

Lunar landing site: Taurus-Littrow Valley.

Number of moonwalks: 3 (7 h 11 m; 7 h 36 m; 7 h 15 m).

Mission duration: 12 days 13 hours 51 minutes.

Time spent on the Moon: 3 days 2 hours 59 minutes.

Number of photographs taken: 3,581, of which 2,237 on the Moon. Color TV transmissions were made (including the liftoff of the LM from the Moon) and color movie footage was also shot.

Quantity of Moon rocks: 110.5 kg (243.6 lb).

Rover: yes, for a total of 35.7 km (22.2 miles).

Notes: The last lunar mission of the Apollo project was the first night launch of a US crew, the longest stay on the Moon and in lunar orbit and as a whole the longest lunar mission. It used the heaviest Lunar Module (1,383 kg (3,050 lb) heavier than the one used for Apollo 11), returned the heaviest load of Moon rocks (five times more than Apollo 11), featured the first visit of a geologist (Schmitt) to another world, took the most photographs, covered the greatest distance in a single Rover excursion (20 kilometers (12.4 miles)), and ventured farthest from the LM (7.6 km (4.7 miles)).

Apollo 17 was also the only mission to investigate the nature of lunar soil by using gravimetric measurements and transmitting radio signals through the ground.

Gene Cernan was the last man to walk on the Moon: he left its surface to reenter the Lunar Module at 5:35 GMT on December 14, 1972. Since then, no one has visited the Moon.

This mission, like the previous ones, also performed a 67-minute spacewalk during the return trip.

Skylab

In 1973 and 1974, three Apollo missions flew on Saturn IB launchers to Skylab, the United States' first space station in Earth orbit. Skylab was a converted S-IVB stage and was launched by a Saturn V on May 14, 1973. These flights provided invaluable science on Earth observations and on the effects of long-term weightlessness on human physiology, setting endurance records (28, 59 and 84 days) for their crews:

– Skylab 2 (May 25, 1973 - June 11, 1973): Pete Conrad, Paul Weitz, Joe Kerwin.

– Skylab 3 (July 28, 1973 - September 25, 1973): Alan Bean, Jack Lousma, Owen Garriott.

– Skylab 4 (November 16, 1973 - February 8, 1974): Gerald Carr, William Pogue, Ed Gibson.

Apollo-Soyuz

The *Apollo-Soyuz Test Project* was a joint flight (July 15-24, 1975) of an Apollo Command and Service Module, launched by a Saturn IB, and of a Soviet Soyuz spacecraft. The two vehicles performed a rendezvous and docking in Earth orbit, allowing their crews (astronauts Deke Slayton, Tom Stafford and Vance Brand; cosmonauts Alexei Leonov and Valeri Kubasov) to meet and demonstrate an unprecedented international collaboration in space.

This was the final flight of an Apollo spacecraft and the last spaceflight of an American astronaut for almost six years, until the first Space Shuttle mission, STS-1, lifted off 5 years and 264 days later, on April 12, 1981.

16.3 Apollo astronauts

This list provides the full name, year of birth and death, age at death, and mission(s) flown of every Apollo astronaut, sorted alphabetically by surname. The role and age during each Apollo mission is also given. Apollo 1 crew information is included as a tribute to their loss during preflight training. *"STS"* references a Space Shuttle flight.

Edwin Eugene "Buzz" Aldrin Jr (1930-) – Gemini 12, Apollo 11 (LMP, 39)

William Alison Anders (1933-) – Apollo 8 (LMP, 35)

Neil Alden Armstrong (1930-2012, 82) – Gemini 8, Apollo 11 (CDR, 38)

Alan LaVern Bean (1932-) – Apollo 12 (LMP, 37), Skylab 3 (CDR, 41)

Frank Frederick Borman II (1928-) – Gemini 7, Apollo 8 (CDR, 40)

Vance DeVoe Brand (1931-) – Apollo-Soyuz (CMP, 44), STS-5, STS-41-B, STS-35

Gerald Paul Carr (1932-) – Skylab 4 (CDR, 41)

Eugene Andrew "Gene" Cernan (1934-) – Gemini 9-A, Apollo 10 (LMP, 35), Apollo 17 (CDR, 38)

Roger Bruce Chaffee (1935-1967, 31) – Apollo 1 (Pilot, 31)

Michael Collins (1930-) – Gemini 10, Apollo 11 (CMP, 38)

Charles "Pete" Conrad Jr (1930-1999, 69) – Gemini 5, Gemini 11, Apollo 12 (CDR, 39), Skylab 2 (CDR, 43)

Ronnie Walter "Walt" Cunningham (1932-) – Apollo 7 (LMP, 36)

Charles Moss Duke Jr (1935-) – Apollo 16 (LMP, 36)

Donn Fulton Eisele (1930-1987, 57) – Apollo 7 (CMP, 38)

Ronald Ellwin Evans (1933-1990, 56) – Apollo 17 (CMP, 39)

Owen Kay Garriott (1930-) – Skylab 3 (Science Pilot, 43), STS-9

Edward George Gibson (1936-) – Skylab 4 (Science Pilot, 38)

Richard Francis "Dick" Gordon Jr (1929-) – Gemini 11, Apollo 12 (CMP, 40)

Virgil Ivan "Gus" Grissom (1926-1967, 40) – Mercury 4, Gemini 3, Apollo 1 (CDR, 40)

Fred Wallace Haise Jr (1933-) – Apollo 13 (LMP, 36)

James Benson Irwin (1930-1991, 61) – Apollo 15 (LMP, 41)

Joseph Peter Kerwin (1932-) – Skylab 2 (Science Pilot, 41)

James Arthur Lovell Jr (1928-) – Gemini 7, Gemini 12, Apollo 8 (CMP, 40), Apollo 13 (CDR, 42)

Jack Robert Lousma (1936-) – Skylab 3 (Pilot, 37), STS-3

Thomas Kenneth "Ken" Mattingly II (1936-) – Apollo 16 (CMP, 36), STS-4, STS-51-C

James Alton McDivitt (1929-) – Gemini 4, Apollo 9 (CDR, 39)

Edgar Dean Mitchell (1930-) – Apollo 14 (LMP, 40)

William Reid Pogue (1930-) – Skylab 4 (Pilot, 43)

Stuart Allen Roosa (1933-1994, 61) – Apollo 14 (CMP, 37)

Walter Marty "Wally" Schirra (1923-2007, 84) – Mercury 8, Gemini 6A, Apollo 7 (CDR, 45)

Harrison Hagan Schmitt (1935-) – Apollo 17 (LMP, 37)

Russell Louis "Rusty" Schweickart (1935-) – Apollo 9 (LMP, 33)

David Randolph Scott (1932-) – Gemini 8, Apollo 9 (CMP, 36), Apollo 15 (CDR, 39)

Alan Bartlett Shepard Jr (1923-1998, 74) – Mercury 3, Apollo 14 (CDR, 47)

Donald Kent "Deke" Slayton (1924-1993, 69) – Apollo-Soyuz (Docking Module Pilot, 51)

Thomas Patten Stafford (1930-) – Gemini 6-A, Gemini 9-A, Apollo 10 (CDR, 39), Apollo-Soyuz (CDR, 45)

John Leonard "Jack" Swigert Jr (1931-1982, 51) – Apollo 13 (CMP, 38)

Paul Joseph Weitz (1932-) – Skylab 2 (Pilot, 41), STS-6

Edward Higgins White II (1930-1967, 36) – Gemini 4, Apollo 1 (Senior Pilot, 36)

Alfred Merrill Worden (1932-) – Apollo 15 (CMP, 39)

John Watts Young (1930-) – Gemini 3, Gemini 10, Apollo 10 (38), Apollo 16 (CDR, 41), STS-1, STS-9

Astronauts who flew around the Moon. Only 24 people, all American white males, have ever left low Earth orbit and flown to the Moon at least once, during Apollo 8, 10 and 13 (circumlunar flights) and Apollo 11, 12, 14, 15, 16 and 17 (lunar landing flights). Seventeen are still alive: Frank Borman, William Anders, James Lovell, Thomas Stafford, Eugene Cernan, John Young, Buzz Aldrin, Michael Collins, Alan Bean, Richard Gordon, Fred Haise, Edgar Mitchell, David Scott, Alfred Worden, Charles Duke, Ken Mattingly, and Harrison Schmitt. Six have died: Neil Armstrong, Charles Conrad, John Swigert, Alan Shepard, Stuart Roosa, James Irwin, and Ron Evans.

Moonwalkers. Only 12 of the 24 circumlunar astronauts walked on the Moon. Eight are still alive: Buzz Aldrin (Apollo 11), Alan Bean (Apollo 12), Edgar Mitchell (Apollo 14), David Scott (Apollo 15), John Young and Charles Duke (Apollo 16), Eugene Cernan and Harrison Schmitt (Apollo

17). Four are no longer with us: Neil Armstrong (Apollo 11), Charles Conrad (Apollo 12), Alan Shepard (Apollo 14), and James Irwin (Apollo 15).

Multiple trips to the Moon. Three astronauts flew to the Moon twice: James Lovell (Apollo 8 and 13), John Young (Apollo 10 and 6) and Eugene Cernan (Apollo 10 and 17). Lovell was the only astronaut to fly twice to the Moon without ever setting foot on it.

16.4 The Saturn V/Apollo spacecraft

Overall dimensions and weight. Height: 111 m (363 ft). Diameter (at the base, not including the fins): 10 m (33 ft). Weight: 2,822 t (6.2 million lb, Apollo 8) to 2,965 t (6.5 million lb, Apollo 16).

First stage (S-IC)

Dimensions and weights. Height: 42 m (138 ft). Diameter: 10 m (33 ft). Weight without fuel: 129,822 kg (286,208 lb, Apollo 15) to 138,451 kg (305,232 lb, Apollo 8). Fully fueled weight: 2,175,939 kg (4,797,126 lb, Apollo 8) to 2,288,088 kg (5,044,371 lb, Apollo 16).

Fuel load. RP-1 kerosene and liquid oxygen, 2,034,664 kg (4,485,668 lb, Apollo 8) to 2,155,071 kg (4,751,120 lb, Apollo 16). Burn rate: 12,437 kg/s (27,420 lb/s, Apollo 13) to 12,741 kg/s (28,089 lb/s, Apollo 15).

Propulsion. 5 F-1 engines (4 gimbaling, 1 fixed). Total rated thrust: 3,401,940 kg (7.5 million lb, Apollo 8) to 3,451,840 kg (7.61 million lb, all other flights).

Second stage (S-II)

Dimensions and weights. Height: 25 m (138 ft). Diameter: 10 m (33 ft). Weight without fuel: 35,356 kg (77,947 lb, Apollo 13) to 40,142 kg (88,500 lb, Apollo 8). Fully fueled weight: 471,114 kg (1,038,628 lb, Apollo 8) to 493,536 kg (1,088,061 lb, Apollo 16).

Fuel load. Liquid hydrogen and liquid oxygen, 430,324 kg (948,702 lb, Apollo 8) to 456,635 kg (1,006,708 lb, Apollo 16).

Propulsion. 5 J-2 engines (4 gimbaling, 1 fixed). Total rated thrust: 510,291 kg (1.12 million lb, Apollo 8) to 521,631 kg (1.15 million lb, all other flights).

Third stage (S-IVB)

Dimensions and weights. Height: 17.8 m (58.5 ft). Diameter: 6.6 m (21.7 ft). Weight without fuel: 9,912 kg (21,852 lb, Apollo 7) to 11,760 kg (25,926 lb, Apollo 8). Fully fueled weight: 116,357 kg (256,523 lb, Apollo 7) to 120,798 kg (266,315 lb, Apollo 15).

Fuel load. Liquid hydrogen and liquid oxygen, 105,866 kg (233,395 lb, Apollo 9) to 108,618 kg (239,462 lb, Apollo 15).

Propulsion. One J-2 restartable engine. Rated thrust: 104,326 kg (230,000 lb).

Command and service module (CSM)

Dimensions and weights. CM height: 3.47 m (11.4 ft). SM height (including engine bell): 7.5 m (24.6 ft). CM diameter: 3.91 m (128.ft). SM diameter: 3.91 m (12.8 ft). Crew volume in CM: 6 m3 (210 cu ft). CM fueled weight: 5,557 kg (12,250 lb, Apollo 11) to 5,840 kg (12,874 lb, Apollo 17). SM fueled weight: 18,413 kg (40,593 lb).

Fuel load. Aerozine 50 (50% hydrazine, 50% unsymmetric dimethyl hydrazine) and dinitrogen tetroxide, hypergolic.

Propulsion. CM: only maneuvering thrusters. SM: one main engine and 16 maneuvering thrusters. SM main engine thrust: 9,298 kg (20,500 lb).

Launch Escape System (LES)

Dimensions and weight. Height: 10 m (33 ft). Diameter: 0.66 m (26 in). Fully fueled weight: 4,042 kg (8,910 lb).

Fuel. Solid compound based on polysulfides.

Propulsion. One main motor, one maneuvering motor and one jettison motor, all solid-fueled. Main engine thrust: 66,678 kg (147,000 lb).

Spacecraft/Lunar Module Adapter (SLA)

Dimensions and weight. Height: 8.53 m (28 ft). Diameter: 6.60 m (260 in) at the base, 3.91 m (154 in) at the top. Weight: 1,814 kg (4,000 lb).

Fuel and propulsion. None.

Lunar module (LM)

Dimensions and weights. Height: 7.29 m (23 ft). Distance between outer ends of legs (deployed): 9.4 m (31 ft). Length of three probes under foot-pads: 173 cm (68 inches). Diameter of the four footpads: 81 cm (32 in). Total surface of four footpads: 20,750 cm2 (3,216 sq in). Cabin volume: 6.7 m3 (235 cu ft), of which 4.5 m3 (160 cu ft) habitable. Weight: 13,941 kg (30,735 lb, Apollo 10) to 16,448 kg (36,262 lb, Apollo 17).

Fuel load. Aerozine 50 (50% hydrazine, 50% unsymmetric dimethyl hydrazine) and dinitrogen tetroxide, hypergolic; 2,365 kg (5,214 lb) in the ascent stage, 8,100 kg (18,100 lb) in the descent stage.

Engines. Descent stage: one, with throttleable thrust (476-4,380 kg; 1,050-9,870 lb) and gimbaling nozzle. Ascent stage: one primary engine, with fixed thrust (1,589 kg; 3,500 lb) and fixed nozzle, and 16 attitude control thrusters.

Saturn V onboard computer (*Instrument Unit*)

Dimensions and weight. Height: 0.91 m (3 ft). Diameter: 6.6 m (21 ft 8 in). Weight: 1,953 kg (4,306 lb).

Lunar Rover

Dimensions and weights. Length: 2.96 m (116.5 in). Width: 2.06 m (81 in). Height: 1.14 m (44.8 in). Wheelbase: 2.28 m (90 in). Weight: 209.6 kg (462 lb) on Earth, 34.8 kg (77 lb) on the Moon.

Top speed. 13 km/h (8 mph).

Propulsion. 4 electric driving motors; 2 electric motors for the steering system of the 4 steerable wheels.

Cost. 38 million dollars for 5 complete vehicles plus three test vehicles and associated training.

Space suits

Weights. Including the PLSS, approximately 81 kg (180 lb) on Earth or 13.5 kg (30 lb) on the Moon. The PLSS alone weighed approximately 27 kg (60 lb) on Earth or 4.5 kg (10 lb) on the Moon.

Apollo onboard computer (CM/LM)

RAM. 4,096 words of 16 bits = 64,000 bit = approximately 8 kbytes.

Clock. 2.048 MHz.

1202 error. Solved by Steven Bales and Jack Garman.

16.5 Moon rocks

Total collected Moon rocks. Approximately 382 kg (842 lb). The heaviest single rock (*"Big Muley"*, Apollo 16) weighs 11.7 kg (25.9 lb).

16.6 Photographs

SO-368 film. Kodak Ektachrome MS color reversal film, ASA 64, 70 mm, double perforation, Estar polyester backing. Used for color photographs outside the LM on Apollo 11.

SO-168 film. Kodak Ektachrome EF color reversal film, ASA 160 (pushed to 1000 ASA for onboard photographs), 70 mm. Used for the ALSCC (stereoscopic lunar surface close-up camera) and for color photographs on all flights except Apollo 11, which used it only for onboard photos.

Type 3400 (HBW) film. Kodak Panatomic-X black and white 70 mm film, ASA 80. Used for the Apollo 11 black and white photographs.

SO-267 (HBW) film. Plus-XX black and white film, ASA 278. Used for photographs outside the LM during Apollo 12 and 14.

Type 3401 (HBW) film. Plus-XX black and white film, ASA 80-125. Used for photographs outside the LM on Apollo 15, 16 and 17.

Magazine. 160 color photographs, 200 black-and-white.

Total of photographs taken on the surface of the Moon. Over 17,000.

Exposure settings. Aperture: f/5.6, f/8 or f/11. Shutter speed: 1/250, except for some photographs with polarization, taken at 1/125.

16.7 The Moon and the Earth

Earth-Moon distance (center to center). Average: 384,403 km (238,857 miles), equal to about 30 Earth diameters. Minimum: 363,104 km (225,622 miles). Maximum distance: 405,696 km (252,088 miles).

Diameter of the Moon. 3,474 km (2,158 miles), 1/4 of the Earth's diameter.

Diameter of the Earth. 12,740 km (7,916 miles).

Orbit around the Earth. Every 27.3 Earth days.

Lunar escape velocity. 2.38 km/s (5,323 mph).

Albedo of the Moon. 0.12. The light reflected by the Moon at first quarter or last quarter, i.e., when half of a sunlit hemisphere is visible from Earth, is only 8% of the light reflected by a full Moon.

Temperature at the surface. Average 107°C (224.7°F), maximum 123°C (253.4°F), minimum -153°C (243.4°F). Minimum temperature can drop to -233°C (-387.4°F) in polar regions that are permanently in shadow. At a depth of 1 m (40 in), the temperature is almost constant at -35°C (-31°F).

Distance of the horizon. 2.4 km (1.5 miles) on the Moon; 4.7 km (3 miles) on Earth.

Duration of lunar day and night. 340 hours each.

Size of the Earth in the lunar sky. About 3.6 times the diameter of the Moon in the Earth's sky.

Brightness of the Earth in the lunar sky. 40 times that of a full Moon.

Contents

Lightning Source UK Ltd.
Milton Keynes UK
UKOW06f1805101215

264506UK00007B/348/P